How to Open a Swiss Bank Account

by James Kelder

Thomas Y. Crowell Company
Established 1834   New York

Manufactured in the United States of America

Library of Congress Cataloging in Publication Data

Kelder, James.
    How to open a Swiss bank account.

    Includes index.
    1. Bank accounts—Switzerland. I. Title.
HG1660.S9K44   332.1'5   75-34285
ISBN 0-690-01033-8

1 2 3 4 5 6 7 8 9 10

This book is dedicated to two men and one woman:

to Harry D. Schultz and Karl Hess for having the courage to write provocative books,

and to my wife, Magda Alfaro Kelder, for having patience.

Acknowledgments

FICTION MAY BE CONSTRUCTED from one man's fantasies. The bricks of nonfiction, though, are information and ideas from many sources; the author is only a mason, using the accumulated material to build a useful structure.

Since many of the sources used for this book provided essentially the same data, few specific references are provided in the text. The opinions and conclusions expressed are my own, as are any inaccuracies. However, I humbly acknowledge my debt to the many researchers and writers whose past efforts have simplified this project.

In particular, I am indebted to Hans J. Bär, Max Iklé, T. R. Fehrenbach, and Leslie Waller for their explanations of the Swiss banking system. The works of Harry Browne and Harry D. Schultz were also particularly helpful in gaining an understanding of the importance of Swiss accounts for Americans.

For information on inflation, the decline of the dollar, and the workings of the foreign exchange markets, I thank Robert Z. Aliber, Robert Lekachman, Sidney E. Rolfe, and James L.

Burtle. For making the subject of Liechtenstein trusts comprehensible, I am grateful to Herbert Batliner, Bruno B. Güggi, and Walter Nuener.

In addition, for their reports, interpretations, or useful information in general, I would like to express my gratitude to the following: "C. M. Allen," René Baxter, Israel Beckhardt, Peter Binzen, James U. Blanchard III, Murray Teigh Bloom, Lewis Chester, Alexander Cockburn, Charles Curley, Edwin L. Dale, Jr., Joseph R. Daughen, Catherine Crook de Camp, James Dines, Jack Egan, Paul R. Ehrlich, Anne H. Ehrlich, Paul E. Erdman, and Rainer Esslen.

Also to Ladislas Farago, Stephen Fay, Howard Flieger, Frederick Forsyth, James P. Gannon, Soma Golden, Renée Grandvoinet, Henry Hazlitt, John Hawkes, Moira Hawkes, Karl Hess, Donald J. Hoppe, Michael C. Jensen, John Kamin, Ian M. Keown, Carroll Kilpatrick, Albert L. Kraus, Gerald Krefetz, Herbert Kubly, George Lardner, Jr., Magnus Linklater, Neil McInnes, James McKeever, Peter Milius, and Robert H. Persons, Jr.

And, for the same reasons, to Franz Pick, Robert L. Preston, William F. Rickenbacker, Robert V. Roosa, Mort Rosenblum, Murray N. Rothbard, James L. Rowe, Jr., Hobart Rowen, Ronald Segal, Leonard Silk, Mark Skousen, "Adam Smith," Julian M. Snyder, Ronald L. Soble, Alvin Toffler, Hans Weber, the late Andrew Dickson White, and George F. Will.

I must also thank Eva L. Meigher of the U.S. Treasury Department, the information office of the Swiss National Bank in Bern, and the New York staff of the Swiss National Tourist Office for providing me with much helpful material. For clarifying particular points, special thanks is also due to Daniel Kellerhals of the Swiss Embassy in Washington.

These acknowledgments would not be complete without expressing my appreciation to the hundreds of Swiss bankers who courteously (and generally anonymously) provided detailed answers to my queries.

To the many friends and acquaintances who confided in me, discussing their personal anti-inflation tactics, I also owe a special debt.

Finally, I would like to thank my agent, David Stewart Hull of James Brown Associates, Inc., and my editor, Nick Ellison, for believing in an idea and making this book a reality.

JAMES KELDER
November 1975

Contents

Illustrations

1
An Introduction

THIS IS A BOOK about Swiss banks, but it is also a book for our times—times of inflation and recession and doubts about the future of the American economy.

As the title promises, this book will tell you how to open a Swiss bank account. There is no need to make a trip to Switzerland. You will learn how to handle the paperwork and make deposits by mail.

It is intended for the average American, who stands to lose the most in the era of economic turmoil and social confusion that has just begun. The emphasis is on personal accounts, to help middle class people protect their savings, the results of a lifetime of hard work.

Americans have long known about the existence of Swiss bank accounts. Until recently, though, they have never considered them pertinent to their investment plans. Now, however, the uncertainties of our economy have turned a financial topic of importance only to specialists into a subject of wide and urgent interest.

As this book discusses how to use a hard currency account in Switzerland to protect personal assets from further depreciation of the American dollar, the reader will also come to appreciate the uniqueness of Switzerland and of the Swiss banking system. The myths surrounding Swiss banking will disappear; in their place will be a new understanding of the meaning of financial security and of the usefulness of Swiss bank accounts in a changing world.

The Mysterious Swiss Banks

For years, Swiss bank accounts have fascinated Americans. Numbered accounts are a cliché of popular adventure fiction. Misconceptions abound: that Swiss accounts are illegal for U.S. citizens, that $100,000 is the minimum for an account. In the popular imagination, Swiss banks are linked with the Mafia, tax evasion, and international intrigue.

The truth is more prosaic—and far more interesting. Many of Switzerland's most respected banks will open an account for $100 or less. American depositors are welcomed by most Swiss banks. Swiss accounts are as legal for Americans as accounts in their hometown bank.

You may be reading this book out of curiosity, because Swiss banks are associated with international finance, with oil sheiks and dictators, with mercenaries and heroin smugglers. If you are, read on. You'll find out how Swiss banks really operate and who their actual customers are. You'll realize why dictators keep their retirement funds in Swiss banks. Numbered accounts, and their true function, will be explained in detail. You'll also be briefed on the formation of Liechtenstein trusts, an even more sophisticated method of hiding the true ownership of a Swiss bank account.

Fear of the Future

You may have bought this book out of fear—fear of what inflation is doing to your money, your savings. Read on and you will learn how a Swiss bank account can act as a buffer between you and the worries of inflation. You'll soon appreciate the usefulness of a Swiss account in protecting your assets when the world financial future is cloudy and uncertain, as it is now.

Traditionally, Americans have shown little interest in having Swiss bank accounts of their own. In the past few years, though, many foresighted Americans have opted for Swiss accounts, and many more are considering placing at least part of their savings in Switzerland. Raging inflation has been the main reason for these new converts. Accounts in Swiss francs or in other hard currencies have proven to be excellent hedges against loss of purchasing power of the dollar.

There are other motivations, too, behind the flow of money to Switzerland. America is definitely changing. Confidence in our political leaders, and in their ability to successfully manage the change, is low. Many of the individuals opening Swiss accounts are seeking a haven for their money beyond the reach of an unpredictable government. They are using Swiss accounts as insurance, to help maintain their personal freedom of action no matter what the future may bring.

Inflation

Inflation is the real reason this book was written. Ten or fifteen years ago, this book would not have been published. Not that the information it contains would have been illegal, or anything like that. Having a Swiss account was as completely legal then as it is now. Back then, however, no American publisher would have felt it worthwhile to bring out such a book; there wouldn't have been enough interested readers to make even a small edition feasible. There was no need, the American dollar was "as good as gold," maybe even better.

Now things are different. The American dollar has had no gold backing at all since August 1971. The dollar is now "fiat" money, paper currency backed only by faith, faith in the U.S. government and its policies. And this faith has been eroding rapidly.

More than faith has been eroding. The annual rate of inflation for 1974 was officially 12.2 percent. A savings account with an interest rate of $4^1/_2$ percent, compounded, just doesn't keep up with a 12 percent inflation rate, also compounded. A long-term certificate of deposit at 7 percent isn't much better. Your money is worth less when it's withdrawn from the bank than when it was originally deposited.

Inflation has become very personal. In the mid-1970s, most Americans are well aware that the dollar is worth much less than it used to be. They are painfully reminded of this fact every time they shop for groceries, for a new car, or for a new anything. Back in the good old days, not so long ago, before Watergate, before the Vietnamese fiasco, before the Arab oil embargo, before the great Nixon impeachment crisis, we had inflation, too. The rate was perhaps 3 percent, just enough to make things interesting. A little inflation gave us a feeling of progress as prices went up.

Before our economy started to change in the early 1970s, few law-abiding Americans had Swiss bank accounts. They felt no need for the extra margin of privacy, security, and flexibility offered by such accounts. The traditional "inflation hedges" served them well.

Weakness of Traditional Investments

The time-honored hedges against inflation, especially common stocks and real estate, worked reasonably well as long as the inflation rate remained low, at 3 percent or less. In the past few years, however, as inflation really began to rage, it has become apparent that standard investments are inadequate protection.

The stock market in particular has been a disappointment to those who counted on rising stock values to keep pace with inflation. For decades, common stock ownership, either directly or through mutual funds, had been touted as a sensible inflation hedge. Advancing stock prices and dividends were expected to offset the gradual loss of the dollar's value through inflation. When the crunch of double-digit inflation came, though, there was little protection in owning common stocks. Stock prices had already collapsed.

In the great bear market of the last few years, investors have been left sitting numbly on the sidelines, wondering what happened to their money. Collectively, in only two years, 1973 and 1974, they suffered an estimated $389 billion loss of stock value on the New York Stock Exchange alone.

Ownership of real estate has proven a somewhat better investment. Property values have kept pace with inflation, at least on paper. But the main drawback has been a lack of liquidity in the marketplace—it has become difficult to convert real estate investments into cash. There are few buyers, and mortgage money has been difficult to obtain. When it has been available, required down payments and high annual interest rates have discouraged many potential buyers.

In the first part of 1975, as indications appeared that the downturn in the economy would soon "bottom out," the stock market showed signs of life. New records for total daily and weekly volume were set on the Big Board. Market indicators, such as the Dow Jones Industrial Average, rebounded significantly from the lows of late 1974. But later in 1975, when it become apparent that recovery from the recession was not going to be either quick or painless, hope for a new bull market faded and stock prices eased back to more realistic levels. Despite a new rally in January 1976 that moved stock prices back toward the levels of a few years ago, there was still much uncertainty.

Whether or not a new bull market began in 1975, a great many people have lost faith in the stock market. A generation of investors no longer accepts the conventional wisdom that common stocks are an inflation hedge. They have abandoned the market to the quick, the nimble, and the professionals. Until a new economic stability is achieved, individuals seeking secure investments and long-term gains to offset inflation will tend to shun stocks.

Traditional Advice

Regardless of the state of the economy and of the stock market, people need investment advice. Managing one's small share of the nation's wealth is a complex problem, if only because of the bewildering choice of investments available. A huge literature on personal investing has developed to meet this need for information. There are literally thousands of books available on the various aspects of personal investing—the stock market, security analysis, real estate, mutual funds, personal financial planning, on all the areas of investing.

In today's economy, these books are generally worthless for the average investor looking for effective guidance. As the world economy changed, as the dollar shifted in its international role, and as our politicians mismanaged U.S. fiscal and monetary policies, the rules of the game became very unclear.

The investment world is now a different ball game. People seeking to protect their assets, to proof their futures against inflation, need coaching more than ever. Unfortunately, most of the investment books on the market were written about an economy that no longer exists. Now these books are only of historical interest. To a reader aware of our national economic situation, such books read like fairy tales about a land that once was and never will be again.

Untraditional Advice

As I write this, I have upon my desk a circular from a book club catering to investors. Thirty-two books are offered; only two or three are still pertinent reading. One is a novel about Swiss banks. The other two are: *You Can Profit From a Monetary Crisis,* by Harry Browne, and *How to Invest in Gold Stocks and Avoid the Pitfalls,* by Donald J. Hoppe.

Browne and Hoppe are two of a group of writers and financial advisers who have been dubbed "gold bugs," "prophets of doom," and the "new Jeremiahs" by the media. Despite such derision, they have found a wide readership among the investing public. The reason is obvious. Their books fill a need, the need for financial advice pertinent to our current economy.

Many of these books have certainly had very melodramatic titles. Admittedly, when such books as Harry Browne's *How You Can Profit from the Coming Devaluation* (his first book), *Panics and Crashes and How You Can Make Money Out of Them,* by Harry D. Schultz, and *How to Beat the Depression That Is Surely Coming!,* by Dr. Robert H. Persons, Jr., began to appear, my personal reaction to the titles was typical. I felt that these gentlemen were somehow unpatriotic. How could they write such books? How could they doubt that the United States was the most powerful nation on earth, its economy depression-proof?

Now I know that they were right in their common basic thesis: because of economic mismanagement, because the money supply has been expanded too far, we are in for a severe and painful shakeout. I personally hope that the situation does not deteriorate as far as they expect, and advise us to prepare for. I hope that they are wrong in their final prognosis, the depths to which our economy will slide. But I have considered the possibilities, and you should, too.

About This Book

This book limits itself to a narrower field of discussion than the more general works mentioned above. One specific investment and survival technique, opening and using a Swiss bank account, is explored in depth. In our past economic situation, a book on selecting the right mutual fund would have made sensible reading. In today's changing economy, a book on selecting a Swiss bank, and the right type of account in that bank, is far more pertinent.

To help in choosing a bank for your account, this book provides a unique feature—chapter 12 contains a listing of over 100 Swiss banks that accept accounts from overseas, the results of a survey conducted especially for this book. Correct addresses of the banks, the types of accounts they offer, and other data are given to simplify the selection process.

Swiss bank secrecy, one of the major differences between Swiss and American banks, is fully discussed. You will discover that privacy in banking matters is an obsession with the Swiss, and protected both by custom and by law. The limitations of secrecy, and its practical uses for Americans, are also explained.

As general background, the evolution of Switzerland as an international banking and financial center is also outlined. Swiss banks are unique in this world; if you are to use them successfully, you should know something about this uniqueness.

In an attempt to explain the utility of Swiss accounts, this book touches on many subjects. Regardless of the reasons for your interest in Swiss banks, you should become much more knowledgeable about a fascinating subject. And perhaps this book will convince you to take steps to protect your future by opening a bank account of your own in Switzerland.

2

Why Does an American Need a Swiss Bank Account?

UNTIL ABOUT 1970, Swiss bank secrecy was the feature that attracted private money to Switzerland from the United States. Naturally, strict banking privacy still has a definite appeal and its own uses. But lately, protecting the purchasing power of their savings from the ravages of inflation has become the primary motivation of most American account holders.

America's dollar is no longer a hard currency. Inflation has destroyed its reputation and much of its value. Once the most favored world currency, the dollar's worth and acceptability have declined markedly. Because of inflation, the dollar will no longer buy what it once would in the marketplaces of the world. As a result, the conversion rate of the dollar into stronger currencies has slipped drastically.

There is every indication that inflation will be with us indefinitely, recurring in waves. On each cycle, higher levels of inflation will be reached and the dollar will slip farther in value. As time passes, thrifty Americans will find that they will be able to buy less goods and services with their accumulated savings.

The dollar can also be expected to decline in relation to more favored currencies. It will take more and more dollars to buy a given amount of any of the harder currencies. The corollary of this, of course, is that a fixed amount of hard currency will gradually buy larger and larger quantities of the ever-cheaper dollars.

The worst effects of inflation can be avoided by practicing a sort of monetary judo, utilizing the dollar's weakening position in the foreign exchange market to offset its loss of domestic purchasing power. With a Swiss account, dollars can be converted to deposits in a hard currency. When needed at a later date, these deposits can be used to buy dollars again. If the exchange value of the dollar in relation to the hard currency has fallen in the interim, the hard currency deposits should then buy enough extra dollars to compensate for the lost purchasing power of the dollar.

Effect of Inflation on Savings

People save for their own reasons. They may build up their savings for security, the proverbial rainy day. They may save to achieve a dream, perhaps a vacation in Europe. Whatever the purpose, savings are postponed spending. Money that could be spent now is accumulated and held for future use.

Savings are essential but they are vulnerable to inflation. Inflation causes a gradual evaporation of the purchasing power of stored dollars; the value of each dollar decreases steadily in proportion to the rise in the general price level. When the savings are finally spent, the thrifty individual will find that his money will not buy as much as it would have at the time it was originally set aside.

Suppose a savings fund were started to satisfy a lifelong dream, a trip to Europe. A ten-day, all-inclusive package tour might now cost $1,000. With a 15 percent rate of inflation, next year the same trip might cost $1,150; two years from now, an identical package would be about $1,325.

If savings were put aside for future living expenses, during retirement perhaps, inflation could lead to a much lower standard of living than planned for. If inflation averages only 9 percent annually, five years from now it will take $15,380 to buy what $10,000 currently buys. After ten years of the same 9 percent inflation, $23,670 would be required to maintain the same modest way of life.

The basic problem is that money put aside as savings is not likely to earn enough interest to compensate for inflation. Interest rates are fixed at artificially low levels by government regulations. Savings accounts yield only 5 to 6 percent, and certificates of deposit commonly generate only $5^3/_4$ to $7^3/_4$ percent, depending upon their term. If inflation runs at a higher rate than the obtainable interest, a saver's buying power is steadily eaten away.

We tend to think of interest as a reward for thrift, a sort of bonus given us by the bank for being a responsible customer. In reality, interest is a service charge that we earn for letting someone else use our money. It is compensation for the temporary inability to spend our money as we please and for the element of risk inherent in every lending situation.

Ideally, savings should earn a return at least 3 to 5 percent greater than the existing rate of inflation. In 1974, the cost of living in the United States rose by 12.2 percent; for the last quarter of 1974, the figure was over 14 percent. To compensate for inflation, savings should have generated at least 16 to 18 percent during this period.

The Dollar Is a Soft Currency

Until 1971, the dollar was a hard currency, "as good as gold." On August 15 of that year, President Nixon decreed that, "temporarily," the United States would no longer convert dollars into gold for the central banks of other nations. Since these central banks were the only holders who could still exchange dollars for bullion, gold backing for the dollar was thus, for all practical purposes, eliminated.

Mr. Nixon, in effect, declared to the world that the United States was insolvent. We would no longer honor the claims against our national gold reserves that our paper dollars represented. We couldn't because there wasn't enough gold in the Treasury's vaults to redeem even the dollars held by foreigners.

What Happened to the Dollar?

Although Nixon was the chief executive who removed the last vestige of gold backing from the dollar, the decline of the American dollar cannot be totally blamed on him. His action was only one step in a process that took almost forty years. The downgrading of the dollar began in 1934, at the beginning of Franklin Roosevelt's long administration. The right of gold ownership was denied U.S. citizens, except for gold jewelry and certain collectible coins; gold certificates were withdrawn from circulation. Gold's official price was raised from $20.67 to $35 a troy ounce, a 40.9 percent devaluation of the dollar. However, Roosevelt allowed the dollar to remain convertible into gold on an intergovernmental basis at the new $35 rate.

After World War II, the American dollar emerged preeminent, the equal of gold. The currency most in demand, it became the great international money. Dollars and gold together formed the reserves that backed most national currencies. For a while, it seemed that the world would never get enough dollars.

By the late 1960s, though, there were more than enough dollars overseas. Foreign central banks were becoming reluctant to retain dollars in their reserves. They started to exercise their privilege to exchange these dollars for American gold. As early as 1968, the United States was redeeming dollars only begrudgingly. In that year, to remove some of the redemption pressure, an international two-tier gold market was established. The American Treasury still maintained a fixed $35 per ounce rate for central banks, but the price of gold was allowed to float freely on the private market. Expectations were that the price of gold would drop on the private side of the market, thereby making foreign governments less anxious to redeem their dollars at the official rate. Instead, the free market price of gold rose and redemption pressure increased.

The year 1971 was a bad one for the dollar. U.S. gold reserves totaled only $10 to $11 billion, but estimates of redeemable dollars in the hands of foreign governments ranged upward to $70 billion. This forced, in August, Nixon's suspension of the redemption of dollars for gold. In December, the dollar was officially devalued by 8 percent, from $35 per troy ounce of gold to $38 an ounce. Although dollars were no longer convertible, even by central banks, devaluations such as this served a purpose. The paper value of the national gold supply was increased, making the Treasury's books look better. Since, in 1971, the world was still on a system of fixed exchange rates, devaluation also lowered the value of the dollar in terms of other currencies, an improvement for trade purposes.

In February 1973, the U.S. government devalued again, for the second time in fourteen months. Gold moved up, and the dollar down, by about 11 percent, to $42.22 per ounce of gold. This was still the official figure in 1975, although the Treasury would not sell gold at this price since gold was trading at about $140 to $150 per ounce on the free market.

As significant as the moves of the American Treasury were the actions of other governments. As doubts arose abroad on the value of the dollar, other nations acted independently to protect themselves. In May 1971, Switzerland, West Germany, Austria, and the Netherlands cut their currencies loose from a fixed relationship with the dollar and allowed them to float upward.

Thus, even before the first official U.S. devaluation, these nations devalued the dollar on their own initiative. In December 1971, the Japanese revalued their yen in relation to the dollar, too. Even after the second official devaluation in 1973, other nations continued to revalue their currencies and devalue the dollar, unilaterally.

Most major currencies are now floating in relation to the dollar. The dollar is worth only what supply and demand dictate in the foreign exchange marketplace. Since the United States has removed the dollar's gold backing, its main supports have been the wisdom and effectiveness of our government. Not surprisingly, foreign governments and currency traders have less faith in our politicians than we do. It appears as though the dollar is in for a rough time for the indefinite future.

The U.S. dollar automatically and immediately became a "soft currency" when President Nixon announced its inconvertibility in August 1971. Since then, over fifteen other currencies have increased in value by more than 10 percent in relation to the dollar. Because of inflationary trends in their economies, however, not all of these currencies offer the prospect of continued appreciation.

The most desirable hard currencies in the world today are those of Switzerland, the Netherlands, and Austria. Swiss francs, Dutch guilders, and Austrian schillings all offer Americans protection from the ills of the dollar. All are currencies of smaller, tough-minded, conservatively governed countries that have maintained strong gold backing for their monies. All have the potential and the reasonable expectation of rising further in value against the dollar.

What Is Inflation?

For the last few years, we have been bombarded with economic news and opinion. Inflation has become a staple of the media. Everyone talks glibly about inflation, and we all recognize the pain in the pocketbook, but what is inflation, really? And what are its causes?

At one time, President Gerald Ford described inflation as "public enemy No. 1." His first official business, two hours after he took the oath of office on August 9, 1974, was to meet with his economic advisers on the inflation problem. Even though, in 1975, his main efforts were devoted to battling recession and plotting his reelection strategy, he seemed to realize that inflation remains the most serious long-term threat to the American economy.

William Simon, current Secretary of the Treasury, in a speech before the Joint Economic Committee of Congress in 1974, summed up the popular opinion of inflation nicely: "Domestically this has become the dominant, overriding—almost overwhelming—fact of economic life. Americans are experiencing their first substantial siege of rapid peacetime inflation. It is a new and most unwelcome experience. They do not understand where double-digit inflation came from and they lack confidence that their government will be able to get the situation under control."

Most Americans would concur. They have seen rising prices wreck their budget plans. The middle-aged and the retired have begun to realize that inflation is robbing them of their savings, the results of a lifetime of hard work. Younger people wonder when they will be able to afford any savings at all. All age groups have seen their expectations of a gradual improvement in their living standards fade.

Inflation is commonly considered to be a period of rapidly rising prices. This is because frequent price increases are the most obvious symptom of inflation. However, there are other important components of inflation that, because they are hidden, are more insidious over the long run.

One old and popular explanation of inflation is "too much

money chasing too few goods.'' A more precise, if less pictur-esque, definition would be: ''Inflation is an economic condition characterized by an excessive increase in the money supply in relation to the supply of goods available, by constant price increases, and by a resultant decrease in the value of the money in use.''

Too Much Money

Individuals seldom have too much money but economies often do, and when they do they suffer from attacks of inflation. People who eat too much of their favorite foods will suffer from indigestion; in this sense, we could also describe inflation as ''monetary indigestion.''

Inflation starts when there is too large a national ''money supply,'' too much money in an economy in relation to the available stock of goods and services. The money supply is the total amount of money available for spending within an econ-omy. It consists of the currency in circulation plus all the de-mand deposits in banks. Currency in circulation is simply all the paper money and coins in the hands of the public. Demand de-posits include both checking account balances and those savings deposits that are freely available, without withdrawal restric-tions.

The size of a nation's money supply is critical; both too little or too much money can cause difficulties. There must be enough money in circulation to facilitate normal business trans-actions, or trade will slow down and the economy suffer. Barter economies, with an insufficient supply of an accepted medium of exchange, are slow-moving economies indeed.

Economists generally agree that, as a rule of thumb, the money supply should grow at about the same rate as the econ-omy. If the gross national product increases by 3 percent in a given year, the supply of money should expand by 3 percent, too. Money is the lubricant of an economy; a machine needs oil to run efficiently, and normal trade requires an adequate money supply. But just as too much grease can cause an intricate piece of machinery to malfunction, too much money can cause problems in an economy.

To illustrate what happens when the money supply expands too fast or too far let us consider the example of a mining boom town, in the far north, isolated during the winter months but stocked with a fair supply of goods. Gold and gold dust are the usual medium of exchange. As the winter grinds along, the mines continue to produce gold, but no more supplies reach the snowbound town. Miners' pokes become heavier with gold as the inventories of the stores and the bars begin to thin out. Competition for necessities and pleasures will drive prices up. The price of meals, pants, whiskey, and bar girls will skyrocket. The economy of the isolated settlement will suffer from inflation until spring, when the thaw will allow goods to move in and gold to be shipped out.

What Is Money?

Money is commonly considered to be the medium of exchange. We think of it as the paper bills in our wallets, "money in our pocket," or the balance in our bank accounts, "money in the bank." Money is our paycheck, a reward for our work; money is a credit voucher, exchangeable for goods or for the services of our fellow citizens. Money is also a store of value, our claim against the future.

Certainly money is one of mankind's greatest inventions, one of the "great leaps forward." Its use allowed trade to expand beyond the limitations of barter, and man to begin to move down the long road of economic development. The use of money was a great advance over fifty baskets of grain for a horse, twenty-seven cows for a piece of land, or a hammer for three lengths of wool and a bag of onions.

Many things have been used as money. Peter Minuet bought all 31.2 square miles of Manhattan Island from the Indians for sixty guilders' worth of wampum, a shell-bead money. Copper ingots, leather hides, and cigarettes have all been acceptable as standards of value in other places and other times. Acceptability as a standard of value is the key thought; money is whatever is commonly accepted as a standard interchange commodity in trade. The desirability of a commodity as a money depends on its characteristics. Whatever is used as money should be relatively scarce, durable, portable, compact, easily stored, divisible into smaller units, and have a use apart from its use as money. If it is scarce enough, and coveted for its other uses, a monetary commodity has an "intrinsic value" quite separate from its monetary value. If its acceptability in its role as money declines, the commodity will retain some value because of its alternate uses.

In the history of our planet, only two substances, gold and silver, have ever been universally accepted as money. No one knows when these precious metals were first used to facilitate trade, although ancient rulers obviously recognized the uses of gold and the value of standardized coinage; gold was coined in uniform weights in Egypt as early as 3500 B.C. Some examples of these ancient mintages survive today in collections, and they still have value, if only as curiosities.

Gold is the only real money, the only standard of exchange valued as highly and accepted as readily today as it has been throughout the ages. Silver has dropped in status and value compared to gold because of the discovery of large silver deposits in the last century. Paper money is a comparatively recent innovation, with a checkered past of only 200 years or so.

It would be an interesting experiment to venture back into ancient times armed with a supply of gold coins and any modern paper currency. Imagine time-traveling to Ancient Rome with a bag of South African Krugerrand gold pieces and a pocketful of American dollar bills. The results are certainly predictable. You could purchase some interesting souvenirs with the gold, perhaps a comely slave girl or two. The currency would only provoke shrugs at best.

Paper Money

Paper currency originated as warehouse receipts for stored gold. Gold in larger quantities is heavy and clearly a temptation to thieves. For reasons of prudence and convenience, it was often left in safe storage with reputable merchants. It was soon discovered that the receipts the merchants gave for the gold could be conveniently used as substitutes for the actual gold. The owner of a storage receipt could claim physical possession of the gold, or he could use the receipt in trade.

The merchants who stored gold for others eventually evolved into specialists, the first bankers. One of their innovations was to issue receipts in smaller, uniform denominations, which was to the receipt holders' benefit. Another innovation, to the bankers' benefit, was to issue receipts for more gold than was actually in their possession. This worked because it had been discovered that all receipt holders were unlikely to claim their gold at the same time. The additional receipts were as acceptable in trade as the original receipts as long as there was enough gold backing to cover the claims that were actually presented for redemption. Occasionally the scheme failed, when doubts arose and too many claims were presented at one time. If not enough gold was on hand to satisfy the demand, the issuing bank collapsed.

Paper currency is only a "money substitute." Its sole advantage over gold is its lighter weight; paper is certainly not a scarce commodity, and it has little intrinsic value. Paper money is as good as gold only when it is convertible into gold upon demand. It can still be safely used, even if not redeemable for gold, if a fixed and known relationship is maintained between the gold backing and the amount of currency issued on the basis of this gold. Paper currency becomes dangerous when it is not backed by gold; instead of a "gold standard," an economy is then on a "paper standard." Once unhindered by the requirement that its product be issued only in quantities bearing some relationship to its gold supply, the issuing agency, be it bank or government, can then usually find reasons to print and distribute ever-increasing amounts of its paper currency.

Governments and Inflation

The relationship between governments and inflation is a simple one: *governments cause inflation*. At least in our modern times they do. Governments have achieved a monopoly on the issuance of money, and when they create too large a money supply, inflation results.

Admittedly, history records inflations that do not fit this pattern. However, these economic curiosities occurred before paper money came into common use. Epidemics sometimes eliminated large portions of a population, leaving the money supply, largely gold and silver coins, intact and too large for the diminished economy. As a result, prices and wages rose rapidly until a new equilibrium was reached. The Black Death of the Middle Ages, when bubonic plague almost halved Europe's population, is an example. Drastic increases in the supply of gold or silver, resulting from either the discovery of new deposits or conquest, have also caused inflation. Spain's seizure and looting of the New World is a classic case. When the Inca and Aztec gold arrived in Spain, the most serious result was a raging inflation. Spain went into a state of national shock from which it is only now emerging, centuries later.

Such accidents of nature or of conquest aside, inflation is caused by governments. Sooner or later, all governments inflate; paper money makes it easy. The scenario consistently follows the same pattern. In the interest of stability and efficiency, the government takes over as the sole issuer of currency. Gradually, it changes the rules, freeing itself from the constraints of common sense. In the United States, a minimum of 35 percent gold backing was once required for Federal Reserve certificates in circulation; in 1945, this gold reserve requirement was lowered to 25 percent; and finally, in 1968, the legal necessity to back Federal Reserve banknotes with gold was totally eliminated.

Politicians are elected to office on the basis of their promises to the electorate. Basically, they offer increased prosperity and additional government benefits to the masses in exchange for votes. To be elected, they must outdo the promises of their opponents; to be reelected, they must make good their own campaign promises; government programs must be enacted; the government must spend.

The problem is that tax revenues can seldom be stretched far enough to pay for all the projects desired. A government must then resort to deficit financing, spending more than it collects in taxes. Whether or not there is enough money to cover the federal expenditures, the government must pay for its programs. Bureaucrats, contractors, suppliers, subsidy recipients, and the elected legislators themselves all want money, not government promises. The ultimate solution is to manufacture money to pay the government's bills.

"Turning on the printing presses" is a common description of the process. In an underdeveloped economy, without checking accounts, it would actually be done that way. New paper certificates would be printed, and the central government would pay everyone with bundles of fresh paper currency.

In developed nations, the process is not that simple, although the consequences are the same. In the United States, most of the economy's money supply exists only as bank deposits; only about 25 percent of our primary money supply is in the form of circulating banknotes or coins. When the American government creates new money, it is pumped into the economy in the form of government checks. This process is handled through the Federal Reserve System, this nation's central bank.

Financing Budget Deficits

A federal budget deficit can be financed in a variety of ways. The workings of the Treasury and the Federal Reserve are so intricate that it would take a book totally devoted to the subject to explain the ramifications of all the alternate methods available. Basically, though, the government can borrow the money or it can create the money. Often it does both at the same time.

The Treasury borrows by issuing several types of interest-bearing paper for both short and long terms. Variously called bonds, bills, notes, or certificates, depending on their size and due dates, these obligations are sold to banks and other investors through the Federal Reserve System. Proceeds from these issues are credited to the Treasury's account with the Federal Reserve; checks are then written against these borrowed funds to help pay the government's operating expenses.

When the federal government's budget deficit is relatively low, as in 1970 when the deficit was only $2.8 billion, this financing method suffices. Funds are readily available on the money market to buy the federal paper. When the amount to be raised is huge, as it tends to be, the nation's banks and institutional investors often cannot easily supply the necessary funds.

The Treasury, in its quest for money, crowds private business out of the money markets; the deficit financing effort tends to absorb funds needed to support normal business activity. In years such as 1968, when the budget shortfall was $25.2 billion, or fiscal 1976, when preliminary estimates put the expected budget deficit at $68.8 billion, other methods of financing are obviously needed.

Although the need is obvious, the methods used are not. The Treasury does not simply have the Federal Reserve print and issue more paper money. Neither does the Federal Reserve buy the government's securities directly. The problem is handled in a more roundabout manner.

Member banks are required to maintain reserve accounts with the Federal Reserve System. These required reserves are set as a percentage of a bank's average deposits, depending on the type of deposit, the class of bank, and the goals of the Federal Reserve. For example, the Fed may set the reserve requirement for checking deposits in a bank located in a metropolitan area at anywhere between 10 percent and 22 percent. However, member banks also have the privilege of borrowing additional reserves from the Federal Reserve when needed. As their reserves increase, they may make additional loans based on any excess in their reserve accounts.

When the Treasury goes to market to seek funds to pay for large budget shortfalls, the nation's banking system is stretched to capacity. The banks must continue to service their regular customers with working capital, inventory, and expansion loans, or the economy will suffer. At the same time, there is heavy pressure to buy the Treasury's offerings. At such times, the Federal Reserve often acts to reduce the strain on the banks by increasing the money supply. Banks are allowed, even encouraged, to borrow funds from the Reserve at what amounts to discount prices. Reserve requirements may also be lowered, freeing funds for the banks to use to make more loans, and to buy the government's securities.

The Federal Reserve System not only sells Treasury obligations, it constantly buys them. Treasury paper is issued in many forms; some issues mature in a few weeks or months, while on others the principal is not due for ten or twenty years. Matured issues are redeemed by the Federal Reserve, but others are bought and held for the Fed's own account. Primarily, this is done to support the market for Treasury securities; the Federal Reserve buys when no one else is willing or able, to protect the market for future issues. However, as the Fed absorbs and pays for surplus Treasury paper, it is also pumping newly created money into the economy. In 1973, the Federal Reserve was holding $80.4 billion in U.S. government obligations, which it counted among its own assets.

In the same year, other agencies of the federal government were holding $125.4 billion in federal securities in their own accounts. The Social Security Old Age and Survivors' Trust Fund, just one of many such funds, was carrying $36.2 billion in U.S. securities on its books. These securities were its major assets; only $291 million was kept in cash deposits. This illustrates yet another way the federal deficit is funded; taxes collected for special purposes such as Social Security are diverted to help meet more immediate general operating deficits.

All of these Treasury securities represent the national debt, which is seldom reduced but only grows and grows. As older series of Treasury obligations reach maturity, they are ''rolled over.'' Their redemption is paid for with the proceeds of newer issues. At the end of fiscal 1973, the public debt had reached $458.1 billion. It has grown since then and will continue to grow by the amount of the annual deficits.

All this ''new money,'' created through the banking system and the Federal Reserve, not only finances the public debt; it is the major source of inflationary pressure in our economy. The government increases the money supply but the supply of goods and services does not increase proportionately. The "new" money competes with the "old" for what is available. Inflation results from a classic "too much money, too few goods" situation.

Inflation Is a Tax

Deficit financing and the inflation it causes may be viewed as an extension of the government's taxing power.

Tax collectors and politicians everywhere recognize that there are limits beyond which a government dares not go in extracting money from its subjects. The government that ignores these limits courts trouble for itself, in the form of rebellion, tax revolt, or defeat at the polls. But politicians are nothing if not shrewd judges of what the public will bear. Rather than push taxes past the resistance point, they resort to budget deficits. Creating money to pay for government expenditures, even though it causes inflation, is much more subtle than collecting additional taxes. Inflation is less direct, its effects are not immediately apparent; elected officials seem to feel that deficit financing is a painless tax, painless at least for them.

Every government must have the ability to raise funds if it is to function at all. Taxes are recognized, if only grudgingly, as a fact of life by citizens of all nations. Resentment builds, though, when taxes become a burden on the economy, when too much is taken by the government and too little is left to the taxpayers. There seems to be a natural law involved. Experts on tax administration have noted that tax evasion becomes much more common when tax levels exceed 30 percent. In the United States, taxes are now just past that point; federal, state, and local authorities together tax away about one-third of the gross national product.

Raising taxes to pay for unpopular causes is another source of potential trouble. Governments have always had difficulty paying for wars, even the popular ones, because they instinctively have hesitated to raise taxes to the necessary levels. Wars that lack popular support make the politicians even more cautious about tax increases.

Roots of the Current Inflation

The obvious example of an unpopular cause is the Vietnamese war. Our late, great adventure in Indochina is also the primary cause of the "Great Inflation" of 1973–1975. In the mid-1960s, as the conflict accelerated and American troop commitments rose sharply, war costs skyrocketed. By 1969, defense expenditures were running $25 to $30 billion a year higher than before U.S ground forces were committed on a large scale.

The booming American economy should have been able to pay the extra costs without undue strain. However, President Johnson had another pet project, his populist "Great Society" programs, designed to placate the minorities and insure Johnson's place in history. The price of both foreign and domestic pacification was more than the federal budget could bear. As early as 1966, the Council of Economic Advisors warned that taxes must be raised. Hesitant in the face of widespread and violent opposition to the undeclared war, Congress and the president stalled. When a 10 percent tax surcharge was finally imposed a year and half later, in 1968, it was already too late and the tax increase too small. The seeds of serious inflation had already been planted in the American economy.

What the total bill for our crusade in Southeast Asia will be, no one yet knows. Almost certainly the cost will at least equal that of our last global war, World War II. The Veteran's Administration alone will be paying Vietnam-era benefits for the next fifty years or more. However, the damage to the economy can be measured. Approximately half the direct costs of the war were paid for by deficits; between 1965 and 1972, the national debt rose by $110 billion, while the money supply increased by $225 billion, a full 74 percent.

By 1969, inflation was running over 6 percent, up from about 2 percent in 1965. Attempts to control it led to the recession of 1969–1970. After President Johnson left office, Nixon's administration attempted to stimulate the economy, then lost control again. Mismanagement, and off-again, on-again price controls only aggravated the problem. By 1974, the economy was suffering from a previously unobserved economic disease, a deep recession, the worst since the 1930s, coupled with Latin American style double-digit inflation. The attending economists were forced to coin a new term, *stagflation,* to classify the phenomena of an inflationary recession.

Recession and Depression

Nothing lasts forever, not even prosperity. Since the Industrial Revolution, boom periods have always been followed by depressions.

America's economy has often been called depression-proof. Maybe, but it depends on what is meant by depression. Formerly, any slackening of business activity or economic growth was termed a depression. The catastrophic slump of the 1930s, however, colored our understanding of the word *depression.* Since then, no American official has dared to use *depression* to describe the periodic low points of the business cycle. Instead, the less menacing word *recession* has become popular. In current usage, a recession is a mild depression, and a depression is a severe recession.

Recession and depression are essentially degrees of the same thing, the natural cure for an overheated economy. Periodically, during an extended period of prosperity, business becomes over-confident and expands too far. In a free market economy, a recession quickly corrects these excesses and the accompanying inflation of an overextended boom. After the economy is shaken down, and the fat trimmed from it, the turnaround comes again in short order. On the whole, after a corrective recession the economy is sounder because of the unhealthy growth, the non-essential and ill-conceived enterprises, that have been excised from it.

The United States, of course, does not have a free market economy. In America today, free enterprise coexists with the welfare state. The government interferes with economic pro-cesses to such an extent that the natural corrective forces of a recession are not allowed free play. To cite just one example, minimum-wage laws place a floor under labor costs. Since sal-aries cannot be adjusted downward to help lower production costs and prices, the labor force must be cut instead, adding to the unemployment roles. Admittedly some legislation, the un-employment compensation laws being a prominent example, serves to dampen the worst effects of a slump. But at the same time such laws also dampen the speed of a rebound from a recession.

How a Swiss Account Protects

There are hard currencies and there are soft currencies. "Hard" and "soft" are only labels, reflecting the accumulated experience of foreign currency traders. The demand for some currencies is "soft" because they are in excessive supply, with more potential sellers than buyers; the consensus of market opinion is that their future price movement will be downward. Other currencies are "hard," by contrast, because the demand for them is usually stronger than the supply; their general price trend is upward. The Swiss franc is hard, and the U.S. dollar, unfortunately, soft.

In this basic difference between the hard franc and the soft dollar lies protection from inflation. Swiss bank accounts are normally denominated in Swiss francs. Liquid assets held as soft dollars are converted to hard currency assets when they are transferred to a Swiss account. Since the value of a hard currency tends to move in the opposite direction to soft currency values, an inflation hedge is created.

In the past few years, this hedge has worked very well indeed for those Americans prudent enough to maintain a Swiss account. As inflation rose from an annual 3 percent in the mid-1960s to 8.8 percent in 1973 and 12 percent in 1974, the value of Swiss franc climbed too.

From 1949 to 1969, the exchange rate between the Swiss franc and the Yankee dollar was stable, maintained within narrow fixed limits. For years, a Swiss franc cost about US$0.2320, and a dollar bought 4.28 to 4.32 francs. After May 1971, when the Swiss allowed their currency to float, this relationship started to change. By mid-1973, the price of the Swiss franc had risen to the US$0.35 range; a dollar could be exchanged for only 2.85 francs. In February 1975, the franc reached a temporary peak of US$0.4185, with the dollar then valued at a scant 2.39 Swiss francs.

As an example of just how well Swiss francs have worked as a hedge against inflation, let us consider the following example. Suppose that sometime in late 1970 US$10,000 was placed in a Swiss bank account. The dollars, when converted, would have created a deposit of 43,100 Swiss francs, at 4.31 francs to the dollar. During the next four years, the francs were left on deposit as price levels in the United States rose by 30 percent. By the end of December 1974, the exchange price of a franc had floated up to US$0.3950, or 2.53 Swiss francs per dollar.

At this point, the 43,100 francs on deposit would buy US$17,025 in American money, 70 percent more dollars than were originally transferred to Switzerland, without even considering the interest earned on the account. Typically, the franc deposit would also have earned at least 3½ percent, compounded annually or semiannually, in a "deposit" account. Earned interest, minus a special Swiss withholding tax on interest (explained in chapter 8), would have added another 4,381 francs, or US$1,728, to the final account balance. Calculated in francs, this interest increment would be 10 percent. Computed in dollars, though, accumulated interest added another 17.28 percent, because the francs earned as interest also benefited from the increase in exchange values.

Swiss francs were much more than a successful hedge. Disregarding interest, the 70 percent appreciation from changes in the exchange rates would have more than made up for the rise in price levels in our dollar economy. Those Americans who took advantage of the opportunity actually made a profit on their money, the difference between the 70 percent increase in dollar value of the franc and the four-year climb in the U.S. inflation rate. Even those Americans who recognized the advantages of hard currency accounts much later have generally made out very well. The dollar value of a Swiss franc account opened as late as January 1974 would have grown by 13.1 percent by the end of 1974, again without considering interest.

Although the value of the franc in relation to the dollar has moved upward drastically over the last few years, the weekly and monthly progression has not always been smooth. The exchange rate tends to move upward in spurts, and franc prices have sometimes dipped as the dollar temporarily regained lost ground. There were also long periods when the dollar–franc rate remained rather stable. Most of the price movement in 1974 came late in the year; in fact, an account opened in late September would have done almost as well as one opened in early January, managing a 12.2 percent gain for three months against 13.1 percent for the full year.

Although accounts in a Swiss bank are usually denominated in Swiss francs, it is possible to open accounts in just about any convertible currency. Swiss francs have performed well, but holders of other hard currencies have made their gains, too. Dutch guilders have appreciated by over 40 percent in the last four years, and Belgian francs by about 35 percent. The West German deutsche mark has also moved ahead by approximately 50 percent at the expense of the American dollar.

How Much to Keep in Switzerland?

Financial survival is the name of the game, the main reason for a hard currency account in Switzerland. Preserving the purchasing power of current assets takes precedence over attempts to make a profit. Any gains achieved in hard currencies, as the exchange rate of the dollar slips, should not be thought of as a "profit" in the normal sense. Depositors should consider themselves fortunate if their hard currency deposits increase in value fast enough to offset the rate of inflation in this country. Sometimes, of course, as happened over the last few years, the exchange rate will move ahead faster than the rate of inflation, producing a bonus "profit."

Swiss banks pay interest, of course, on savings-type accounts. Later in this book, when the reader is considering the interest rates on specific account types, he must be careful to maintain his perspective. It may very well be possible to obtain 9 percent interest on a time deposit in a Mexican bank, or a point or two more interest at a hometown bank. But the Mexican peso is as soft as the U.S. dollar, locked in an unchanging ratio with the dollar, with no possibility of exchange rate gains to offset inflation. The gain in interest becomes insignificant when measured against the loss of purchasing power dollars, and dollar-pegged currencies will suffer when U.S. inflation runs 10 percent, 15 percent, or more.

A Swiss account should be thought of primarily as a hedging operation. A hedge is an investment made to counterbalance the risk of another investment. With a hedge, an investor is betting both ways; if either investment shows a loss, the other posts an equal gain. As dollars fall, the Swiss franc rises; and, of course, the hedge works in reverse, if dollars rise at the expense of Swiss francs. Once the principle of hedging is understood, consideration can be given to the size of the amount to be held in a hard currency account.

To take full advantage of a hedge, both sides of the investment should be balanced. For this reason, a good starting point would be to consider dividing the available liquid assets equally between "hard" and "soft" investments, keeping approximately half in dollar-denominated investments and placing the rest in hard currency deposits or related inflation hedges. Liquid assets are those that can be converted quickly to cash or its equivalent, and spent when the need arises. They include cash, checking and savings account balances, certificates of deposit, Treasury certificates and savings bonds, and, of course, common stocks and bonds. Gold and silver coins, gold bullion, and gold mining shares are liquid assets, too, but they are "hard" investments because their value tends to move in opposition to the dollar's.

It is neither practical nor convenient to put all of one's funds into a Swiss account. Of necessity, some money must be retained in this country, to meet routine expenses, and as a reserve fund to meet contingencies that must be paid for on short notice. In deciding what balance between hard and soft investments to establish, careful consideration must be given to personal circumstances. What are the sources of personal or family income, and how secure are they? What are anticipated needs and plans for the future? How large an investment fund and an emergency reserve have been accumulated over the years?

To function adequately as an inflation hedge, however, a significant portion of total liquid assets must be committed to hard currency or gold-related investments. If only 10 percent of all available liquid assets were allotted to hard investments, perhaps in Swiss franc deposits, only an equivalent amount of the remaining dollar-denominated investments would be covered by the hedge. With only a 10 percent hedge, 80 percent of total assets would be unprotected from a loss of buying power in the event of more inflation. The closer the balance of investments, the more conservative the hedging operation.

But regardless of all other considerations, an individual should distribute his investments in a way that makes him feel comfortable. One depositor might feel secure with 75 percent of his available funds in hard currency deposits, because he believes strongly that the dollar will get progressively weaker. Another might feel exposed if he transferred over 25 percent of his money to Switzerland. Each reader will have to make his own decisions, but hopefully this book will provide enough information to make the decision easier.

When to Bring Your Money Back

There are two simple answers to the question of when to transfer your money back from Switzerland: (1) when you need it, and (2) when it's safe.

Funds deposited in Switzerland can be drawn upon as needed. For example, if money were needed to pay a large medical bill, and the family's emergency savings were kept in Swiss francs, there should be no hesitation to use what's needed. After all, the funds are there to pay for unforeseen crises. In the meantime, the savings have been safer than if kept in dollar deposits.

Retirees and others who find it necessary to live off their accumulated capital can arrange to draw upon their Swiss deposits on a regular basis. A Swiss bank can be instructed to send a fixed sum, say $1,000, each month for living expenses, while the bulk of the capital remains in Switzerland, its purchasing power protected from the dry rot of dollar inflation. Some types of Swiss accounts have restrictions on the amounts that can be withdrawn without notice; these limitations are discussed in detail in chapter 9. Forewarned, and taking anticipated needs into consideration, a depositor can choose an account type compatible with his access needs.

The second answer, "when it's safe," deserves a fuller explanation. "Safe" means when the American economy and the foreign exchange rate of the dollar have stabilized, when the threat of continued high inflation recedes, and when the dollar's convertibility into gold is restored, at least for foreign central banks. It may be a long time before these conditions come to pass. The world economy is in a period of adjustment that may last until the end of this century. There is little prospect that the U.S. dollar will soon become a hard currency again; the Treasury remains adamantly antigold and anticonvertibility. The U.S. government shows no sign of living within its means, so there will be more heavy budget deficits and more inflation. It will probably take an economic lesson of the proportions of the Great Depression to trigger the necessary reforms.

What Lies Ahead?

It is not necessary to be either a prophet or an economist to predict what the economy will be like over the next few years.

The seeds of our economic future are already in the ground; eventually, after they sprout and the crop matures, we will all eat what big government has planted. It is only necessary to know the type of seed to know the future.

One of the characteristics of a democracy is that there is no central direction; a consensus is arrived at only slowly, if at all. Fortunately, the debate over what economic policy to follow, the argument on what type of seeds to plant, is carried on publicly. In mid-1975, as the economy begins to come out of the latest recession, Congress and the executive branch are controlled by different political parties. President Ford and his Republican administration seem to view inflation as the major threat; they claim to prefer a course of monetary and fiscal restraint, holding federal spending and the money supply down even at the price of a slower recovery. The Democrats who control Congress, on the other hand, want to stimulate the economy as quickly as possible to provide jobs for unemployed voters at any cost. The result is a lack of direction, an indecisiveness, that is destroying America's economy.

As of now, last year's crop has not yet ripened. In fiscal 1975, the budget year that ended on June 30, 1975, big government planted a deficit of $44.2 billion, the largest *peacetime* budget deficit ever. As this is being written, the planting for fiscal 1976 has just begun. A budget deficit of $68.8 billion has been predicted; President Ford would like to hold it to $60 billion, but the director of the Office of Management and Budget, James T. Lynn, has warned that congressional spending programs now being considered could drive the 1976 federal deficit up to a whopping $88 billion. Not until the end of the fiscal year will we know the true figure. Regardless, it will certainly be the largest deficit in our 200-year national existence; the prior record was a deficit of $53.8 billion in 1943, at the peak of World War II spending.

These two huge budget shortfalls, for 1975 and 1976, are

being planted in a fertile field, an economy that has just produced a record crop of inflation. The leftovers from the past harvest are still with us; according to most estimates, inflation for 1975 will average at least 7 to 8 percent. Unemployment is still holding at about 9 percent nationally, and, at the best, is only expected to decline to 5 percent by 1980.

What lies ahead for 1976 and 1977 is already fairly obvious. By early 1976, business activity will be showing definite signs of improvement. The increase in the money supply caused by the $44.2 billion deficit financing of fiscal 1975 will cause the rate of inflation to begin to climb again; inflation will probably be running at 10 to 15 percent by the end of 1976. In an election year, the pickup in business activity will be good news for the politicians, and the renewal of double-digit inflation, very bad news.

In 1977, inflation can be expected to reach new highs, with the average rate probably moving up from the 10 to 15 percent range to a faster 15 to 20 percent later in the year. The expansion of the money supply, caused by the earlier $60 to $80 billion budget shortage, will make this almost inevitable. By mid-1977, the economy will begin to show definite symptoms of distress again, as inflation squeezes business profits, shrinks consumer buying power still further, and adds to the ranks of the unemployed. As inflation begins to really roar, the government will attempt to regulate it out of existence, perhaps with wage and price controls, certainly with a tighter monetary policy.

By 1978, the U.S. economy will be in trouble, in the really deep water; a rate of inflation from 20 to 25 percent is a definite possibility. Projecting this far ahead is tricky because a lot depends on how the government reacts to the problems of 1976 and 1977. If federal spending is cut, it may trigger a recession. If not, and there is another huge deficit for fiscal 1977 (Oct. 1976 to Sept. 1977), inflation will cripple the economy. (The

Office of Management and Budget has already predicted that the deficit for fiscal 1977 will be somewhere between $34 and $80 billion, depending upon what programs Congress enacts during fiscal 1976.) Looking ahead from 1975, a recession would seem to be the main event scheduled for 1978, except that when it comes it will be an unmistakable depression. Unemployment will rise from a probable 1976–1977 national average of 7 to 8 percent to new highs of 10 to 15 percent, if a downturn comes in 1978.

If such predictions as these are not pleasant to read, neither are they a pleasure to make. It would cause this writer little pain if they were 100 percent wrong, if the federal government would suddenly come to its collective senses and restrain itself from interfering with the natural strength of our economy. However, to expect this to happen within the next two or three years is to be unduly optimistic. At best, the reader can hope that the above projections are only partially right, that inflation and unemployment reach only half the levels predicted.

Hyperinflation

Depressing as is this scenario of renewed double-digit inflation and another bad recession, there is an even gloomier prospect. If the federal government panics, and tries to spend its way out of a future depression, there is a fair possibility that runaway or hyperinflation may be triggered. "Runaway" inflation is Latin American style inflation, with purchasing power being lost at a 25 or 40 or 75 percent annual rate. "Hyperinflation" is three- or four-digit inflation, running 150 or 600 or 1,400 percent annually; it is the ultimate destroyer of economic confidence, of currencies, of the middle class, and of governments.

Deficit spending to prime the economic pump and to stimulate business activity is an established government tactic. In a traditional depression, when an economic turndown and high unemployment rates are accompanied by a drop in price levels, an increase in government spending may help; the inflation it causes will likely be mild, a small price to pay for a bit of prosperity. The danger is that our economic slowdowns are now "inflationary recessions," featuring high levels of unemployment coupled with double-digit inflation. Pumping huge budget deficits into an already inflated economy may put more people back to work, but it is also like pouring gasoline onto a fire; inflation is likely to explode with new vigor.

Runaway inflation could become chronic if it became institutionalized. If the idea of a more or less permanent state of inflation became widely accepted by the public, private attempts to mitigate the worst effects of inflation would lead to automatic compensators being built into the economy. Wage and raw material contracts would be "indexed," so that payments routinely increased as general price levels rose. If such practices became widespread, they could be a source of continual pressure, causing inflation to spiral endlessly upward upon itself.

As runaway inflation progressed, there would be a need for an ever-larger money supply, because of the greater sums involved in routine trade. If additional liquidity, more money, were not supplied by the Federal Reserve and the banking system, it would tend to choke off the economy, probably quickly causing a serious depression. If the money supply were enlarged enough to facilitate trade at the new price levels, the new money would, in itself, add more fuel to the inflationary fires.

As runaway inflation progresses, with price increases running at perhaps 50 to 70 percent, industries providing essential services, such as the utilities, and even state and local governments would be forced to the brink of bankruptcy by rising costs. In such a situation, the national government would be asked to intervene, to finance their survival. In a sort of foretaste of possible future events, the U.S. government has already been approached in at least two cases. Special legislation was passed to enable the federal government to guarantee loans for the Lockheed Aircraft Corporation; New York City was initially turned down when it sought $1 billion in aid from Washington. But if the nation were threatened with massive trauma from the simultaneous financial collapse under the weight of inflation of important segments of the economy, such as the banking system or the network of local governments, Congress would likely respond very quickly with therapeutic infusions of newly created money. Conceivably, such a last-ditch effort could pump hundreds of billions into the economy within a very short period, doubling, even tripling the money supply within a year or so.

Runaway inflation is bad enough, but hyperinflation is worse. We have already had one short and very mild burst of runaway inflation, in the last quarter of 1974, when retail prices were being increased every month of two; in the supermarkets it was common to find new price labels covering the old. When hyperinflation strikes, money depreciates so rapidly that merchants are forced to mark their prices up weekly, even daily. In the last stages of hyperinflation, there is a mad scramble to buy something, anything of value, before even more purchasing power is lost. Eventually, a hyperinflated currency becomes completely worthless, when people are no longer willing to accept paper money in trade; barter becomes common until a new currency is substituted for the old.

What is the likelihood of America's economy being stricken with runaway inflation or hyperinflation? It is difficult to say, but I would make a guess that there is at least a 30 percent chance of a serious outbreak of runaway inflation, at a 40 to 50 percent rate or more, in the coming ten years, after one of the next two downturns of the business cycle. Hyperinflation is far less likely, though not impossible. A reasonable guesstimate would place the odds at 5 percent or less for its occurrence within ten years. However, the possibility that our currency will be revalued and replaced within fifteen to twenty years is much higher. It does not take hyperinflation, three-digit inflation, to destroy a currency's value; several years of 10 to 15 percent inflation, or a few years at a 25 to 50 percent rate can do the job, too. When inflation has driven the dollar to the point where a loaf of bread costs $12.50, an average worker is paid $4,000 a week, and $500 bills are common pocket money, a new currency can be expected. A revaluation at this point might readjust value so that twenty old dollars would equal one new dollar, bringing bread back to sixty-three cents a loaf and a worker's salary to $200 again.

Future Swiss Franc Values

Obviously, no matter how accurate the prior predictions, or whether or not hyperinflation ever destroys the dollar, some means of protecting the value of reserve assets is still needed. There are alternatives to hard currency hedges, of course, the most notable being gold, but they are outside the scope of this book.

How much protection will hard currencies offer against inflation in the future? Swiss francs and a few others have proven effective so far, but how will they fare over the long term or during the next few years?

Over the long term, the ultimate value of the dollar in relation to other currencies will be determined primarily by its gold backing. It is possible to estimate the potential appreciation of another currency against the dollar by comparing the available gold reserves of the two currencies against the amount of the currencies in circulation.

As of August 20, 1975, the United States' gold stock stood at

$11.6 billion and its money supply (currency plus demand deposits) at $294.8 billion; thus the dollar's gold backing was 3.93 percent. In contrast, the Swiss franc was backed by gold at slightly over 20 percent, the Austrian schilling and Dutch guilder by about 15 percent, and the German mark by roughly 10 percent.

Based on these figures we can estimate the future potential exchange value of the hard currencies likely to provide the best inflation hedges. In each of the following projections, the August 1975 exchange value is given, then the currency's estimated ultimate value, and finally the appreciation possible against the dollar expressed as a percentage. The West German deutsche mark has the potential of moving from its August 1975 price of US$0.3877 to about US$0.9960 for a 250 percent gain. Austria's schilling can move from US$0.0550 to US$0.2440, or about 440 percent; and the Dutch guilder from US$0.3793 to US$1.65, a possible 435 percent. Switzerland's franc has the greatest estimated upside potential, from US$0.3730 to US$2.08, for an eventual 550 percent gain.

Although these figures are exciting, it must be emphasized that they are only an estimate of the possible outer limits of these currencies' long-term movement against the dollar. They represent the real reason, though, why the U.S. Treasury officially opposes any proposals to return to a gold standard. Eventually, if some sort of monetary stability is ever to be achieved, it will be necessary to link the dollar to gold again. It can only be hoped that, in the meantime, the federal government does not dissipate its remaining gold reserves; when the time comes, they will be needed to support a new gold-backed dollar.

For a variety of reasons, it is unlikely that foreign exchange prices will approach their potential limits until the world returns to something resembling a gold standard. First of all, a sudden move to currency values at these levels would be very disruptive to world trade; exports of the hard currency nations would simply dry up. For example, a modestly equipped Volkswagen "Rabbit" sedan, now about $3,500 in the United States would jump in price to $8,750 if the mark became worth 99.6 cents; similarly, a gold Rolex wristwatch from Switzerland that only a few years ago retailed for about $580 and now sells for $1,000 would be a prohibitive $5,500 in American jewelry stores. Secondly, even the hard currency nations are having trouble with their economies in the worldwide recession; Germany, for one, has been running budget deficits in an attempt to stimulate her economy. As these nations increase their money supplies, the percentage of gold backing for their currencies drops, cutting their potential for appreciation against the dollar.

Over the short term, the next few years, the exchange value of the main hedge currencies will probably be influenced primarily by their "relative purchasing power" compared to the dollar's. This concept is explained more fully in chapter 13, but basically it means that as inflation cuts the buying power of the dollar, the dollar's foreign exchange value will fall relative to the currencies of nations that have inflation under better control.

From 1975 until late 1976, the exchange rate for the Swiss franc will most probably remain in the US$0.37 to US$0.40 range. The Swiss have decided that they can live with the dollar priced at 2.5 francs, and the franc at forty U.S. cents or less. They are likely to try to keep the franc from rising above this level; this period would seem to be an opportune time to acquire Swiss francs.

By late 1976 or early 1977, when double-digit inflation returns to America with a vengeance, the Swiss franc is likely to push through the US$0.40 resistance point, gaining 8 to 10 percent over its mid-1975 value. Because of the risk of importing inflation if it continues to attempt to hold the dollar–franc exchange rate down, the Swiss government will eventually be forced to let the exchange value of the franc rise.

By late 1977, Swiss francs have a good chance of being priced near US$0.45, 12 percent above their early 1977 value and 20 percent over the mid-1975 exchange rate. If inflation in the United States continues, or if it spurts into the 20 to 25 percent zone, the probability is high that the Swiss franc will approach US$0.50 by 1978.

Exchange values for Dutch guilders and Austrian schillings are likely to parallel the movement of the Swiss franc, but with slightly lower percentage increases. The Dutch are members of a European "joint float" (again, see chapter 13) which will have a dampening effect on guilder price movements; the Austrian schilling is not as widely recognized as the Swiss franc as an inflation hedge. The future of the West German deutsche mark is more problematic; much depends on how successful the Bonn government is at holding the line on inflation. If it succeeds in keeping it below the 1975 rate of 6 percent, the mark stands an excellent chance of advancing against the dollar, too.

A Long-Term Problem

History is a one-way road. We can look back and see where we've been, but if we've gone astray it is impossible to retrace our steps to take the smoother path. From where we stand in time, it is easy to recognize the mistakes that have weakened the dollar and now threaten our future security. These errors, though, are now the province of economic historians; there is nothing you or I can do to revise the past.

Only the future need concern us now. Inflation seems likely to be with us for some time to come; the only sensible course is to try to minimize its effects on our personal lives. Financial survival is the new game, and, whether we like it or not, we are all players for the duration. It is likely to be a long game.

Because there are risks in using hard-currency hedges, and what seem to be even greater risks in remaining with dollar-denominated investments, it is likely to be an interesting game, too.

3

Some More Reasons for a Swiss Account

HERR T. NEEDED A SWISS BANK ACCOUNT to survive. In the 1930s, he was a prosperous Vienna coffee merchant—and a Jew. He was also foresighted. He heeded the early signs of trouble and took steps to protect himself.

In July 1934, Dollfuss, the chancellor of Austria, was killed by Austrian Nazis in an unsuccessful *putsch,* an attempt to take over the state. Herr T. who also owned coffeehouses, was a coffee wholesaler and importer. Twice a year, he journeyed to Latin America to buy coffee. On his next buying trip, he made certain arrangements with his long-time business associates, coffee exporters in Colombia. They agreed to overbill him, to charge him higher than market price for his coffee. The overcharge was then transferred to Herr T.'s secret Swiss bank account.

By March 1938, when Hitler annexed Austria to Germany, Herr T. was ready. When he left on his next regular coffee buying trip, his wife and children stayed behind in Austria, but took a spring vacation in the Tyrol, the western Austrian Alps.

With a local guide, his family walked across the mountainous border into Switzerland, where Herr T. was waiting. A portion of his Swiss assets was easily transferred to a bank in Mexico City. The entire family followed.

After a time in Mexico, Herr T. and his family received a visa to the United States. When I knew him in New York in the late 1950s, Herr T. was not as prosperous as he had once been in Vienna. The property he had to leave behind in Austria had been confiscated by the Nazis. But Herr T. and his family were alive.

To Herr T., it was a matter of life or death to have some money in Switzerland. To the Swiss bankers, it was just another banking transaction. Herr T. violated the laws of the Third Reich, and probably of Austria as well, but he didn't break any Swiss statutes. Neither did the Swiss bankers.

There is an important lesson to be learned from the story of Herr T., a lesson that the most astute people of many nations know well. When a national government begins to become repressive, when it imposes currency restrictions, when inflation becomes rampant, or when the early signs of political instability appear—that is the time to have assets safely in Switzerland.

Money in Exile

For centuries, the Swiss have provided asylum for capital fleeing disorder in its home country. In 1685, after the Catholic King Louis XIV revoked the Edict of Nantes that guaranteed religious freedom, French Protestant Huguenots fled France. Many took refuge in Geneva, bringing their money with them. And to this day, the French establishment still keeps a substantial portion of its assets safely in Switzerland.

German money flooded into Switzerland after the First World War. Two generations later, Germans, ever wary of inflation, are steady customers of Swiss banks in Basel and Zurich. Italian money, fleeing the inflations and governmental ineptitude chronic to Italy, hides in Swiss Lugano. Arab businessmen and politicians tuck away a little bit for a rainy day in Swiss accounts. Latin Americans with money prefer the safety of Switzerland to the risks of devaluation and changing regimes in their own countries. A few clever East Europeans and Russians, mostly high-level bureaucrats, have managed to get some hard currency hidden in Swiss banks.

Lately American money has begun the trek to the Alps. Those Americans who opened accounts between 1970 and 1974 have already profited from devaluations and a weakening dollar. For the majority of Americans, however, Swiss bank accounts have always been tinged with an aura of illicitness. Generally when the American press has mentioned Swiss accounts it has been in connection with some sort of knavery. Indeed, in the 1950s and early 1960s, the prime reason for an American to have a Swiss account was to take advantage of Swiss bank secrecy. The U.S. economy was ripe with legitimate business opportunities, and the dollar was sound. Some American companies dealing internationally, and expatriates who lived or worked permanently abroad, kept money in Switzerland for convenience. However, Swiss bank public relations aside, probably most Americans who had Swiss accounts in those days were involved in tax evasion, hiding assets from court proceedings, or making an end run around U.S. securities laws.

Beyond Any Government's Reach

American authorities, especially the tax authorities, undoubtedly wish that Switzerland would simply disappear. Money in Switzerland is effectively outside their control. Their opinion is shared, no doubt, by the tax authorities of many nations, whose citizens have caused their liquid assets to flee to a safer land.

The pattern of capital flight has occurred throughout history. As conditions deteriorate within a given nation, more and more money is sent outside its borders and converted to harder currencies. As the economy continues to sicken, the government enacts additional laws and regulations. This only causes a more rapid demoralization; asset outflow increases. In desperation, severe measures are applied to stop the flight of capital.

The government of revolutionary France seduced itself into an early and ill-fated experiment with unsupported paper currency. This money, called "assignats," crippled France with inflation; by 1793, conditions were chaotic. A law was passed that provided the death penalty for Frenchmen who made overseas investments. This monetary mess was not cleaned up until Napoleon took the country back to gold coinage and pay-as-you-go financing.

The inflation that plagued Germany after World War I was perhaps the most astronomical inflation of modern times. As a result, in the 1920s many Germans kept money outside of Germany. After Hitler came to power in 1933, German citizens were ordered to declare their foreign holdings. If they didn't and were caught, the penalty was death. Hitler used the Gestapo to help his people comply.

Swiss Accounts Are Legal

Because of a bad press, and because the Internal Revenue Service now asks about foreign bank accounts on the annual tax return, a large portion of the public believes that Swiss accounts are illegal for American citizens or residents.

This is a misconception. At the current time, there is no law prohibiting foreign bank accounts for Americans. However, the Treasury Department has been able to put regulations into effect requiring U.S. citizens and residents to disclose overseas accounts on their income tax returns. This explains the little box on the back of the IRS Form 1040 which asks: "Did you, at any time during the taxable year, have an interest in or signature or other authority over a bank, securities, or other financial account in a foreign country . . . ?" The taxpayer is supposed to check off yes or no.

This query is a beautiful example of administrative intimidation. Foreign accounts are completely legal, but the average taxpayer is being led to conclude that there is something illegitimate about having an account in a foreign bank.

If the taxpayer checks yes on his 1040, a copy of Form 4683 must then be completed and filed as part of the tax return. This form, the "U.S. Information Return on Foreign Bank, Securities, and Other Financial Accounts," is reproduced here for your information. (See illustrations 3–1 and 3–2.).

Whether or not an individual should answer truthfully on his tax form is an interesting question. Harry Browne advises his readers to do what makes them feel comfortable. It really depends on the reason for having the account. I can only say read on, and when you must make this decision at tax time, let your conscience and your common sense be your guide.

The same Treasury regulations that require Americans to report foreign accounts also contain provisions that require residents to report transmittal of more than $5,000 overseas. The report of receipt of similar amounts from other countries is also required.

The enabling legislation is Titles I and II of Public Law 91–508, the Financial Recordkeeping and Currency and Foreign Transactions Act of 1970. To quote from a Treasury Department summary of the implementing regulations, effective July 1, 1972:

> The issuance of these regulations is a further step in major efforts directed toward frustrating organized and white collar criminal elements who use secret foreign accounts to conceal substantive

Form **4683**
(Rev. Sept. 1973)

Department of the Treasury
Internal Revenue Service

U.S. Information Return on Foreign Bank, Securities, and Other Financial Accounts

▶ Attach to your tax return.

For the calendar year 19........ or other taxable year beginning ...., 19......, and ending ...., 19.......

Complete this form showing your relationship during the taxable year to one or more bank, securities or other financial accounts in foreign countries. Use additional sheets if necessary.

Name(s) as shown on return	Tax identifying number (Social security number or employer identification number if other than individual)	Check type of return
		☐ Individual
		☐ Partnership
NOTE: Ownership of 50% or less of the stock of any corporation which owns one or more foreign accounts is not a "financial interest" in these accounts and need not be reported by the shareholder. Accounts in a U.S. military banking facility operated by a U.S. financial institution are not foreign accounts and need not be reported.		☐ Corporation
		☐ Small business corporation
If you wish, you may also submit any other information or explanation not required by this form concerning your interest in or authority over an account.		☐ Fiduciary

Part I Check all appropriate boxes. See instruction F for definition of "financial interest." Use additional sheets if necessary.

1. ☐ I had signature authority or other authority over one or more foreign accounts, but I had no "financial interest" in such accounts (see instruction I). Indicate for these accounts:

   Name and tax identifying number (if any) of each owner ....

   Address of each owner ....
   (Do not complete Part II for these accounts.)

2. ☐ I had a "financial interest" in one or more foreign accounts, but the total maximum value of these accounts (see instruction H) did not exceed $10,000 at any time during the taxable year. (If you checked this box, do not complete Part II.)

3. ☐ I had a "financial interest" in 25 or more foreign accounts. (If you checked this box, do not complete Part II.)

4. ☐ I had a "financial interest" in one or more but fewer than 25 foreign accounts, and the total maximum value of these accounts (see instruction H) exceeded $10,000 during the taxable year. **(If you checked this box, complete Part II.)**

Part II Complete this part ONLY if you checked item 4, and provide information in items 5 through 10 for each account. Please use a separate Form 4683 for each account or use your own schedule to provide this information.

To avoid duplicate reporting on accounts owned by a corporation, partnership, or trust required to file this form, you may follow the procedure in instruction J by checking this box ☐ and completing the statement on the back of this form.

5. Name in which account is maintained	6. Name of bank or other person with whom account is maintained
7. Number and other account designation, if any	8. Address of office or branch where account is maintained

9. Type of account. (If not certain of English name for the type of account, give the foreign language name and describe the nature of the account. Attach additional sheets if necessary.)

   ☐ Savings, demand, or checking   ☐ Securities   ☐ Other (specify) ....

10. Maximum value of account (see instruction H)

   ☐ Under $50,000   ☐ $50,000 to $100,000   ☐ Over $100,000   ☐ Unable to determine (attach explanation)

Instructions

A. Who Must File a Return.—Each United States person who has a financial interest in or signature authority or other authority over a bank, securities, or other financial account in a foreign country at any time during a taxable year must report that relationship for each taxable year. Do this by checking the appropriate box on the Form 1040, 1041, 1065, 1120, 1120-DISC, 1120L, 1120M, or 1120S you file for the taxable year and by filing with that return an information return on Form 4683 for that year.

B. United States Person.—The term "United States person" means (1) a citizen or resident of the United States, (2) a domestic partnership, (3) a domestic corporation, and (4) a domestic estate or trust.

C. Account in a Foreign Country.—A "foreign country" includes all geographical areas located outside the United States, its possessions, and Puerto Rico.

Report any account maintained with a branch, agency, or other office of a bank (except a military banking facility as defined in instruction D) or broker or dealer in securities that is located in

a foreign country, even if it is part of a United States bank or other institution. Do not report any account maintained with a branch, agency, or other office of a foreign bank or other institution that is located in the United States, its possessions, or Puerto Rico.

D. Military Banking Facility.—Do not consider as an account in a foreign country an account in an institution known as a "United States military banking facility" (or "United States military finance facility") operated by a United States financial institution un-

(Continued on back)

Illustration 3–1: IRS Form 4683 (front)

der designation by the United States Treasury to serve U.S. Government installations abroad, even if the United States military banking facility is located in a foreign country.

E. Bank, Securities, or Other Financial Account.—The term "bank account" means a savings, demand, checking, deposit, loan, or any other account maintained with a person engaged in the business of banking. It includes certificates of deposit.

The term "securities account" means an account maintained with a person who buys, sells, holds, or trades stock or other securities for the benefit of another.

The term "other financial account" means any other account maintained with any person who accepts deposits, exchanges or transmits funds, or acts as a broker or dealer for future transactions in any commodity on (or subject to the rules of) a commodity exchange or association.

F. Financial Interest.—A financial interest in a bank, securities, or other financial account in a foreign country means an interest described in either of the following two paragraphs:

(1) A United States person has a financial interest in each account for which he is the owner of record or has legal title, whether the account is maintained for such person's own benefit or for the benefit of others including non-United States persons. If an account is maintained in the name of two persons jointly, or if several persons each own a partial interest in an account, each of those United States persons has a financial interest in that account.

(2) A United States person has a financial interest in each bank, securities, or other financial account in a foreign country for which the owner of record or holder of legal title is: (a) a person acting as an agent, nominee, attorney, or in some other capacity on behalf of the U.S. person; (b) a corporation in which the United States person owns directly or indirectly more than 50 percent of the voting stock or more than 50 percent of the total value of shares of stock; (c) a partnership in which the United States person owns an interest in more than 50 percent of the profits (distributive share of income); or (d) a

trust in which the United States person either has a present beneficial interest in more than 50 percent of the assets, or from which such person receives more than 50 percent of the current income.

G. Signature or Other Authority Over an Account.—

Signature Authority.—A person has signature authority over an account if he can control the disposition of money or other property in it by delivery of a document containing his signature (or his signature and that of one or more other persons) to the bank or other person with whom the account is maintained.

Other authority exists in a person who can exercise comparable power over an account by direct communication to the bank or other person with whom the account is maintained, either orally or by some other means.

H. Account Valuation.—For items 2, 4, and 10, the maximum value of an account is the largest amount of currency and non-monetary assets that appears on any quarterly or more frequent account statement issued for the applicable taxable year. If periodic account statements are not so issued, the maximum account asset value is the largest amount of currency and non-monetary assets in the account at any time during the taxable year. Convert foreign currency by using the official exchange rate at the end of the taxable year. In valuing currency of a country that uses multiple exchange rates, use the rate which would apply if the currency in the account were converted into United States dollars at the close of the taxable year.

The value of stock, other securities or other non-monetary assets in an account reported on Form 4683 is the fair market value at the end of the taxable year, or if withdrawn from the account, at the time of withdrawal.

For purposes of items 2 and 4, if you had a financial interest in more than one account, each account is to be valued separately in accordance with the foregoing two paragraphs.

If you had a financial interest in one or more but fewer than 25 accounts, and you are unable to determine whether the maximum value of these accounts exceeded $10,000 at any time during

the taxable year, check item 4 (do not check item 2) and complete Part II for each of these accounts.

I. United States Persons with Only Authority Over but No Interest in an Account.—Except as provided in the following paragraph, you must state the name, address, and tax identifying number (if any) of each owner of an account over which you had authority, but if you check item 1 for more than one account of the same owner, you need identify the owner only once.

If you check item 1 for one or more accounts in which no United States person had a financial interest, you may state on the first line of this item, in lieu of supplying information about the owner, "No U.S. person had any financial interest in the foreign accounts." This statement must be based upon the actual belief of the person filing this form after he has taken reasonable measures to ensure its correctness.

If you check item 1 for accounts owned by a domestic corporation and its domestic and/or foreign subsidiaries, you may treat them as one owner and write in the space provided, the name of the parent corporation, followed by "and related entities," and the tax identifying number and address of the parent corporation.

J. Avoiding Duplicate Reporting.—If you had a financial interest (as defined in instruction F(2)(b), (c) or (d)) in one or more accounts identified in item 4 which are owned by a domestic corporation, partnership or trust which is required to file Form 4683 with respect to these accounts, in lieu of completing items 5 through 10 for each such account you may check the box in the introduction to Part II and fill in the statement below.

K. Providing Additional Information.—Any person checking one or more boxes of Part I of this form, when requested by the Internal Revenue Service, shall provide information concerning each account reported in Part I that is necessary to determine such person's Federal income tax liability.

L. Penalties.—For criminal penalties for failure to file a return or to supply information, and for filing a false or fraudulent return, see sections 7203 and 7206 of the Internal Revenue Code.

Statement (Pursuant to Instruction J) Relating to a "Financial Interest" in Foreign Accounts Owned by a Domestic Corporation, Partnership or Trust

I had a "financial interest" in one or more foreign accounts owned by a domestic corporation, partnership or trust which is required to file Form 4683.

Name and tax identifying number of each such corporation, partnership or trust ....

Address of each such corporation, partnership or trust..

(Do not complete items 5 through 10 on the front of this form for these accounts.)

Illustration 3–2: IRS Form 4683 (back)

violations of drug smuggling, securities and gambling laws, as well as untaxed income generated by these and other illegal activities. The regulations are designed to benefit both foreign-related and domestic law enforcement efforts without burdening legitimate commerce. It should be emphasized that the regulations impose no restrictions on the free flow of funds into and out of the United States.

The regulations will:

Require all persons maintaining foreign bank or securities accounts to disclose that fact on their Federal income tax returns, and to maintain adequate records of such accounts;

Require all persons transporting, mailing, or shipping from the United States to a foreign country, or receiving from without the United States, currency or bearer instruments in excess of $5,000, to report such transactions to Customs. . . .

Freedom

Swiss banks offer a greater measure of privacy, security, and flexibility than American banks. But what does this mean to the average American considering placing some of his money in a Swiss institution?

Basically, it means more freedom, freedom from additional government interference in private affairs. Inflation may be the primary reason for having a Swiss account, but Swiss bank secrecy remains the main defense against future restrictions that may be enacted by a nervous officialdom.

Freedom from additional restrictions is more important than it may seem now. Historically, as a currency has started to decline in value, governments have placed more and more limitations on their citizens' freedom to invest their assets abroad. The trend is already apparent in this country. Additional restraints can be expected.

Transfer Restrictions

No matter what form further future restrictions may take, they will have a common aim. Their goal will be to keep private assets inside this country, denominated in dollars, and securely within the reach of the federal government.

Restrictions on the transfer of money abroad seem almost inevitable at some future date, as the government tries to bail itself out of its accumulated mistakes. A hard-currency account may provide shelter against the worst effects of inflation, but only if you can get some money safely to a foreign bank. Once strict exchange controls are instituted, transferring funds will become exceedingly difficult.

Foreign bank accounts are still allowable, but frowned upon. For the time being, our government is relying on the implication that foreign accounts, especially in Swiss banks, are somehow illegal.

It is not to be assumed, however, that the Treasury Department is content with the current regulations. The existing regulations are a compromise. In 1969, when the current law was under consideration by Congress, the Treasury pushed for stricter limitations. As originally proposed, the act would have made secret accounts illegal, and would have limited the amount allowed to be taken out in one year to only $10,000.

Strongly opposed to the projected regulations were the major banks. Their argument, that the excessive recordkeeping required of them would constitute "undue hardship," apparently fell upon sympathetic ears in Congress, and the final legislation was only a watered-down version of the original proposal.

As our economy deteriorates further, fewer profitable investments will be available in the United States. The inertia of the people, their natural reluctance to send money overseas, will be overcome. When the word finally reaches the boondocks, when the money flowing abroad is mainly from the middle class, the government will certainly react with harsher restrictions. The lobby for tighter controls within Treasury and Internal Revenue will then probably prevail.

Public Law 91–508, discussed previously, is not the only pertinent legislation on the books. Substantial portions of Executive Order 6560, dated January 15, 1934, are still effective. Franklin D. Roosevelt, then the president, issued this order under powers granted him by reason of national emergency. It's a complex order, but basically "every transaction in foreign exchange . . . by any person within the United States, is hereby prohibited, *except under license* therefor issued pursuant to this part."

This Executive Order gave broad powers to the secretary of the Treasury to either tighten or ease the restrictions. Currently, they are quite loose. Some time ago, a general license was granted to everyone, "authorizing any and all transactions in foreign exchange, transfer of credit, and exports of currency." But farther on in the fine print it states, "The regulations in . . . the general license granted in this part may be modified or revoked at any time."

Interpretation: What the government has taken away, it has given back, but can take away again at any time, in whole or in part. The order remains on the books, but temporarily inactive. Without further legislative action, it can be activated again by the secretary of the Treasury.

What future restrictions can be expected on the transfer of funds overseas? Well, I can only speculate. The Treasury Department has some clever people, adept at the art of writing "wherefores," "limitations," "hereby prohibiteds," and "provided, howevers" into new regulations.

I would guess that future legislation or regulations would contain some provisions like these. That U.S. nationals with foreign accounts would be required to grant the government a "waiver of secrecy,'' allowing federal agents access to foreign bank records. That funds sent abroad would be more closely limited as to the amount allowable. That only very limited sums could be taken abroad when traveling. Eventually, foreign bank accounts might be flatly prohibited for private parties.

How far would the rules go? It would depend on the future economic situation, and on how high a panic level was reached within the government. Certainly, the death penalty won't be imposed, as long as some semblance of our democratic system remains.

The Right to Travel

As a people, we have long taken the right to travel for granted. We can envision few restrictions. When and if transfer restrictions are imposed, though, they will undoubtedly be part of a package that includes limitations on the amount of money a traveler can take out of the country with him.

As an example of how exchange controls might affect an American's ability to travel, let us consider an English example. England is the source of our most precious legal rights. The English are known as champions of personal liberty. Not so, however, when taking currency abroad is concerned.

In the 1950s, when I was living in England, I knew an executive who wanted to take his family on a grand tour of Continental Europe. He felt that the experience should be part of his two daughters' educations. As English residents, however, each member of the family was allowed to take with him only about the equivalent of $15 in currency and a very limited amount of traveler's checks. They couldn't go far on that, which was the whole intent. They weren't supposed to go, but the statutes couldn't actually say that Englishmen were not allowed to travel.

Fortunately, this gentlemen was a finagler, and worked for an international company with branches all over Europe. He arranged his family's vacation with several of his coexecutives on the Continent. In France, his French colleague paid the family's way; in Spain, another company representative financed the Spanish part of the tour; in Italy, similar arrangements prevailed. Within a few months after the family's vacation was over, these representatives all visited London, where they were reimbursed, and their families royally wined and dined. This individual found a way around the rules, as some resourceful and well-placed people will always do. In a truly free society, without unnecessary governmental restrictions, such skullduggery would not be needed.

Over twenty years later, the British are still closely limited as to the amount of money they can take out of the country with them. "Exchange control" is still in force. Vacationing Britons are now permitted to leave with only £25 (about $53) in British currency and £300 ($630) in foreign currencies. Many other countries have similar limitations. Japanese tourists, for example, are permitted only about $1,500 in traveling money.

Americans are fortunate in that they can still travel quite freely, even if the dollar doesn't buy quite as much overseas as it once did. To insure their ability to travel, though, prudent people will have funds available outside of the United States.

Investing Overseas

Economic problems are largely caused by government policies. The burden and the blame, however, always fall upon the people, shifted there by new restrictive regulations. Typically, rather than trim a balance of payments deficit by cutting government spending overseas, an attempt is made to reduce personal spending on travel and on private investments in other nations.

In 1963, to discourage Americans from investing in foreign stocks and bonds, the American government introduced the interest equalization tax. This levy, 11.25 percent on the purchase price of foreign stocks, effectively deterred citizens from seeking investment opportunities in other nations. Fortunately, on January 30, 1974, the tax was eliminated. During the ten years it was in force, however, the government continued to spend billions overseas. Hundreds of billions of dollars were wasted in Southeast Asia alone. During these same years, American investors were prevented, by the same government, from profiting in a worldwide investment boom.

As the world economy changes further, there will be recurring opportunities to profit from foreign investments. Alas, there is no guarantee that the U.S. government will not repeat its mistakes, and prevent its citizens from participating in a new boom. With a precedent in hand, the probability is high that, sometime in the coming years, similar restrictions will again be slapped on overseas investments.

A Swiss account is the perfect tool to help maintain your right to invest internationally. Not only will your investment funds be beyond the reach of a capricious government, but Swiss banks can handle investments for their customers in just about any publicly traded security in any country in the world.

Currency Changes

There are all sorts of interesting tactics a government can resort to in an economic panic situation, in an attempt to reassert its control over the economy and the people. One possibility is a change in the national currency.

The U.S. "greenback" has been around for many years. It will not be in circulation forever. Someday, maybe sooner than we think, maybe not in our lifetime, Americans will have a different currency.

The design of the new bills is unimportant. What is important is that a currency change is often accompanied by a revaluation or by limitations on the convertibility of the new issue.

Revaluation, by changing the type of money in circulation, often follows runaway inflation. When a government has totally destroyed the value of an existing currency by issuing such ridiculous amounts of it that its worthlessness is apparent to everyone, then it is forced to issue a new type of paper money. Ten thousand of the old dollars might equal 100 of the new, and hopefully better, dollars in such a revaluation.

Currencies are changed quite often. About fifteen years ago, France went from the "franc" to the "new franc." The old franc had slipped, and was worth roughly 400 to the U.S. dollar. Under the new valuation scheme, one new franc became worth 100 of the old ones, or about four to the dollar. This French example is only a minor, two-decimal-place revaluation. Germany has issued a new currency after both world wars, each time denominating downward many decimal places.

The United States has altered its circulating currency twice within common memory. Gold certificates were withdrawn from public use in 1934, and, in the 1960s, certificates redeemable for silver were removed from circulation. Increased quantities of Federal Reserve notes were issued as replacement currency.

A currency change could also be used to create an "internal" money, for use only within the territorial limits of the United States. Such paper bills could not be used to purchase international transfers, nor be convertible to other currencies overseas. Their use would effectively stop the further flow of assets to lands with sounder currencies.

For years, there have been recurring rumors that the government has already had a redesigned, replacement currency secretly printed. Perhaps, although I believe it more likely that this gossip has its roots in long-standing Civil Defense preparations. It is reasonable to presume that the authorities have stockpiles of a distinctive emergency money hidden away, for use in the aftermath of a nuclear war.

In any case, anyone with a large hidden stash of our current money risks more than steady erosion of value caused by inflation. When currency replacement time finally arrives, it will be announced suddenly. Large quantities of undeclared greenbacks will become difficult to convert into the new money, without explaining their origins. Again, assets in Switzerland, "hot money" or not, will be relatively unaffected by the red tape that may be part of a future currency switch.

Plain Old Privacy

Freedom from unwarranted intrusion into private affairs is another sound reason for a Swiss bank account.

In our society, the relationship between an individual and his physician or lawyer is considered a privileged one. In Switzerland, banking matters are also private and confidential, both by custom and by law. Protecting a depositor's privacy is a specialty of Swiss banks.

In the United States, there are no effective banking secrecy laws. Just about anyone can find out the approximate amount in your bank account, and the government can determine your balance to the penny. If someone walks up to a teller at your bank and inquires about your account balance, they will be told that such information is confidential. But that's about as far as an American bank will go to protect your privacy. There are no real safeguards, especially where the government is concerned. When you write a check, retail stores will often check your balance before letting you take possession of the merchandise.

They call your bank, give the account number and name, and ask if there are sufficient funds to cover the check. In such cases, the caller is often told that the balance runs in the "low three figures," or the "high four figures," etc. By not giving the exact balance, I imagine the banks feel they are maintaining a customer's privacy.

When you apply for credit, you are asked to name the banks where you have your checking and savings accounts. Banks are reluctant to provide information to credit investigators, but such information is sometimes obtained indirectly, with the lender's bank seeking the data from the borrower's bank. Such tactics are often used to explore credit ratings in business deals, and by divorce lawyers, potential employers, or insurance companies.

Government Prying

Federal government investigators can do much more. The Internal Revenue Service has been called the "American Gestapo" because of its broad powers. Most banks cooperate all too fully with Internal Revenue's investigators. An IRS agent can obtain your exact balance, review the checks drawn on your account, examine just about anything felt necessary.

For years there have been reports that Internal Revenue investigators have conducted "fishing expeditions" into bank records. Tax evaders sometimes open accounts under false names. In pursuit of this hidden money, it is necessary to have a "John Doe" subpoena drawn up, since the name on the suspect account is not known. Such a legal order then allows the IRS agent to root through all the bank's account records looking for the hidden account. In the process, the confidentiality of all the accounts inspected is violated. How many agents involved in such a search, do you think, will use the opportunity to note the details of other accounts that show interesting patterns of activity? For later investigation, of course.

To compound the indignity, this practice recently became legal. On February 19, 1975, the U.S. Supreme Court decided a test case in the government's favor. The *New York Times* summarized the decision the next day with a story headlined, "High Court Grants I.R.S. Wide Access to Bank Files." We can expect one thing from this ruling, that now such tactics will become much more common.

The IRS not only has the power to investigate bank accounts, it has the power to seize them. In case of unpaid taxes, or even a controversy over the amount of taxes due, Internal Revenue has the ability to apply a lien to an account. This is a very powerful tool. The taxpayer often has no choice but to settle; any checks drawn against an account covered by an IRS lien must automatically be returned unpaid by the bank.

Internal Revenue is not the only government agency with the power to investigate your financial affairs. The Federal Bureau of Investigation, the Securities and Exchange Commission, and many other federal and local law enforcement agencies can probe your banking and brokerage accounts with very little trouble.

Tax Evasion

Swiss accounts are still very useful tools for those Americans who may wish to take advantage of bank secrecy to try to evade part of their tax liability. An increase in tax evasion seems inevitable as citizens become more disenchanted with their government. In the last few years, Americans have been treated to a spectacle of ineptness and corruption at the top. Their faith in government received another blow when Richard M. Nixon scandalized us all with his imperial attitude toward paying his personal taxes.

Americans do not have the world's heaviest tax load. That dubious honor goes to Israel and to some of the Scandinavian countries. However, there is one essential difference. Israel's taxes are used for its own needs, primarily a heavy defense budget. Norway's and Sweden's levies are spent largely on programs of social welfare, such as free medical care, for their own people. America's taxes, in contrast, are increasingly wasted abroad, on useless foreign wars and on supporting foreign governments unpopular with their own people.

To many Americans it seems likely that taxes will continue to rise and the army of bureaucratic drones will steadily increase in size. To those who want to arrange their own informal tax cut, I can offer luck but not much advice.

First of all, you will need some financial maneuvering room, a way to work some assets free of the system. Withholding taxes limit the ability of most wage earners to juggle things in their favor. Secondly, you will have to understand the tax system. American tax collectors are the most efficient in the world, the envy of many governments. Collection may rely on what the IRS terms "voluntary compliance," but this compliance is enforced by audits, by stiff penalties, and by occasional use of informers.

There's one consolation for anyone considering evasion, though. I would judge that many people no longer would consider tax evaders to be moral lepers, the way they would have a few years ago. The "my country, right or wrong" philosophy has been severely weakened by lack of moral leadership at high levels.

There is a great deal of sentiment already for genuine tax reform and for a reduction in the size of our government. If inflationary pressures persist and genuine reforms do not come soon, tax evasion may become more than just an exercise in financial self-preservation. It may become a popular form of civil disobedience.

To Summarize

Basically, a Swiss bank account is protection against the future and what the future might bring. The world economy is in a state of change. What our society will be like after a new world pattern evolves is uncertain. There is a high probability that it will feature continued inflation, stricter regulations, and less personal liberty.

Regardless of changing times, an individual must still do his best to prepare for the future. A Swiss bank account will be a help in maintaining some freedom of action in the face of future restrictions.

With improved communications worldwide, the rate of change has speeded up. Events that formerly took years to ripen and occur are now completed in months. It took hundreds of years for the Roman Empire to decay and collapse. England ceased to be a world power in little more than a generation. America's decline could happen in ten years or less.

As this is written, conditions are not yet critical. There is still time to act. The next negative signal will be renewed inflation or tighter exchange controls. As the situation slips further, transfer restrictions will almost certainly become reality; the only uncertainty is in the timing. Will controls be applied six months, or two years, or ten years from now? Any prediction would only be a guess.

The only sure thing is that the time to open a Swiss account is now, before it becomes extremely difficult to transfer funds out of this economy.

4

Switzerland and the Swiss

TO UNDERSTAND THE SWISS BANKING SYSTEM, it is first necessary to know something about the Swiss, as a people and as a nation. Swiss banks are only part of the total Swiss system, but they reflect in purest form Swiss attitudes toward life in general and money in particular. The Swiss are a practical, hardheaded people. They expect efficiency, conservatism, and secrecy from their banks, and they get it.

Switzerland is a unique country. It has been said that if Switzerland didn't exist it would have to be invented. Somewhere there must be a neutral corner, a safe place, a country untouched by the wars, the troubles that periodically plague our planet. There must be a place where money can be secure, safe from ideologies and from government shortsightedness.

Switzerland is just such a place. It was invented by the Swiss as their own haven, where they could go about their business untroubled by the wars and other irrationalities that have swept Europe for the past 700 years. Switzerland is a successful invention, a prosperous and secure country. How prosperous and how successful can easily be judged; its per capita savings are the highest in the world, and its unemployment rate the lowest.

The International Savings Bank Institute recently reported, according to *The New York Times,* that the Swiss keep more money in savings banks than the people of any other nation. As of the end of 1973, the average Swiss had $4,987 in savings deposits. By comparison, the average for the United States was $3,247, and, for Western Europe as a whole, only $1,728.

"Unemployment rate" is perhaps the wrong phrase to use for Switzerland. Swiss statistics give the actual number of people who are out of work, rather than a percentage figure. In September 1974, there were only sixty-nine jobless individuals in all of Switzerland. As a percentage of population, this would work out to about .0000106 percent. In October 1974, the Bureau of Labor Statistics estimated U.S. unemployed at 5,513,000, 6 percent of the labor force, or approximately 2.5 percent of the total population. By June 1975, the American unemployment rate had climbed to over 9 percent of the work force, with 8.5 million workers jobless. If the Swiss "rate" prevailed in the United States, we would have only a total of about 2,300 unemployed here.

Such statistics are not accidents, but rather the result of a long series of deliberate decisions made by the Swiss people over the past several hundred years. This chapter will briefly review Swiss history and discuss the current Swiss situation. When we understand the Swiss system, we will have come a long way toward understanding Swiss banks and their usefulness.

The Alps

Individuals are largely products of their environment. So are nations, and Switzerland is no exception. Switzerland's national character is largely a result of its location in the Alps. Faced with the task of forcing a living from a basically hostile environment, the Swiss developed characteristics similar to many mountain peoples the world over. They are, and have been for centuries, hard-working and thrifty, conservative and very independent.

Switzerland today is a nation of about 6.5 million people. Its area is only 15,944 square miles, smaller than forty-one of the American states. For comparison, it is only about 40 percent the size of Kentucky, which has 40,395 square miles. Distances in Switzerland are short: 117 miles from north to south, and 209 miles east to west. The mountains and the valleys of the Alps occupy about 60 percent of its land area. Three-quarters of the Swiss live in the cities and towns of central Switzerland, between the Alps which stretch across the southern part of the country, and the Jura mountains which run along the northwestern border with France.

Only a small portion of Switzerland's land is suitable for agriculture, and only the central lowlands and the lower Alpine valleys are inhabitable. The rest is mountain, rock, glacier, or lake. No valuable exploitable mineral resources, such as coal or iron ore, have been found in Switzerland. Despite the poverty of their natural resources, the Swiss have raised themselves to prosperity and world power by diligently capitalizing on their chief resource, an almost impregnable location.

The Importance of Location

Switzerland is one of the most important crossroads of Europe. Germany borders it to the north, and Italy on the south. To the west is France, and to the east, Austria and the tiny principality of Liechtenstein.

Long before these nations existed, the ancestors of the Swiss sat on the strategic passes through the Alps. In ancient and medieval times, the only way over the Alps was through the mountain passes. There are several important Alpine passes, none of them really easy routes. Among the better known are the Little St. Bernard pass at 7,177 feet, the Great St. Bernard at 8,111 feet, the Simplon at 6,950 feet, and the St. Gotthard pass at 6,395 feet.

To traders and to the rulers of the surrounding territories, these Alpine passes have always been quite important. They learned quite early that it was desirable to be on good terms with the mountain people who controlled access to the passes. Perhaps they remembered Hannibal, the Carthaginian general. In 218 B.C., he led an army from Spain to Italy to attack Rome on its home grounds. During the fifteen days it took to move his troops and his famous elephants across the Alps, Hannibal lost 15,000 men to snowstorms, to landslides, and to hostile mountain tribesmen, who undoubtedly triggered many of the landslides.

Early History

An alternate Swiss name for Switzerland is the "Confederatio Helvetica," or the Helvetian Confederation. The Helvetii were an ancient Celtic people, part of the Gauls, who inhabited what is now western Switzerland. About 100 B.C., they started a mass migration to southern France, defeating a Roman army in the process. This was a big mistake; in 58 B.C., the Romans, under Julius Caesar, slaughtered about 200,000 Helvetii in central Gaul. The survivors returned to western Switzerland, where they became subject to Rome.

Although Julius Caesar conquered all Gaul, the Romans never really extended their administrative control over the regions that now comprise Switzerland. Controlling the routes through the Alps, to the provinces of "Gallia Transalpina," or "Gaul over the Alps," was apparently sufficient for the Romans. High up in St. Bernard pass, pieces of an old Roman road can still be seen; Martigny, in the canton of Valais, stands on the site of the old Roman outpost of Octodorum, which protected Roman access from the St. Bernard pass to the Rhône Valley and Gaul beyond. With the exception of Rhaetia, now the canton of Grisons in southeastern Switzerland, the Romans were seemingly content to ignore the stubborn tribesmen in the mountains.

It was during the later days of the Roman Empire that the roots of modern Switzerland's four official languages were put down. Latin dialects, similar to those used in Gaul, became the common language of the people living in western Switzerland. These dialects developed parallel to those of the French; the Swiss in this area, from Geneva to Bern, today speak a fairly standard French. Germanic tribesmen, the Alemani, moved south of the Rhine into central and eastern Switzerland; their descendants now speak German, or more precisely Schwyzerdeutsch, the Swiss variant of standard German. On the southern slopes of the Alps, the locals spoke Latin dialects which eventually evolved into the Italian now spoken in these cantons. In Rhaetia, the one Alpine area where the Romans maintained a strong presence, some Swiss today speak a language called Romansh, derived from the Latin–Rhaetian dialect.

As the Roman Empire disintegrated, parts of Switzerland came under the control of various petty feudal lords. However, it remained a frontier region, with the mountain districts under only a very loose control. The mountain people were predominantly freemen, certainly not the serfs common to the flatlands of Europe.

The Hapsburgs and Confederation

Around 800 A.D., for the first time since the fall of Rome, Europe was unified politically and administratively under the

Holy Roman Empire. Charlemagne, king of the Franks, ruled what is now France, Belgium, Holland, West Germany, and Austria. Once crowned Emperor by the Pope, he expanded his control eastward to the Oder River, south into northern Spain, and down into the Italian boot.

As an effective political system, the Holy Roman Empire lasted only about twenty-five years. After Charlemagne's death, because of his son's ineptitude, and because of the ambitions of his feudal vassals, the system started to crumble. Political unity soon ceased to exist, as petty lords, dukes, counts, barons, even bishops and abbots, struggled to seize and hold what they could.

By the tenth century, in the aftermath of the Holy Roman Empire, the Hapsburg family began to be a power in the upper Rhine Valley. Their family seat was the castle of Hapsburg, on the Aare River, now part of the Swiss canton of Aargau. By the twelfth century, the domains of the counts of Hapsburg included large portions of what is now central Switzerland.

The inevitable disputes over taxes and justice arose. In the thirteenth century, the sturdy inhabitants of a few mountain valleys took the first step on the long road that culminated in Switzerland as we now know it. On August 1, 1291, representatives of the district of Schwyz joined with their neighbors of Uri and Unterwalden and signed the Oath of Eternal Alliance. Their mood was well expressed in a sentence from the pact, "With one voice do we swear and promise not to tolerate in our valleys the dominion of foreign overlords." Thus began the Swiss Confederation. Eventually, the Confederation began to be referred to as Schweiz in German, derived from the name of the birthplace canton.

Defending the Confederation

Guerrilla warfare began as the Hapsburgs attempted to reassert their authority. As might be expected in such a situation, the natives came out ahead, fighting for their personal freedom on their home grounds. A major attempt to quell the rebels failed when, in 1315, the army of the Hapsburg Duke Leopold I was soundly defeated at Morgarten.

With success came recruits to the cause. The confederates were joined by Lucerne in 1332, Zurich in 1351, Zug and Glarus in 1352, and Bern in 1353. Now there were eight cantons in revolt. The Hapsburgs evidently felt that they could not afford to lose so many taxpaying districts; under Leopold II, they sent a force to subdue the Confederation. Again, the confederates demonstrated the superiority of their infantry and crossbowmen over the armored knights sent against them. The rules of chivalry were no match for a bolt from a crossbow, or a pike in the hands of a determined Swiss farmer. The Hapsburgs were defeated, and Leopold killed, at Sempach in 1386. After another defeat at Nafels in 1388, the Hapsburgs finally signed a twenty-year peace treaty with the confederates in 1394.

Expanding the Confederation

Emboldened by its successes, the Confederation went on the offensive, embarking upon a policy of expansion. In 1415, the eight allied cantons attacked the Hapsburgs and took the old city of Aarau from them. Soon they added Thurgau to their spoils, making both vassal states. In 1474, the French King, Louis XI, arranged a final peace between the Hapsburgs and the Swiss. Impressed by the confederates' military might, Louis XI then persuaded them to side with him against his rival, Charles the Bold of the Burgundians. War with Burgundy ended quickly in 1477, when after several defeats at the hands of the Swiss, Charles the Bold was killed while fighting them at Nancy.

Territory to the south was soon added to the Confederation. Using a dispute over cattle trading as an excuse, Swiss expeditions moved south over the St. Gotthard pass. At Giornico, in

1478, a small Swiss force of 600 men humiliated a 15,000-man Milanese army, first confusing and then routing them with a sharp attack at the tactically right moment. After these successes, more cantons joined the Confederation. About 1481, Fribourg and Solothurn were accepted, and soon afterwards Basel, Schaffhausen, and Appenzell became members of the alliance.

The prestige of the Swiss military machine had grown steadily since confederation. As French allies, they had destroyed the ambitions of Burgundy, and bloodied the forces of Milan, gaining territory and loot as their reward. But, about the year 1500, the Swiss broke their alliance with the French and became the allies of the Duchy of Milan, from whom they had previously seized some fiefs.

The Beginning of Neutralism

In 1512, another Confederate army crossed the Alps and marched south onto the plains of Italian Lombardy. Time and time again, they defeated the French forces there. Finally the Swiss captured the city of Milan and reinstalled Maximilian Sforza as Duke of Milan. At Navaro, the following year, a French army lost 8,000 men and all its supplies and artillery to the Swiss.

Such successes on foreign battlefields may have been sweet to the Swiss, but they were a major irritant to the French. A new French King, Francis I, apparently decided that enough was enough; he dispatched a large force of 60,000 men, well equipped with artillery, to face the Swiss in Italy. In 1515, they engaged 20,000 Swiss at Marigano.

On the second day of a two-day battle, the French kept the Swiss infantry phalanxes busy with cavalry attacks, until they finally ranged in with their artillery. The Swiss infantry, deadly with its massed pikes against cavalry, took a severe pounding from the French fieldpieces. Withdrawing in order with their wounded, the Swiss left the field of battle, soundly defeated.

Never stupid, the Swiss withdrew back over the Alps. Having faced the "modern" artillery of the times, they realized that their forces could no longer compete on the battlefields of Europe. The thirteen confederated cantons renounced all intention of ever again using their armies to play European power politics. They settled down to work, to trade, and to become prosperous.

The Mercenary Era

To help prosperity along a bit, however, the Swiss began to export their military manpower.

Swiss democracy and Swiss military power have always been supported by its freemen, exercising their duties to vote and to serve as soldiers. Traditionally, all male citizens were required to furnish themselves with arms and to participate in militia exercises. Voting and military duties were interlocked; in many cantons and communes, men who were too poor to equip themselves for military service were denied the right to vote.

For centuries, Swiss youth were given organized premilitary training prior to actual militia service. Communal and cantonal militias held field exercises during the periods when they were not actively campaigning. Full military equipment was kept ready in each male citizen's home. Because of this, the confederated Swiss cantons had perhaps the largest pool of trained soldiers in Europe.

Swiss farming has always been marginal at best. With a scarcity of good land and a short growing season, the Swiss valleys could not support their growing populations. The small towns of the era could absorb only a few of the extra people from the mountain regions. As a consequence, Switzerland became a recruiting ground for the armies of Europe. The Swiss young men were sturdy and healthy, and already trained as infantrymen. With few prospects at home, they flocked to the role of professional soldiers for pay. Neutrality became an advantage; the Confederation found that so long as the Swiss as a nation did not participate in the wars of Europe, both sides were eager to hire Swiss troops. Soon Swiss mercenaries became a tradition throughout Europe.

Generally, the Swiss fought as separate units under Swiss officers, flying their cantonal flags. They fought bravely and professionally, and, a novelty for the times, never switched sides in the middle of a war. However, according to their working rules, they would not fight against other troops from the Confederation. When Swiss units met Swiss on the battlefield, they greeted each other with cheers and friendly greetings, but would not engage.

The only other time the Swiss ever balked at battle was when the agreed-upon pay was late. A French folk saying, "Pas de sous, pas de Suisses," or "No money, no Swiss," dates from this era. The French should know; it is estimated that between 1477 and 1830, a million Swiss soldiers fought as mercenaries for the various French regimes. The bodyguard troops of the French kings were traditionally Swiss. During the French Revolution, the Swiss palace guard of Louis XVI defended Tuileries Palace, with heavy losses, against the attacking revolutionary mob. Professionalism prevailed, however, for after the Revolution Swiss regiments continued to serve in the armies of Napoleon.

During this period, the earnings of the export soldiery helped Switzerland to prosper. Many of the quaint houses that adorn the older parts of the mountain towns date from these years and were built with gold earned on foreign battlefields.

Consolidation at Home

After they withdrew to the Alps in 1515, the Swiss con-
sciously adopted a policy of neutrality. The three hundred years
from 1515 to 1815 were a period of consolidation, during which
the Swiss nation matured, developing from a loose defensive
confederation into a cohesive republic. These were not entirely
peaceful years; several serious internal problems had to be resolved. But, in general, Swiss energies were devoted to the development of commerce and trade.

Gradually, the larger trading centers, such as Bern, Basel,
Lucerne, and Zurich, grew and came to have more influence in
Swiss affairs than the less populous and less prosperous mountain and forest cantons. As the Protestant Reformation arrived in
Switzerland, it was eagerly embraced by the trading folk of the
towns. Some of these small cities became citadels of the new
faith. Zurich banned Catholicism in 1523, and Geneva, though
not officially then part of the Confederation but an independent
republic, became almost the Vatican of Calvinism. However,
the more isolated rural areas remained staunchly Catholic.

Because of religious and political differences, conflict eventually broke out between the cantons. Sometimes religion was
only an excuse: ambitious Bern seized and annexed the canton
of Vaud from the House of Savoy, on the pretext of protecting
the people of Vaud from religious contamination. Eventually,
though, the religious differences were resolved, with only a few
minor battles. Of the thirteen cantons then in alliance, six became officially Protestant, while seven remained Catholic. The
most important aspect of this entire period is that the Swiss
Confederation stayed together; the Swiss developed the habit of
patching up any differences that arose between the cantons. For
the sake of unity and strength, the Swiss were seemingly able to
develop a great deal of tolerance.

The cement that finally bonded the alliance together, however, came from outside the Confederation.

The French Revolution

Switzerland, as a close neighbor of France, was one of the first infected by the revolutionary ideas of liberty, equality, and fraternity as the thoughts put forth in the Declaration of the Rights of Man spread across Europe like some great epidemic. Political excitement caused confusion and a breakdown in confederate affairs. In early 1798, the people of Vaud, a vassal state of Bern since the middle 1500s, revolted and formed an independent "Lemanic Republic."

Two months later, French armies invaded Switzerland. They annexed the independent "Republic of Geneva" to France, and replaced the Confederation of thirteen cantons with a puppet government, called the Helvetic Republic. This ill-conceived regime, doomed to failure from the start, endured for only five years. By 1803, Napoleon Bonaparte had consolidated his position in France to such an extent that he could afford time for Swiss affairs. He abolished the unworkable Helvetic Republic, restored the Confederation, establishing a federal legislative body, the "Diet," in the process. Six new cantons, all former vassal states, Vaud, Aargau, Thurgau, Grisons, St. Gallen, and Ticino were also made part of the renewed Confederation.

As Napoleon's hold over Europe began to weaken, an Austrian army of 160,000 moved onto Confederation territory. Emboldened by the presence of Napoleon's enemies, in 1813 the Swiss Diet broke the ties binding it to Napoleonic France. In 1815, after Bonaparte's defeat and abdication, the Congress of Vienna was held to reorganize Europe. One of its major goals was to eliminate the confusion over national boundaries caused by a decade of Napoleonic conquest. Switzerland's territorial limits were firmly established: Geneva, Neuchâtel, and Valois became Swiss, bringing total membership to twenty-two cantons. A new federal pact, governing the Confederation, was drawn up by the Swiss Diet and approved by the nations assembled in Vienna.

The Congress of Vienna forced Switzerland's solidification into a nation. Perhaps more importantly, the Congress gathered in Vienna also officially recognized Switzerland's status as a permanently neutral state.

The Swiss Political System

The federal pact of 1815, drafted under pressure from the Congress of Vienna, was finally replaced by a new Swiss constitution in 1848. This, in turn, was extensively revised in 1874, when its deficiencies became clear. Despite some amendments since, the Swiss political system still functions under the constitutional arrangements of 1874.

Any Swiss will proudly tell you that the Swiss constitution was modeled after the constitution of the United States. There are some similarities, the inspiration is obvious, but the differences are dramatic; the Swiss constitution is a pragmatic instrument that gives the Swiss people exactly what they want, a limited government.

There are three basic levels of government in Switzerland: the federal government, the cantons, and the communes. Cantons might be considered the equivalent of American states in function, except that in size they more closely resemble the typical U.S. county. Communes function at about the level of an American township.

As modern nations go, the powers of the Swiss federal government are extremely limited. All governmental powers remain at cantonal or communal level, except for foreign policy, civil and penal codes, national defense, postal services, general economic policy (which includes the national currency), and the federal railways. The federal government has some taxing power, in the form of a defense tax, and a levy on income from interest and dividends.

Switzerland's legislative body, the Federal Assembly, or *Bundesversammlung,* consists of two houses. The National Council, or *Nationalrat,* corresponds to our House of Representatives; its members are elected directly by the voters, one representative for each 22,000 people. The equivalent of our Senate, the Council of States, or *Standerat,* has two members for each canton. Both houses meet in Bern, the seat of the national government.

Though the bicameral legislature resembles the American Congress, Switzerland's executive branch is a far different matter. Executive power is vested in a Federal Council, called the *Bundesrat* in German. Members of the Federal Council are elected by the Federal Assembly for four-year terms; each of the seven members of this council is responsible for a separate government department. Each year, the Federal Council selects one of its members to be the vice-president; at the end of a one-year term, the vice-president automatically succeeds to a one-year term as president. In practice, the presidency is rotated among the members of the Council, who consider the president as only the "first among equals."

Most Swiss would be hard pressed to provide you with the name of their current president, since he is not elected directly by the people, and is treated with little ceremony by the public. No official residence is provided for him, and there are no executive limousines or helicopters, either; the president rides to work on a streetcar or bus just like every other Bernese officeworker.

Each Swiss canton is very much a sovereign republic, with its own constitution, legislature, and executive branch. There is a strong tradition of cantonal independence; until the Swiss constitution of 1848 became effective, each maintained its own army and issued its own money. The Swiss federal government has little power to interfere with the cantons; their affairs remain very much under the control of the cantonal governments. Cantons collect taxes from their residents, and control education, the police, and public health.

The basic political unit of Switzerland remains the commune, as it has for centuries. There are 3,095 separate Swiss communes. In ancient times, because Switzerland is so mountainous, each mountain valley, each small town, was completely responsible for its own welfare. Independence and self-sufficiency were important; there was little communication with other communities, none at all during the worst winter months. Neighbors became dependent upon neighbors for mutual survival. Communes elect their own magistrates, by direct vote, and enact their own local rulings. They remain responsible for local taxes, schools, water supplies, road construction, and other local matters.

Surprisingly for a modern nation, the communes control Swiss citizenship. Every Swiss is a member of the commune of his birth. If he later moves, and perhaps decides to run for public office in his adopted commune, he must transfer his citizenship. This is not an automatic procedure; the new commune will often require a donation to a communal charity before accepting him as a burgher. Foreigners who decide to become Swiss citizens must first be accepted as a resident and a member of a specific commune. Only after commune approval, and this is again often conditional upon a substantial charitable contribution, will the federal government issue a Swiss passport.

In some cantons, open-air parliaments are still held to elect officials, and to approve budgets and taxes for the coming year. At these *Landsgemeinden,* voters exchange vows with the elected magistrates; the magistrates swear faith to the people and the voters swear that they understand and will uphold decisions made at the meeting. The Landsgemeinden are ancient political customs, dating back to the founding of the Confederation in the thirteenth century.

The Power of the Voters

Since the right to vote has been inextricably bound up with the duty to bear arms and to defend the Confederation, until recent years only male Swiss have had the privilege of voting. Women have only been allowed to vote, and then solely in federal elections, since 1971. Though most cantons have since adjusted their voting rules to conform to federal election procedures, in some rural cantons female Swiss are still not allowed to cast votes in local elections.

The power of Swiss voters goes far beyond just selecting their representatives. The Swiss people can effectively curtail their government's ability to enact unpopular legislation, or to expand its power, by exercising two special constitutional rights, those of initiative and of referendum. "Initiative" gives the people the power to enact laws directly, bypassing the Federal Assembly. Any Swiss citizen who obtains the signatures of 50,000 voters can force a proposed law to be put to a direct national vote. If a majority of the voters approve the proposed legislation, it becomes the law of the land.

"Referendum" gives the people the opportunity to veto and repeal any law enacted by the regular legislature. To force a referendum, only 30,000 signatures are needed; and these, like those required for an initiative, are usually gathered with the help of an interested organization. Once the necessary number of signatures has been obtained, the controversial law must be submitted directly to the voters for approval. Majority disapproval wipes the act from the books.

The rights of initiative and referendum, and the relatively low percentage of voter signatures necessary to bring an issue to the polls, give the Swiss people a tool to keep the federal government in its place. The mere existence of these provisions forces the legislature to consider public reaction to any new measure affecting personal liberties.

Neutrality and the Swiss Army

Americans find it difficult to comprehend neutrality. We tend to take sides in any conflict, anywhere; neutrality almost seems immoral to us. Sometimes, as we are now doing in the Middle East, we provide aid to both sides in a conflict and call that neutrality. The Swiss consider this sort of thing a very silly business. As a nation, they have managed to remain neutral in every war since 1515. They just consider war a waste of energy and resources.

Switzerland's neutrality is of a special type, however, perhaps more understandable to Americans. Sometimes nations are neutrals only because they are unable or unwilling to make essential military expenditures. Not so the Swiss; they are believers in Teddy Roosevelt's famous dictum, "Walk softly and carry a big stick."

Swiss neutrality is based upon military power; Switzerland is perhaps the world's most militaristic nation. Despite her small size, she maintains one of the largest national armies in Europe. In twenty-four hours, the Swiss could field an army of more than 600,000 troops, armed with modern weaponry.

To man an army of this size, the Swiss rely on their tradition of universal military service. Every Swiss male is required to serve in the army from age twenty to about age fifty. Active duty begins at twenty, when a Swiss youth reports for basic training, which is intensive and lasts 120 days. After basic, he returns to his home town, taking his uniform, his full field equipment, and his weapon (a fully automatic assault rifle) with him.

Each soldier is assigned to a tactical unit, based in his home town. From age twenty to thirty-two, his assignment is to a first-line combat unit, part of the elite force. These units undergo twenty days of active-duty training each year. Between the ages of thirty-three and forty-two, he belongs to a *Landwehr* unit; and from forty-three to fifty, to a *Landsturm* unit. The *Landwehr* and *Landsturm* are support and local defense troops, who also receive periodic active-duty refresher training.

The Swiss army is unusual in another respect—it has no generals. Colonel is the highest rank an officer can reach, except in the event of a general mobilization. Then the Federal Assembly elects a general to serve as commander-in-chief for the duration of the national emergency. Switzerland's last general was General Guisan, who led the Swiss army during its most important test, World War II.

Hitler and the German general staff undoubtedly considered invading Switzerland. They had conquered France, and Italy was a Nazi ally; Austria, another neighbor of the Swiss, had actually been annexed to Germany. Switzerland remained an island in a German sea. The Swiss, however, faced the Germans down. On the day that England declared war on Germany, the Swiss army was already fully mobilized, with every soldier and unit in their assigned positions. The Swiss maintained defensive positions on their borders and remained on military alert until VE Day. The Germans made many bad decisions during the war, but they made the right one about the Swiss. They decided that Switzerland, given the advantage of defense and terrain, was just too tough a country to invade successfully.

After the war, Switzerland continued to maintain the strictest neutrality. Unlike many World War II neutrals, she did not join the United Nations; Switzerland today remains one of the few nations in the world not a member of the UN General Assembly, even though the Swiss participate in some activities that are now under UN sponsorship such as the international postal union and UNESCO, the United Nations Educational, Scientific, and Cultural Organization.

The Swiss Ethic

Historians agree that the Protestant Reformation led to the development of capitalism and the modern world as we now know it. The Reformation was a great revolution in religious thinking, that swept Europe in the sixteenth century, attacking the basic teachings of the then dominant Roman Catholic church.

When the Reformation arrived in Switzerland, the Swiss were in a receptive mood. Like many Europeans of the time, the Swiss resented taxation to support the church, the large amounts of tax-free land held by the church, and submission to a distant papal authority. Moreover, the practical Swiss were skeptical of the Roman Catholic Church's doctrine that suffering on earth somehow piled up merit in heaven; they never really believed that the poor and the meek would inherit the earth.

Martin Luther is credited with beginning the Reformation. A German priest, he became upset over the selling of indulgences by the church to finance the construction of a new cathedral. In 1517, Luther nailed his famous theses, challenging church doctrine, to a church door. His ideas spread, were debated upon everywhere, and, quite importantly, encouraged reformers elsewhere. One of these, John Calvin, was a Frenchman who began to preach the Reformation in Geneva in 1536. Elected city preacher by the town magistrates, he compiled a systematic Protestant confession of faith, wrote a catechism for Geneva, and advocated several extreme reforms. Eventually, he revised the city laws and organized a theocratic government that controlled almost every aspect of Geneva's life.

Calvin's importance, though, lies in the doctrines he preached. His core doctrine was a form of predestination; God selects some individuals for salvation, and rejects others, for reasons known only to God. Success in business came to be looked upon as evidence of God's grace. Calvin also attacked the Catholic strictures against usury, the practice of collecting interest on loans, which opened the way for Protestants to specialize in banking.

Calvinism spread from Geneva in many directions. One of Calvin's disciples, John Knox, carried it to Scotland and to England. It was transported to America, especially New England, by the Puritans and other groups. Calvinistic doctrine strongly influenced what we call today the "Protestant Ethic."

Switzerland's most important reformer, however, was Huldreich Zwingli, a contemporary of Luther. Born of Swiss peasant parents, Zwingli had been a parish priest in Glarus. In 1518, he became *Leutpriest,* or people's priest, in Zurich. Zwingli was an independent thinker, considering other reformers' ideas but developing his own doctrine for the Swiss. He agreed with Luther on the uselessness of the Pope and the Roman church bureaucracy, and on the virtues of diligence and simple living. His doctrines, however, went further and evolved into a rational Protestantism that appealed to the Swiss.

Zwingli's dogma might properly be called the "Swiss Ethic." Simply put, his philosophy goes something like this: Diligence and work are necessary virtues, the rewards of work are holy; prosperity is a sign of God's favor, wealth is a sign of God's special favor; honesty is the only way to conduct business; you only get what you pay for, and you should expect to pay for everything; God owes you nothing, but poverty offends God; there may or may not be a hell, but you should live as though there is; sometimes it may be necessary to sin, but you should not enjoy it.

Zwingliism was a practical doctrine, for a practical people. He began to preach his philosophy in sermons given in Zurich's Grossmunster church in 1519. Response from the Zurichers came quickly. By 1523, just about everyone was converted, and the city formally accepted the Reformation. Interestingly, all the changes were accomplished without strife, by votes of the city council. The Catholic mass was replaced with a much simpler service; relics and images of the saints were burned; ceremonial processions were eliminated; priests and nuns were released from their vows. Zwingli himself became a married man.

Although the townspeople, especially the merchants of the Confederation, accepted Zwingli's doctrines and the Reformation wholeheartedly, the more conservative forest cantons did not. They upheld their faith in the Roman Catholic church. There were two battles between the Catholic and newly Protestant cantons. In the second of these fights, at Kappel in 1531, Zwingli was killed. Peace soon followed, the agreement being reached that each canton would choose its own religion.

Swiss Attitudes

It is probably safe to say that the vast majority of the native-born Swiss have an attitude toward life and work that parallels what we have called the Swiss Ethic.

T. R. Fehrenbach, in his book, *The Swiss Banks,* said that "After Calvin, people in Evangelical lands would still be poor . . . but they could never again pretend that they were proud of it." The Swiss have a right to be proud; by work, by the continued application of their special ethic, they have raised themselves from an isolated and resource-poor nation to a position of prosperity as one of the most powerful small nations on earth.

Because money is the reward for work, which is a virtue in its own right, the Swiss have a tremendous respect for money. Their attitude differs somewhat, though, from those of other European peoples who also respect money. The Germans, for example, cherish money for what it will buy. Americans do, too, but we also pursue it because it leads to status and to power. The Swiss seek money and husband it as an end in itself, more for security than for spending or status.

Swiss admire men who respect money, who know how to preserve it, who work hard, and are honest. Perhaps the most respected men in Switzerland are their bankers. If the Swiss have raised money almost to a religion, then their bankers are the high priests of the cult.

Naturally, the Swiss must spend money to live. When they do, since they value money so highly, they expect their money's worth. Almost nothing in Switzerland is despised so much as shoddy goods or poor workmanship. To help maintain the quality they expect, the Swiss enforce high standards in every craft and business.

The Swiss and Foreigners

The Swiss expect thoroughness, diligence, and prudence from others, and they know that other Swiss expect the same from them. Social pressure to conform, to work steadily, save money, live conservatively, and be law abiding is quite high in Switzerland. Switzerland is a small country, and every Swiss knows that he is being watched by the others, his behavior judged by the unwritten but strict standards of the community. The Swiss, however, do not apply the same standards of conduct to non-Swiss. Seemingly, they are more tolerant of imperfections in foreigners.

Trying to determine how the Swiss feel about Americans is difficult. We look upon Latin Americans as interesting and colorful people, with great potential, but handicapped by their culture and history. We view with dismay their lack of discipline, their inefficient governments and economies. We feel that if only they learned to be more like us, how much better life would be for them. It is a humbling thought, but I suspect that the Swiss feel the same about us as we feel about the Latin Americans. They respect some of our accomplishments, but abhor our tendency to go on crusades and to give away so much "foreign aid" in an attempt to convert the world to democracy. If anything, the Swiss believe more strongly in democracy and capitalism than we do. They prefer, though, to convert by example rather than by gifts or by force.

5
Switzerland as a Financial Center

SWITZERLAND HAS ATTAINED A PROMINENCE in international banking that was unforeseen by the Swiss themselves. It should not have surprised them, however. Given the advantage of hindsight, it now seems almost inevitable.

International financial centers must develop naturally. They cannot be legislated into existence, although many governments have tried. Generations are needed to lay the necessary foundations of faith and confidence.

Basically, Switzerland won its reputation and its banking business by default. A crossroads location in central Europe and a conservative, money-respecting people were definite assets. Switzerland's long history of neutrality and independence was also important. But the decisive factor was that, over hundreds of years, in a process of selection by elimination, only the Swiss maintained their financial integrity. In other European nations, banks collapsed under speculative schemes, and governments bankrupted their peoples with wars and inflations. Switzerland remained an island of stability despite the chaos that often surrounded it.

Geneva and the French

It has been said that the Swiss profit from other people's misfortunes. A better way to put it is that the Swiss thrive on other government's mistakes. The case of the French Huguenots illustrates this perfectly.

After 1685, when the French king revoked the Edict of Nantes, religious intolerance returned to France and life rapidly became intolerable for the French Protestants. In France, banking was essentially a Protestant specialty. When the Huguenots fled into exile, a large part of the Parisian banking community emigrated to Geneva. By 1709, Geneva was a recognized banking center, with at least a dozen well-established Huguenot banking houses. The Geneva banks handled transactions through a network of other exiled Huguenot bankers, often blood relatives, who were active in London, Amsterdam, Lyon, and Marseille.

Once safe from persecution in Geneva, the immigrant bankers continued to do business with France. During the Spanish War of Succession from 1701 to 1713, they were important suppliers of funds to France's Louis XIV. Later they profited handsomely from heavy investments in French government securities.

An example of the Geneva bankers' attitude toward the French was their response when France's royal government found it necessary to refinance the national debt. In 1770, France began to issue rent-bearing bonds, backed by the royal lands. Something like annuities, these obligations paid "rent," or interest, only during the lifetime of the original registered bondholder; the amount of rent paid each year was based on an estimated average life expectancy of fifteen years. More sophisticated than the royal financial advisers, the Geneva banks soon devised the "Geneva System" to augment the yield from these securities. Bonds were bought in the names of healthy young girls, who could be expected to have a life expectancy of much more than fifteen years. These desirable bonds were then resold to the banks' customers. Soon, the Geneva banks were collecting about 12 million livres annually from the French, on an investment estimated at 100 million livres.

Early Zurich Banking

Banking began in Zurich in a much more home-grown way. As in much of Europe, the early banks were simply depositories for the safekeeping of gold and silver. As north–south trade routes developed through the Alps, money-changing also became important. After 1515, when the cantons of central Switzerland began to export mercenaries to all of Europe, banking was often concerned with their pay. It was one thing to soldier in Italy or France, and another to get the proceeds safely back to the folks at home. In 1570, for example, Charles IX of France dismissed a Swiss mercenary force after a campaign but unfortunately did not have the money to pay them. The towns of Zurich, Bern, and Fribourg bailed the king out, advancing him the money to pay off his Swiss infantry. Zurich's share of the loan, arranged by the town government, was 150,000 livres, for two years at 5 percent.

Banking in Zurich often had this sort of civic flavor to it. In the early 1700s, Zurich was a town of only 10,000 people. It must have been well managed, however, for there were recurring budget surpluses. In 1727, the town council invested part of their excess funds in 100,000 guilders worth of English government securities.

Today, banking is Zurich's main industry. At the time, however, few banking institutions existed. To fill the gap, in 1755 the town government organized an "interest commission," authorized to accept deposits and to invest the funds abroad. In what was certainly an interesting arrangement, this government body was called Leu & Company, after a Mr. Leu, the city treasurer. Leu & Co. offered 3 and 3½ percent bonds to the public and invested the proceeds in Austria, France, and the Americas. In an era of slow communications, difficulties naturally arose in the servicing of some of these distant placements. As a result, in 1798, the bondholders instructed Leu to begin to phase out the foreign investments with as little loss as possible; most of the capital was repatriated to Zurich and reinvested within Switzerland.

Formation of the Swiss Credit Bank

A new type of bank had evolved in France about 1852. Called the Crédit Mobilier, it was designed to "mobilize" the savings of the people to help finance industrial development.

As the rest of Europe started to industrialize rapidly, the small city of Zurich began to feel its isolation behind the Alps. The need for a large bank was recognized; some elements of the business community suggested that a German bank, the Allgemeine Deutsche Kreditanstalt, be invited to open a Zurich branch. Alfred Escher, a businessman and politician of prominence, was the leader of a group who rejected the idea of a German bank for Zurich. In 1856 he organized a Swiss bank patterned after the French Crédit Mobilier. Called the Schweizerische Kreditanstalt in German, and Crédit Suisse in French, it became the Swiss Credit Bank in English.

Escher's group provided part of the capital themselves, but offered 9,000 shares, worth 4.5 million gold francs, to the public. Zurich had grown but its population was still only about 20,000. Escher's stock offering was an astounding success; in only three days, the people of Zurich subscribed for 436,539 shares, worth 218,269,500 gold francs. Escher's good reputation had brought the money out of hiding; some of this gold had probably been buried for hundreds of years, for lack of decent investment opportunities.

The proceeds of the offering were quickly put to work. According to its charter, the Swiss Credit Bank could do much more than just accept deposits and make standard loans. It was allowed to form other companies and run them for its benefit, or to buy into existing enterprises. The new bank could trade in merchandise, gold, or securities for its own account. Financing the Gotthard tunnel project, which brought the railroad to Zurich, was one of its first major investments. Soon, the new bank was busy organizing insurance companies, and helping to finance industrial enterprises in the surrounding cantons. By 1890, it was already investing overseas in a major way; as an example, it helped form the Swiss–Argentine Mortgage Bank.

Escher had demonstrated that capital could be raised from the Swiss. The rapid success of Credit Suisse led to the formation of similar banks in communities all over the Confederation.

The Swiss Franc

A stable, fully convertible currency is of prime importance to an international banking center. Although Switzerland's banking tradition is long established, the Swiss franc has a much shorter history. Until the middle of the nineteenth century, a bewildering variety of coinage was in daily use. Most cantons and towns issued their own money, and foreign coins were also used in trade. "Anything round circulates" is a traders' saying from this period.

With the federal constitution of 1848, the Swiss franc became the official monetary unit of the Confederation. However, the franc continued to be issued at cantonal level. At times, up to thirty-six different banks issued their own bank notes and coinage. A truly national currency did not develop until 1907, when the newly established Swiss National Bank became the sole bank of issue.

The Swiss franc is a sound currency. Soundness of any currency is determined basically by the amount of gold held as backing for the currency in circulation. As of September 1974, Swiss franc bank notes were covered 67 percent by gold, calculated on the intergovernmental rate of $42.22 per ounce. By law, Swiss franc paper money must have a gold cover of at least 40 percent. At times, it has risen much higher, with the gold reserve exceeding the bank notes in circulation; in 1961, for example, gold coverage actually reached 150 percent.

The Swiss National Bank

Switzerland was one of the last industrial nations in Europe to form a central bank. The Schweizerische Nationalbank began operation in June 1907, charged with the responsibility of issuing the national currency and acting as the central clearing house of Swiss banks.

Though the bank is organized as a corporation under a special federal law, the Swiss government does not own any of its shares. All the National Bank's stock is held by the cantons, by cantonal banks, and the public at large; private shareholders must be either Swiss citizens or Swiss corporations. Two main offices are maintained. One, in Bern, houses the general administrative functions and the departments dealing with currency and the federal government. The other, in Zurich, handles commercial banking matters and auditing activities.

Getting Ready

With the establishment of a national currency and a central issuing and clearing bank in 1907, the banking infrastructure was essentially in place; Switzerland was ready to become an important world financial center. In the years between 1856, when the Swiss Credit Bank was created, and the turn of the century, many new commercial banks were formed as joint stock corporations and several new cantonal banks were organized. As experience was gained, Swiss banking practices became standardized, resembling the practices of all the other European banks of the period.

Swiss banking gradually became integrated into the larger European financial community, although at this stage the Swiss were not a really important part of the European banking system. Switzerland remained in the shadow of the great nations surrounding it, yet each year Swiss banks continued to grow, participating in more and more international placements.

The Turning Point

World War I marked the beginning of a new era for Europe and for the Swiss. Before 1914, European wars had been fought on a limited basis. Army fought army, with the civilian populace conducting their business pretty much as usual, unless they were unfortunate enough to live on a battlefield. Wars ended when the national treasuries ran out of money.

Now it became nation against nation, with entire populations and all their resources mustered for the effort. Thirty-two nations participated in the 1914–1918 war. When the struggle ended, well over 10 million soldiers and civilians were dead, and hundreds of billions of dollars worth of property had been destroyed or spent on the war effort.

Throughout it all, the Swiss remained at peace. It was not a period of prosperity for them, though, for Switzerland was cut off from its normal trade and business partners during the conflict. But the Confederation emerged with its reputation intact, even burnished a bit; the Swiss had demonstrated that their armed neutrality would survive even continental madness.

After the war, an era of revolutionary change began, as governments toppled, new nations were created, and boundaries realigned. National currencies became worthless, and were replaced by others. Germany was required to pay reparations of 132 billion marks to the victorious Allies. To help ease the pain of these reparations, the German government inflated its currency until the mark became worthless. In 1922 and 1923, the inflation rate in Germany was 14,000 percent. By August 1923, one gold mark equaled 1 trillion paper Reichmarks. The Russian, Polish, Austrian, and Hungarian peoples suffered through hyperinflation, too, as their monies became valueless.

To those Europeans not yet bankrupted by their governments, Switzerland began to look like the promised land. Capital from all over Europe flowed into the Swiss banking system. Private individuals moved their hard assets to the safety of Swiss banks, often smuggling money or gold across frontiers to do so. Corporations transferred control of their foreign subsidiaries to newly formed Swiss holding companies. Since Switzerland is a small nation, only a limited portion of this foreign money would be reinvested within Swiss boundaries. Swiss banks began to reinvest the funds abroad, becoming increasingly involved in international finance.

The Rise of Fascism

Hyperinflation and a worthless currency are always followed by the collapse of the irresponsible government. Unfortunately, the replacement regime is usually authoritarian; loss of freedom is the common penalty for a nation's economic folly. In Germany, Adolf Hitler rose to national leadership on the heels of the worst inflation in modern times. The Nazi party recruited its members from among the millions of German unemployed.

After 1933, when he came to power, Hitler initiated a conservative economic policy. A moratorium was placed on the transfer of funds from Germany. Foreign accounts were forbidden to Germans, under pain of death. Coupled with the Nazi persecution of liberals, democrats, and Jews, these restrictions only underlined the desirability of having some assets in Switzerland. As Hitler moved into Austria and Czechoslovakia, foresighted Europeans, including those Germans who were still able, rushed emergency funds into Swiss accounts. Secrecy rapidly became the most important attribute of the Swiss banking system.

The strength and conservatism of Swiss banks were tested to the utmost; the transfer moratorium effectively cut the flow of funds from Swiss investments in Germany. In a test of their liquidity, Swiss banks still allowed their German depositors to withdraw funds for return to Germany or for disposition elsewhere. Despite many problems, the Swiss banking system maintained the confidence of its foreign customers in a very difficult situation.

World War II and the Aftermath

As Hitler's armies blitzed their way across Europe, the Swiss kept their own peace, maintaining an alert, armed neutrality. Again, as in World War I, these were hard years for Switzerland, cut off from most of her trading partners.

When the conflict ended in 1945, Switzerland and its banking system remained intact. There were complications, however, with the prewar investments of the Swiss in Germany and other European countries. A few banks which had heavy holdings in German mortgages and industrial enterprises found themselves in serious trouble; their investments were no longer assets, but, instead, now mostly heaps of rubble. Two of Switzerland's largest banks, Basel's Trade Bank and Zurich's Federal Bank, were badly weakened by the loss of their German investments. As a result, they failed; their questionable foreign assets were separated from the salvageable Swiss investments, which were then taken over by more solvent institutions.

The Postwar Period

In the 1950s and 1960s, foreign banking interests began a large-scale move into Switzerland. Prominent foreign banks opened Swiss branches, new Swiss banks were formed with foreign money, and majority interests were purchased in established Swiss banks. By 1968, the Swiss Federal Council estimated that 102 Swiss banks were owned or controlled by foreigners.

Before the Second World War, of course, a few foreign banks had been active in Switzerland. The French Crédit Lyonnais and the Banque de Paris et de Pays-Bas (Paribas Bank) were among the most notable. The American Express Company, which operates banks outside of the United States, was the only American-controlled institution.

Foreign-controlled banks were opened in Switzerland after the war for many reasons. Many of the American banks organized Swiss branches primarily to service American companies doing business in Europe. Switzerland also became a base from which to participate in Eurodollar bond offerings (see chapter 13), or to avoid home country restrictions on overseas investments.

Since the war, Zurich has become perhaps the most important world trading center for gold. After World War II, the Swiss got off to an early start, trading again in gold as early as 1946; London revived its gold market only in 1954. For reasons of convenience, much of the gold coming onto the world market from South Africa is physically distributed through Switzerland, even though the British have financial control over the mines. The Swiss government places no restrictions on the import or export of gold, and private ownership of gold in all its forms has always been legal. Each of the three biggest banks in Switzerland has its own gold refinery. The lack of inhibiting restrictions, the availability of processing facilities, and the international scope of Swiss banking, all have helped Switzerland to dominate the gold trade. The importance of the gold market has, in turn, enhanced Switzerland's reputation as an international financial center.

Although the Swiss banks have become increasingly involved in international banking and finance in the thirty years since 1945, they have tried to remain as independent as possible. The Swiss are generally cooperative in international economic matters, but they have declined to enter into arrangements that bind them to follow the lead of other perhaps less rational governments. For this reason, Switzerland is not a member of the World Bank nor of the International Monetary Fund.

Regulation of Swiss Banking

Swiss attitudes toward government being what they are, Swiss banks have suffered far less interference in their affairs than the banks of other nations. For years, Swiss banks operated with little federal regulation. Nevertheless, probably as a result of its experience in the 1930s, Switzerland finally codified its banking traditions. The result was the Federal Banking Law of 1935.

This legislation established the Federal Banking Commission, which is charged with overseeing compliance with the law. Basically, all Swiss institutions that accept deposits are subject to the banking law; the banking commission has the right of final decision if a question arises as to whether an institution is a bank or not. To establish a bank requires the permission of the commission. It must satisfy itself that a projected bank has sufficient capital (SFr 2 million is now the minimum), and that the planned bank will have adequate facilities and systems to cope with the type of business anticipated. The experience and background of intended management personnel are also scrutinized carefully.

In 1971, the banking law was revised somewhat. One of the apparent motives was to give the banking commission tools to help restrict the number of foreign-controlled banks being opened in Switzerland. Under the new rules, permission is granted to form a foreign-controlled Swiss bank only when the other nation allows the establishment of Swiss banks in its jurisdiction. In addition, a Swiss-owned bank opened in the other country must not be required to operate under conditions more stringent than it would in Switzerland itself. Obviously, if these requirements are strictly interpreted and enforced, there will be very few foreign banks opened in Switzerland in the future.

If the money of a bank's depositors seems threatened, the banking commission has the power to send an observer to inquire into all of a bank's management and operational aspects. If necessary, the commission may withdraw a bank's permission to operate and start the liquidation proceedings.

Periodic statements of financial condition, such as balance sheets and profit and loss statements, are required of all banks. Such reports must also be made available to the public, except in the case of private banks. All banks must furnish statistical reports to the Swiss National Bank. However, this information is kept confidential. Details on a particular bank are never published; when studies on the banking industry are issued by the National Bank, the data is provided only in summarized form, consolidated by type of banks.

Swiss bankers believe that maintaining adequate liquidity is more sensible than merely meeting fixed reserve requirements. The banking law reflects this attitude; it specifies minimum ratios of capital and liquid assets to liabilities for the various types of banks. To insure adherence to these rulings, the banking commission supervises the auditing of Swiss banks. Private outside auditors are used; they must also meet certain net worth and experience requirements set by the commission. These auditors submit their findings to the inspected bank's board of directors. Only when serious financial problems or violations of the banking laws are uncovered, are the auditors required to report the audit results to the banking commission.

Much of the regulation of the Swiss banking industry is carried out by the banks themselves, acting jointly through their trade organizations. The most important of these is the Swiss Bankers' Association, which acts as the industry's main liaison with the Swiss government. Its membership consists of bank officers who represent most of the banks of Switzerland. This association has also sponsored several "conventions," under which most banks have agreed to standardize conditions and fees for the major banking services. There is also a Swiss Private Bankers' Association, an Association of Cantonal Banks, one for Swiss Regional and Savings Banks, and others of more specialized interest. Very few banks do not have a membership in one or more of these trade associations.

Self-regulation extends to areas usually reserved for the government in other nations; for example, interest rate limitations are set by regional bank associations rather than by the Swiss National Bank or the banking commission. These interbank agreements would certainly be illegal, described as "in restraint of trade" in the United States. In Switzerland, however, order in the marketplace is valued more highly than the Anglo-Saxon notion of fair play and competition. Such interbank arrangements are considered a normal and sensible way to do business.

Although self-regulation has undoubtedly strengthened the Swiss banking trade and increased its profitability, it is probably best viewed as a typical Swiss solution. It is the Swiss bankers' answer to the problem of avoiding the alternatives, either a banking system in trouble from unbridled competition, or a system saddled with bureaucratic restrictions.

Leslie Waller, in his book *The Swiss Bank Connection,* says that the Swiss banking system "is perhaps a textbook model of what the free and pure-minded pursuit of capital gain will produce if left to form its own structure." Other nations' banking systems, by contrast, could be considered mutants whose natural growth has been warped by the arbitrary interference of their governments. And, on that thought, let us go on to consider the various types of banking houses to be found in Switzerland.

6

Types of Swiss Banks

SOME OFFICERS OF AMERICAN SAVINGS BANKS probably envy their Swiss counterparts. Swiss savings banks offer checking accounts to their depositors, something the American institutions have been trying to do for years.

This minor dissimilarity between the two systems points out a far more important difference. Savings banks in the United States are not able to provide checking services for only one reason, the U.S. government forbids it. The Americans would if they could, but the Swiss do because no one says they can't.

Swiss banks are often described as "universal" banks that offer their customers one-stop financial service. As a generalization, this is accurate. Nevertheless, there are differences between Swiss banks. Not all banks care to engage in all types of banking transactions; their size, their ownership, and their legal structures vary considerably.

Swiss banks are usually classified into seven types: "big" banks, cantonal banks, savings banks, private banks, local banks, loan associations, and "other banks." In addition to

102

these seven categories of banks, the Swiss also have a well-organized postal checking system that supplements the banking system but is not truly a part of it.

The Big Banks

Only five banking houses, commonly called the "Big Five," are included in this category. They are the Union Bank of Switzerland, the Swiss Bank Corporation, the Swiss Credit Bank, the Swiss People's Bank, and Bank Leu.

The three largest, Union Bank, Swiss Bank Corporation, and Swiss Credit, are the "Big Three." One of their common characteristics is that their branches are to be found everywhere in the Confederation, in almost every decent-sized town. The Big Three are commercial banks par excellence, truly universal banks, providing their Swiss and foreign customers with every required financial service. Because of their size, they tend to dominate most areas of activity in which they participate. The Big Three are the most active foreign exchange dealers in Switzerland, the largest stock brokers and bullion merchants. Since their charters do not restrict them to pure banking, they have subsidiaries active in gold refining, consumer loans, and mortgage lending; they run the largest mutual funds and real estate trusts. Their captive accounting organizations provide auditing services to other banks. All three are publicly owned corporations whose shares are traded on Swiss stock exchanges.

Although these big banks loom large in the Swiss banking world, it must be remembered that Switzerland is a small country. In any international listing of banks by size, all three would fall somewhere about fortieth to fiftieth place. At the end of the first quarter of 1975, the Swiss Credit Bank had admitted assets of over 32 billion Swiss francs. By comparison, the largest bank in the world, California's Bank of America, is about three times this size. Regardless, the Big Three have an international reputation that far outweighs their relatively modest size.

The Union Bank of Switzerland, Schweizerische Bankgesellschaft in German, is the largest of the big banks. It was created in 1912 by a merger of the Bank of Winterthur and the Bank of Toggenberg. Headquarters for the Union Bank is now in Zurich. In the United States, it has a branch in New York and representative offices in Chicago and San Francisco.

The Swiss Bank Corporation has its main offices in Basel. It grew from a loosely organized syndicate of Basel private banks that called itself the *Bankverein,* or bank corporation. In the 1870s, this group formally became a banking house, called the Basler Bankverein, to head off a move to set up a major foreign bank in Basel. It later merged with the Bank Corporation of Zurich and the Swiss Union Bank of St. Gallen. Now called the Schweizerischer Bankverein, it has continued to grow by taking over smaller banks. The process is apparently still going on; in preparing the listing of Swiss banks for chapter 12, I ran across two small-town banks that proudly informed me they were now part of the Swiss Bank Corporation.

We have already met Alfred Escher's Crédit Suisse, the Swiss Credit Bank. After its organization in Zurich in 1856, this bank, too, expanded by merger and the takeover of local banks. It now has 112 Swiss branches. Like other members of the Big Three, it is active abroad, with offices in major cities worldwide. In the United States, Crédit Suisse's branches are located in New York and Los Angeles.

The People's Bank of Switzerland, commonly called the Swiss Volksbank or Schweizerische Volksbank, is ranked among the Big Five only because of its Confederation-wide banking network. It has about 106 branches, but only approximately one-quarter of the assets of the Swiss Credit Bank. Originally organized as a bank to serve the "common people," the Volksbank grew and gradually evolved into a full-fledged commercial bank.

Like the Volksbank, Bank Leu is much smaller than any of the Big Three. Bank Leu is ranked as a big bank primarily because of its history; it dates its formation to 1755, over a century before any of the Big Three became active. Bank Leu has only fourteen branches; several of the cantonal banks and the newer foreign-controlled banks can claim much larger assets. Originally the semi-official "interest commission" of Zurich, it became a private mortgage bank in 1822, developing later into a full-service commercial bank.

Cantonal Banks

Cantonal banks are banks which were formed by the cantonal authorities. Termed a *Kantonalbank* in German, and a *Banque Cantonale* in French, there are now twenty-eight of them. Their assets represent an estimated 20 to 25 percent of the total assets of the Swiss banking system; some of these banks are much larger than the smaller two of the Big Five.

Capital for these cantonal banks was generally furnished by the cantonal governments. In a few cases, notably in the cantons of Zug and Vaud, the banks have private shareholders as well. The cantonal banks were all established in the century between 1816 and 1917. In the years before the Swiss National Bank was opened in 1907, they were banks of issue, a source of the coins and currency used in their respective cantons.

Most of the cantonal banks now operate as general commercial banks, but a few are primarily savings or mortgage institutions. Often cantonal banks maintain branches in the main towns of their cantons. They are heavily involved in mortgage financing, in providing loans for local businesses, and in helping to fund local governments. Most cantonal banks accept accounts from overseas. Indeed, they offer a special advantage; there is no deposit insurance in Switzerland, but the deposits in the majority of cantonal banks are guaranteed by the cantonal governments. When this is the case, their stationery will be marked either *Staatsgarantie* or *Garantie de l'Etat*.

The Private Banks

An American visitor would easily recognize many of the bank buildings in Swiss cities by their familiar look. Modern facades with the bank name and logo boldly displayed, and the sturdy commercial fortresses of a half-century ago are both as common in Switzerland as in the United States. But there are banks in Switzerland, substantial banks, that spurn glass and chrome doors or the massive entranceways of a palace. These are the private banks, usually discreetly hidden away, with only small, polished metal plaques to mark their existence. Inside, business is conducted in private soundproof offices, not at a desk on an open public business floor. Often their offices are tastefully furnished with antiques and portraits of their founders.

Period furniture is not really an affectation for these banks. At heart, private banks are themselves antiques, a carryover from the past. Wegelin & Company, private bankers in St. Gallen, date their foundation back to 1741. Geneva has several banks that have been active for more than 150 years; Ferrier, Lullin & Cie., for example, was formed in 1795, and Lombard, Odier & Cie., only three years later.

Private banks are not incorporated. Under Swiss law, they may be organized only as proprietorships or partnerships. The principals, the partners in a private bank, are not employees, they are the owners. As such, their risk is not limited to the bank's capital and reserves, as is the liability of an incorporated bank. When private bankers make a business decision, they are responsible to the full extent of their personal resources.

All private banks are subject to the Swiss Federal Banking

Law. Normal periodic audits are required, but private bankers are not required to make public their statements of financial condition; in return they may not advertise for deposits nor solicit new business in any way. They are not even allowed to post their interest rates in their windows to lure in an occasional customer from the street.

Under Swiss law, private banks must operate under the name of a principal, an unlimited partner. If the family dies out, if no heirs of the same surname come into the business, the bank's business name must be changed or the bank must close its doors. For this reason, and because it is often easier to raise capital as a corporation, the number of private banks has been steadily declining. Records indicate that in 1903 there were 266 private banks in business. By 1964, only sixty private houses survived. Nine years later, in 1973, their numbers had fallen to just thirty-nine.

Sometimes a private bank just fades away, transferring its customers to another institution. More often, it becomes a joint stock company, or continues under new ownership; sometimes, it does both. Bank von Ernst & Cie., AG., was formerly a private bank in Bern; now it is incorporated, and is a wholly owned subsidiary of an English financial group.

Although the private banks are declining in number, those that remain seem quite vigorous. Because they do not publish statements, and since statistics on the private houses are not included in the National Bank's annual report on the banking system, it is difficult to judge their size. It is generally agreed that the private banks are more of a factor in international finance than in the internal Swiss banking business. Most of their money comes from outside the Confederation and most leaves Switzerland again to be reinvested in other nations. The size of the private banks can be estimated only from their activity on the stock exchanges, the number of their employees, and their participation in large loan syndicates. Hans J. Bär, in his study,

The Banking System of Switzerland, estimated that the assets of all private banks total about 3 billion Swiss francs.

In considering the size of any Swiss bank, including those that publish financial statements, the question of "admitted assets" always arises. Swiss bankers do not include managed assets, the investment portfolios they control for their clients, in their reported figures. Since private banks specialize in portfolio management, their true power is probably many times their estimated assets. Herr Bär gives, in the 1973 edition of his book, a guesstimate of SFr 40 billion as the value of the marketable securities controlled by the private banks. This is about 20 percent of the total securities held by the entire Swiss banking system.

In Switzerland, where there is no aristocracy, but where respect is gained only through hard work, wealth, and civic virtue, the private bankers are counted among the true patricians. They have an influence in Swiss banking circles much greater than might normally be expected; traditionally, only private bankers are elected as president of the Swiss Bankers' Association (which includes members from all types of banks), as heads of the major stock exchanges, or as president of the Association of Swiss Stock Exchanges.

Savings Banks

In Switzerland, all banks invite savings deposits, and savings banks offer checking-type accounts to their customers. The distinguishing mark of a savings bank is that it is organized primarily to promote thrift in its community. Other types of banks seek depositors to generate funds to use in making profitable loans. Savings institutions are less profit minded; their investments are made mainly with the objective of earning enough income to cover the interest due to their depositors.

Although savings banks are generally community oriented, many are quite willing to accept business from overseas. Their primary advantage to an American lies in the greater variety of savings plans they offer.

A savings bank is a *Sparkasse,* or an *Esparnikasse,* in German. In French, it is properly a *Caisse d'Epargne,* although many savings institutions just call themselves a "bank" or "banque." Sometimes a *Kreditanstalt* may be a savings bank, too.

Mortgage and Local Banks

At best, the classification of Swiss banks by type is an extremely arbitrary business. Since the banks engage in so many types of banking, and since their mix of business changes over the years, the categories tend to overlap. Mortgage banks and savings banks are an example. They are basically the same type of savings institution. Savings banks usually have a large portion of their money invested in mortgages, but mortgage banks are considered to be those institutions which hold over 60 percent of their assets in mortgage paper.

A mortgage bank is called a *Hypothekenbank* in German, and a *Caisse Hypothecaire* in French. A *Spar-und Leihkasse* is a savings and loan bank, which is essentially the same thing.

"Local" banks are mostly country banks. They provide a mixture of services: savings accounts, current accounts, loans, and mortgages for the people of their communities. Some maintain only one office, while others have branches in neighboring towns. Many local banks originated as community savings banks and gradually evolved into small-town commercial banks.

The "Other" Banks

The Swiss National Bank began to issue banking statistics and to classify banks by type as the result of the Federal Banking Act of 1935. "Other" banks are basically banks that do not fit neatly or conveniently into any of the other six categories. Before the Second World War, they were mostly "ex-private" banks, houses that had changed their legal structure from a partnership arrangement to a more modern corporate form.

Since the war, this has been the fastest growing category of Swiss bank. In 1957, there were only fifty-six "other" banks. They had increased in number to 169 by 1968; by the beginning of 1972, there were 193 banks in this classification. The growth in the number of "other" banks has more than made up for the loss of private banks.

The National Bank, in its breakdowns, now distinguishes between two types of "other" banks, those that are Swiss-owned and those that are controlled by foreigners. The Swiss-controlled institutions are largely the former private banks that have become corporate, joint stock banks. Some of the foreign-controlled houses were established as newly created Swiss corporations; others were once Swiss-controlled and have been purchased by non-Swiss interests.

The rapid profusion of foreign-controlled banks has caused much consternation among the Swiss banking fraternity. Giant American banks, led by the First National City Bank of New York, have opened several branches since 1963. Chase Manhattan Bank, the Bank of America, Morgan Guaranty Trust, and the First National Bank of Chicago are among those who have entered the Swiss market. The Dow Banking Corporation is the offspring of the American chemical firm of the same name. Even smaller regional American banks have established footholds in Switzerland; the Bank of Indiana opened the Banque

Indiana Suisse and the Northern Trust Company became a part owner of the Banque Scandinave en Suisse.

Russia opened the Wozchod Handelsbank. The British expanded their activity, with the Guyerzeller Zurmont Bank and Keyzer Ullman joining such long-established banks as the Société Bancaire Barclays (Suisse). The Bank of Tokyo and Fuji Bank serve the Japanese.

Arab and Israeli banking interests saw Switzerland as the land of opportunity, too. The Arab Bank (Overseas) was established in 1962. Bank Leumi Le-Israel (Schweiz) is part of the Leumi group, which also controls Bank Leumi Trust Company in New York City. The Israeli-controlled Banque pour le Commerce Suisse-Israélien has very rapidly become one of the largest of the new banks, with assets of over a billion Swiss francs.

Swiss bankers have always tried to keep their industry non-competitive, and as profitable as possible. Needless to say, the large-scale intrusion of foreign banking into the Swiss system upset the status quo. Competition increased, as the foreign banks struggled to establish themselves quickly. The American-controlled institutions in particular were careful to avoid agreements or situations that might lead to future antitrust problems with U.S. regulatory agencies.

There were manpower problems, too. The Swiss believe in full employment with a vengeance; permission for foreign nationals to work in Switzerland, except as menials, is very difficult to obtain. As a result, foreign banks were unable to utilize many of their own nationals in their Swiss operations. Charges were often made that the new foreign-controlled banks were raiding Swiss banks to obtain qualified people. There are probably quite a few younger Swiss bankers who, as a result of the scarcity of Swiss managers, moved up in the ranks years ahead of schedule.

Other problems arose, too, because of the shortage of seasoned management. United California Bank in Basel, AG., the Swiss subsidiary of the large Los Angeles bank, collapsed in 1970, primarily because of a lack of internal controls. The bank had lured some Swiss middle management personnel from such established houses as Bank Hoffman, but it apparently did not get all the expertise it needed. Hans Bär, among others, has speculated that perhaps the failure could have been avoided if United California had been allowed to supply its Basel unit with the management talent it needed.

Despite such problems, on balance the influx of foreign banks would seem to have done Swiss banking more good than harm. Although the Swiss do not view competition in the same light as Americans, many Swiss bankers would probably admit that the foreigners have helped to make their industry more progressive. The new banks have also given Zurich and Geneva, where most of them are located, added international importance as banking centers.

The Loan Associations

The seventh type of Swiss bank is the local loan society, usually called a *Raiffeisen Bank* in German. They resemble the familiar American credit union, and are important in communities too small to support a full-fledged bank.

Individuals become members of their local Raiffeisen cooperative by buying a membership for SFr 200. Secured loans and mortgages are available to members of the cooperative; savings and current accounts as well as certificates of deposit are offered to the local people regardless of whether or not they are members. These cooperatives have no local employees except for a part-time cashier, who keeps office hours in his own home. There are two national associations of these local loan societies, each of whom maintains a headquarters that acts as a central bank for the local units. The dominant association, with its main office in St. Gallen, has a membership of 1,148 affiliated groups, and total assets of over SFr 1.2 billion.

Because of the community-oriented nature of their business, these loan societies are of no importance to a nonresident. Of course, if a reader is lucky enough to become a full-time Swiss resident, then he might want to join his local Raiffeisen bank.

The Giro System

Special checking accounts, designed for the payment of small bills by the average householder, are unknown in Switzerland. Swiss banks offer "current accounts," which are similar to regular checking accounts, but they are intended for larger sums than are involved in the typical family's budget. Instead, the Swiss pay their small bills by means of an unusual, but very efficient, *giro* system that is run by the Swiss postal service.

This postal giro system is not part of the regular banking setup, but instead supplements it. Individuals, companies, stores, and all banks maintain postal giro accounts in their own names. To pay a bill, the account holder fills out a simple giro transfer form which instructs the post office to transfer the sum involved from one giro account to another. The giro system has evolved to such an extent that stores and physicians send special blank giro forms along with their statements. Bank deposits can also be made by means of giro transfers without making a special trip to the bank; a depositor makes his bank deposit at the nearest post office, paying the money directly into his bank's giro account. Most banks with a Swiss clientele print their *Postcheckkonto* number on their letterhead and on their statement forms.

The Swiss National Bank also maintains a parallel giro system that interlocks with the postal giro system. All banks have accounts in this system, too. The National Bank's giro arrangement is utilized to make payments between Swiss banks; it makes it unnecessary for the banks to keep clearing accounts with each other.

7

Swiss Bank Secrecy

CONTRARY TO POPULAR PRESUMPTION, the Swiss did not adopt a policy of bank secrecy to attract foreign depositors. Strict secrecy is certainly the best-known feature of Swiss banking, but it is not a clever promotional scheme; its origins are rooted in the attitudes of the Swiss people toward personal privacy.

Banking secrecy is undeniably a lure for foreign money, and not only the Swiss realize this. Other nations have tried, with mixed success, to use bank secrecy to promote business for their banks. Lebanon, for one, has copied many features of the Swiss banking code. Numbered accounts are available in Panama, the Bahamas, Singapore, Uruguay, and Hong Kong. Even Communist Hungary now offers secret, tax-free savings accounts to residents of the Western world.

Imitation may be the sincerest form of flattery, but unfortunately imitation can only go so far. Establishing an international money haven is far more difficult than merely enacting a local copy of the Swiss banking laws. The reputation of Swiss banks for secrecy is based not only on the law, but upon the customs and philosophy of the banking profession and upon Switzerland's long history of stability, neutrality, and genuine democracy. Banking secrecy may become more believable in some of the countries that have copied the Swiss code in a hundred years or so, if they still exist as independent nations.

Secrecy as Custom

Banks of all nations conduct business with as much privacy as they can manage. In most countries, however, the banks are not able to keep banking transactions secret from their governments. In practice, the bureaucrats' propensity to investigate bank records overrides any citizen's right to financial privacy.

In the twentieth century, governments everywhere have become much more centralized and powerful. Alone among modern industrial nations, the Swiss have maintained a limited government. Because of this, they have managed to retain their basic right to personal privacy. In most other nations, the bureaucrats have triumphed, at the expense of personal liberty.

But the Swiss custom of privacy in banking matters springs from deeper roots than the urge to frustrate bureaucratic probing. The Swiss live under steady psychological pressure. Always they are expected to be prudent and conservative, to work hard and be thrifty. There is little escape from social pressure to conform; Switzerland is a nation of small towns and small cities, and the Swiss seldom move. Their neighbors know them well and observe their behavior constantly. T. R. Fehrenbach, author of *The Swiss Banks,* has suggested that the Swiss cherish banking privacy for this very reason, as a respite from the constant watchfulness of other Swiss.

Secrecy as Law

Banking secrecy may have its roots in the attitudes of the Swiss toward personal financial privacy, but banking secrecy is also the law of the land. The traditions of privacy and discretion have been codified and made the primary working rule of Swiss banking.

Switzerland's secrecy laws are defensive, the result of pressure from other governments whose concept of individual liberty does not coincide with that of the Swiss. The secrecy laws are a direct reaction to the attacks on Swiss banking secrecy by Hitler's Third Reich.

When Hitler achieved power in 1933, Germany was in economic turmoil. He rapidly took total control of the economy, placing a moratorium on the transfer of German funds abroad and issuing regulations that forbade German nationals to keep bank accounts outside of Germany. Efforts began to force citizens to repatriate any money they might have abroad.

Much of this money was in Switzerland. The banks of Zurich and Basel, in particular, had long had a substantial German trade. Most of this business was of an ordinary commercial nature, but there were thousands of nervous Germans who maintained secret personal accounts.

It became the task of Reichsführer Heinrich Himmler's Gestapo to seek out information on Swiss accounts that had not been declared by their German owners. They approached the assignment with their usual energy and efficiency. Mail and cable communications with Switzerland were monitored; German bank records of years past were carefully examined for leads. Soon Gestapo agents were in Zurich, armed with lists of suspected violators and of the banks where the hot money might possibly be located.

These agents did not need the sort of legally admissible evidence that an Anglo-Saxon judge might require. All the Gestapo sought in Switzerland was mere confirmation that an account existed. Inside Germany, it could then easily detain, interrogate, intimidate, and even torture the account holder to extract whatever additional information it needed. Once the account details were known, it became simple to instruct the Swiss bank to return a German depositor's funds to Germany.

Several tactics were used to penetrate the protective screen of silence that Swiss bankers used to protect their customers. The most common was to enlist the cooperation of bank employees. Friendship, sex, or money reportedly induced a few low-level clerks to provide account numbers, names, and other data on German depositors. Another ruse was to openly attempt to make a deposit worth a few thousand dollars in the name of a suspect German national. If the teller accepted the money, or even if the bank's officers hesitated unduly before refusing the deposit, it was unfortunate for the poor German who was being checked out.

The Nazi field men enjoyed modest success for a while; Swiss bankers were simply unprepared for this type of intelligence gathering effort. German depositors, accompanied by a silent Gestapo escort, soon appeared at the banks to withdraw their funds. In other cases, strangers from Germany presented properly executed documents and signatures giving them access to the accounts. Phone calls and telegrams, using authentication phrases previously agreed upon, ordered deposits sent back to Germany. Knowing that many of these withdrawals were being made under Gestapo duress, the Swiss bankers hastily changed their rules. Business was not discussed with German depositors, nor their funds handed over, if another person accompanied them. Instructions by cable, by phone, or by letter were not honored until confirmed personally in Germany by a Swiss diplomatic or business representative.

This underground war continued for about a year. Swiss

bankers found themselves in an unenviable position, playing a life or death game in which their German depositors usually lost. The contest reached a peak in 1934, when the Nazis publicly tried and executed three Germans for having secret Swiss accounts. Perhaps the Nazis intended to use these unfortunates to demonstrate to other Germans just how serious their regime was about undeclared foreign funds. If they did, it backfired on them. The secret struggle between Swiss banks and the Gestapo quickly became front page news in Switzerland. The Swiss people became indignant, demanding that something be done to frustrate the Gestapo. Public opinion caused the National Assembly, which was even then considering a new banking code, to react sharply.

The result was article 47 of the *Bundesgesetz über Banken und Sparkassen*, the banking law of 1934. For the first time, the Swiss tradition of banking secrecy had teeth in it, very sharp teeth. Article 47 made violations of secrecy a criminal offense rather than a civil matter.

In many countries a customer may sue for damages under civil law if his banker violates the confidence of the banking arrangement. Under the new Swiss law, prison terms and heavy fines became the penalty for violators. Bank officers and employees, authorized agents, representatives of the Swiss Banking Commission, and bank auditors are all subject to the law. So is anyone who "tries to induce others to violate professional secrecy." Violators may be punished with jail terms of not more than six months, or fines of up to 50,000 Swiss francs.

Clumsiness is no excuse under the law, either. The regulations provide penalties even when secrecy is broken inadvertently, through negligence. The proscription against breaking professional silence also remains intact even when an individual is no longer connected with the banking profession in any way.

Article 47 is unusual not only because breaking bank secrecy is considered a criminal offense; perhaps its most unique feature is that Swiss government agencies enjoy no special exemption under the law. Several nations have some sort of legal provision for banking secrecy, but none, except Switzerland, go so far as to provide protection from their own government. In Switzerland, a banker would actually be in violation of the law if he discussed a customer's account with the head of the Swiss National Bank. A government employee could be prosecuted if he even asked for information. It is interesting to note that article 47 does not specifically define banking secrecy. There are cantonal banking laws, though, that predate the federal laws of 1934. Article 47 basically reinforces and strengthens the local laws, without superseding them.

There have been several court decisions which have served to clarify and broaden the interpretation of bank secrecy; several accepted rules have emerged. Unless he has specific permission from a depositor, a banker violates the law even if he simply acknowledges that there is an account. If a bank officer has any question as to the correct course of action under the law, he has the duty to refuse to give any information at all. Secrecy covers more than such routine matters as bank accounts and securities purchases; the umbrella of banking secrecy protects the privacy of all discussions and business meetings held in the bank. This is why Swiss banks are normally insistent that all matters pertaining to the formation of corporations or trusts be transacted on the bank's premises.

In Switzerland, taxes are considered to be a routine matter best handled between a taxpayer and his local tax collector. Authorities expect that every Swiss will pay his taxes and by and large the Swiss do. Tax problems are not normally pursued through the courts. Income tax is not even withheld from salary checks. Swiss governments have never claimed the authority to vigorously pursue tax violators, and certainly not the right to inspect bank records. Besides, the voters would veto any attempt in that direction anyway.

Banking secrecy also enjoys the protection of article 273 of the Swiss Criminal Code. This provision makes it illegal for anyone to make "trade secrets" available to foreign governments or organizations; banking secrets are considered trade secrets under the law. When German pressure on Swiss banks was at its most intense in 1934, the new banking code containing the secrecy law was not yet in effect. Instead, article 273 was used to punish those who collaborated with the Gestapo. Several bank employees were jailed as a result. This section of the criminal code is now used mainly to prevent industrial and business espionage.

Numbered Accounts

Numbered accounts are the best known and most copied feature of Swiss bank secrecy. Actually, they are more of a special arrangement than a distinct category of account. Savings accounts, checking-type accounts, or investment management accounts can all be set up as numbered accounts.

A numbered account is simply any type of account where the routine bank records are maintained under a code number rather than under a customer's name. This system is used to prevent clerical workers or bank auditors who routinely have access to account records from learning the identity of an account owner. This does not mean that the account is completely anonymous; no bank will ever open a numbered account without knowing the name, address, and something about the depositor's background. However, information linking the account code number with the customer's true identity is kept locked away in a vault. Access to this data is restricted to two or three senior bank officers.

Obviously, normal signatures are not practical under a numbered arrangement. When a written authorization is needed to instruct the bank, the customer signs the account number in script. For cabled communications, an innocuous alternate code phrase is often substituted.

In the days before banking secrecy was written into the banking law, numbered accounts were an added security measure against the indiscretion or subversion of bank employees. A clerk could not be bribed to match a number and a name because such information was kept beyond his reach. Nowadays, some banks feel that article 47 has made numbered accounts an unnecessary precaution. Nevertheless, they are popular with the Swiss themselves. Since most communities are quite small, it is common for the Swiss to have relatives or acquaintances working in the banks that they must patronize. For the sake of discretion, to prevent such people from knowing their true financial situation, many Swiss prefer to use a numbered arrangement.

Although numbered accounts are intriguing, they are really not needed by the average depositor with only a modest-sized bank balance, honestly acquired. Many banks, in fact, discourage the frivolous use of numbered accounts by foreigners, by requiring larger minimum balances for such arrangements.

The Limits of Secrecy

Both numbered accounts and regular accounts enjoy the routine protection of Swiss bank secrecy, but banking privacy does have its limits. Federal and cantonal laws clearly allow access to bank records in certain specified instances. A Swiss bank may be required to provide account records to the courts, in bankruptcy or inheritance proceedings, and in criminal cases.

Cantonal courts may obtain information to assist in settling bankruptcy cases, both domestic and foreign. However, the account details are kept secret by the court. The material provided by the bank is seen only by the judges, not by the lawyers for either side nor by other individuals who may be involved in the litigation.

Inheritance cases are a problem area. The law requires that a bank must provide information on an account belonging to a deceased depositor, if requested by all the heirs. But the law also requires a banker to maintain his usual silence if even one heir objects to the information being made available to the others. Since normally there is a great deal of jealousy between claimants, and since it is often difficult to determine the rightful heirs, there have been many inheritance cases filed in Swiss cantonal courts.

A complicating factor is that Swiss banks may not allow depositors to designate beneficiaries in case of death. Instead, they usually require a power of attorney that grants someone else alternate signature power over an account. Such a power of attorney, under Swiss law, remains effective even after the death of the account holder and has the same practical effect as naming a beneficiary. Often, before relatives arrive to claim what they consider rightfully theirs, the money in an account maintained by the deceased has already gone to the person holding such signature power.

There has been speculation that such a problem arose with the Swiss accounts of Eva Perón of Argentina, who died in 1952. She was reputed to have had several accounts in Geneva. Her husband, Juan Perón, then the dictator of Argentina, was never able to reclaim much of this money; Eva simply had not given the banks powers of attorney in her husband's name. The world will never know who Mrs. Perón favored with signature power and with most of her money, but later in this chapter the reader will get some idea of where these funds might have gone.

Swiss courts also have the legal right to obtain pertinent information from Swiss banks to aid in the prosecution of criminal cases. The courts will also cooperate with foreign authorities in such matters, if a treaty of mutual assistance exists. Aid may not be given foreign governments in obtaining information in cases that involve political, foreign exchange, or tax violations. There are no Swiss laws restricting foreign exchange transactions, and taxes are administrative rather than legal matters in Switzerland. In refusing assistance in these cases, the Swiss are only denying foreign regimes the powers they already deny their own government.

Swiss authorities will only assist foreign governments if the alleged criminal act is also a violation of Swiss law. Counterfeiting, fraud, forgery, bank robbery, and embezzlement are among the types of crimes that the Swiss are very happy to help solve. Since banks are sacred to the Swiss, they find crimes against banks particularly abhorrent. In one instance in the 1950s, Swiss authorities and bankers were delighted to help locate money stolen in a Canadian bank robbery.

Sometimes foreign authorities unnecessarily complicate things for themselves. In the Billie Sol Estes case, about $7 million of the proceeds of his famous liquid-fertilizer swindle were supposedly missing after his trial and conviction. Texas and U.S. federal law enforcement officials reportedly believed that a good portion of this money might be in Swiss accounts. Since fraud was involved, the Swiss would normally have cooperated in recovering the money, if any of it were indeed in Switzerland. The U.S. tax collectors, however, applied a tax lien against all of the missing funds. This automatically made it impossible for the Swiss government to assist; the case now involved tax evasion, which is not a breach of the law in Switzerland.

Clifford Irving's Mistake

Swiss banks have long had a bad press in the United States. Periodically, some grand confidence scheme collapses and finds its way into the newspapers. Readers are scandalized by the details of how the organizers of the unsuccessful plan attempted to hide their loot in Switzerland. Inevitably, the general public links Swiss bank accounts with international swindlers, con artists, and clever people gone astray.

The "Autobiography of Howard Hughes" scandal of 1971 is a classic of the genre. Clifford Irving, an established writer with a then modest reputation, convinced his publisher that he had met Howard Hughes. The reclusive billionaire had supposedly agreed to allow Irving to ghostwrite his autobiography. Beguiled by the prospect of tremendous profits from this venture, the McGraw-Hill Book Company paid a huge advance to obtain Mr. Hughes' signature on a book contract. Unfortunately, Hughes' signature on this agreement had been faked, presumably by Clifford Irving. So had several hours of taped interviews and a remarkable nine-page letter that handwriting experts agreed was in Hughes' own hand.

Three checks made out to "H. R. Hughes" and totaling $650,000 were paid into a current account opened at the main Zurich office of Crédit Suisse. Naturally, "H. R. Hughes" was not the legendary Howard Robard Hughes, but was instead a mysterious "Helga R. Hughes." For a while, neither the bank nor the publishing house suspected fraud. The account had been opened routinely by a blond, German-speaking woman who presented a Swiss passport to verify her identity and signature. The checks that found their way back to McGraw-Hill's accounting department were endorsed with an "H. R. Hughes" that matched the signature on the book contract in their files; and, of course, McGraw-Hill did not yet suspect that the Swiss "H. R. Hughes" was a woman.

Eventually, just before publication, the complex scheme unraveled. Perhaps bedazzled by their potential take, the conspirators had made two serious mistakes. First, they had misjudged Howard Hughes. He had not appeared in public in years, but there was no guarantee that he would remain silent in the face of an unauthorized "authorized" autobiography. If nothing else, Internal Revenue pressure for taxes on Hughes' presumed share of the book proceeds would have forced him to disown the book.

Secondly, while the plotters studied Hughes' life with painstaking care, they apparently did little research on Swiss bank secrecy. Certainly, they did not fully understand its limitations. When a document, signed by the real Hughes, testifying that he had not personally endorsed a check in over ten years, was presented to the Zurich police, an intensive Swiss investigation began. Bank secrecy no longer applied; a crime, forgery of a bank instrument, had been committed in a Swiss bank. Officials of Crédit Suisse willingly assisted the Zurich police. Tellers were questioned, records examined, deposits and withdrawals tallied. "Helga R. Hughes" was soon revealed to be Edith Irving, Clifford's Swiss-born, blonde wife.

Although Mrs. Irving eventually cooperated with the police investigation, Swiss authorities sentenced her to prison, where she spent fourteen months. Clifford Irving, faced with a mounting mass of evidence against him, first confessed and then pleaded guilty to the charges in the New York courts. For his part in the affair, he spent sixteen months in an American penal institution.

Leslie Waller, writing on the Hughes affair, has speculated on what steps the Irvings could have taken to keep themselves under the protection of Swiss bank secrecy. He has suggested that they could have somehow cashed McGraw-Hill's checks to "H. R. Hughes" elsewhere and then simply banked the proceeds in Switzerland; if they had done so they would not have committed a crime in Switzerland. Most of the $650,000 deposited to the Crédit Suisse account was quickly withdrawn again, as cash, by Edith Irving. Less than $500 was left as a token balance. Part of the money was then redeposited in other banks under another name, some of it reportedly at the nearby Union Bank of Switzerland. In the ensuing fuss, only Crédit Suisse, the bank that accepted the original checks with forged endorsements, was obliged to break bank secrecy.

Uncle Sam vs. the Swiss

In the Irving affair, the Swiss cooperated with American authorities, but occasionally some Swiss bankers with long memories must wonder why. Gestapo pressure was bad enough, but the greatest threat ever to the Swiss banking system has come from the United States government.

American pressure was applied to the Swiss because of Switzerland's special relationship with Germany. The Swiss have never been ardent admirers of German politics, but, as neighboring states, Switzerland and Germany have always been natural trading partners. Swiss money has often been invested in Germany, and German money in the Confederation. After World War I, when the Weimar government lost control of the German economy, many large German business enterprises moved their liquid assets to the safety of Swiss banks. Holding companies, formed as Swiss corporations and managed by banks in Basel and Zurich, were used to conduct the international business of German cartels. The stability of the Swiss franc, and the lack of Swiss foreign exchange controls, effectively insulated German overseas business from the chaos in the fatherland.

After Hitler came to power, German corporate funds were joined by those of foresighted private persons of property. Much of the Gestapo's effort to repatriate German funds was directed at this private money. Cartel assets were generally left alone, both because much of Hitler's early financing had come from the industrialists and because the activities of the holding companies were basically in the interests of the German state. In the decades since the war, it has also become apparent that some of the funds carried in the name of German companies were actually Nazi party money, "contributed" to the party but left on deposit abroad in the name of the original account holder.

As World War II began, the Allies adopted a policy of economic warfare against the Germans. In April 1940, although the United States was not formally at war with the Axis powers, President Franklin D. Roosevelt signed Executive Order No. 8389. This gave the U.S. Treasury Department authority over German property in the United States and the power to restrain the business activities of German citizens and others who might be fronting for them. To implement this order, the Treasury began to compile a blacklist of firms suspected of or known to be doing business with Germany. Because of Switzerland's normally heavy trade with Germany, eventually 1,300 Swiss firms were blacklisted.

As the world headed toward total war, capital from many nations began to flow into the United States. Switzerland's federal government sent its gold reserves to New York as a precaution, in case the Germans invaded the Confederation. Swiss banks packed off their dollar reserves, their securities portfolios, and their gold stocks to the New York branches of the Swiss big banks for the duration. By 1941, Swiss assets in the United States were estimated at $1 billion.

In the eyes of the U.S. Treasury, this Swiss money was suspect. They believed that a large portion of it was actually German money, hiding behind the neutral Swiss flag, and perhaps some of it was. Since Swiss banks in New York operated under American banking laws, Treasury agents could and did force them to open their records for inspection. However, New York account records revealed little. The Treasury agents found, as they should have expected if they had been more knowledgeable about Swiss banking practices, that every Swiss asset in New York was carried in the name of a Swiss bank.

Frustrated in its first attempt to crack Swiss bank secrecy, in June 1941 the American government retaliated by freezing all Swiss assets in the United States. Even the Swiss federal gold holdings were frozen, although they obviously did not belong to the Nazis. Throughout the war, the Americans continued their efforts to get the Swiss to reveal the true owners of the frozen accounts and securities kept in New York.

In December 1944, as the war in Europe approached its conclusion, a delegation of Swiss bankers came to the United States to discuss a solution to the stalemate. Treasury officials refused to meet with them on the grounds that they were not Swiss government officials. The Americans stubbornly ignored the fact that, under Swiss secrecy laws, the Swiss government was forbidden to even seek information on the banks' customers. Only the bankers, of course, had any information about German accounts in Swiss banks.

Confidential talks continued in Switzerland between special representatives of President Roosevelt and the Bern government. In early 1945, a compromise was finally reached. The Swiss government would freeze all known German assets, cut off the remaining trade with Germany, and ask the Swiss banks to determine by themselves which of the assets in New York were actually German-owned. Before the banks could complete their survey, though, Germany surrendered and U.S. Treasury agents followed the Allied troops into Germany. The T-men seized German bank and corporate records and interrogated bankers and accountants.

In late 1945, the Swiss announced the results of their bank-conducted hunt for Swiss-held German assets; they had identified holdings worth only a quarter of a billion dollars. In contrast, the U.S. Treasury claimed, based on its probing of German domestic records, that the total should be a full billion dollars, four times the Swiss estimates. To compare with the tally, the Swiss authorities requested access to the material gathered by the Americans. The Treasury rejected this approach and instead pushed for permission to examine Swiss bank records. Naturally, the Swiss refused, and the standoff continued.

Germany was by now totally under the control of the Allied armies. In October 1945, the Four Power Control Council, the de facto supreme government of conquered Germany, promulgated Public Law No. 5. This edict claimed for the allies ownership of all German government property and control over all private German assets, both inside and outside of Germany. The Swiss became indignant. They considered the Allied edict arbitrary; to them, it was a threat to their status as a sovereign nation, and illegal under international law, at least as far as private German property was concerned.

There was probably not as much Nazi money in Switzerland as was commonly thought. Among the true believers, the National Socialist party members, transferring assets abroad was considered a breach of faith in the Third Reich. Swiss accounts could be fatal, too, for party members were not immune to Gestapo observation. Only in the last days of the war, when the Reich's collapse was inevitable, did discipline collapse and the Nazi rank and file attempt to get some funds across the Swiss border. It was generally too late, although some high officials had been successful earlier. After the war, the Swiss quickly moved to locate and return property that had been stolen by the Nazis. Theft is a crime in Switzerland, and the proceeds of theft are not protected by bank secrecy. Reichsmarschall Herman Göring, the Luftwaffe commander-in-chief, had sent looted paintings to Switzerland and sold them through a Swiss art dealer. The Swiss government confiscated this art work from the Swiss residents who had bought it and returned the art to its rightful owners, museums throughout Europe. Nine million dollars found in Göring's personal accounts were also seized and returned to Germany.

As has since been discovered, much of the Nazi money that the Americans were seeking was simply not in Switzerland and never had been. In *Aftermath,* a recent book by Ladislas Farago, the disposition of part of the Nazi party's secret funds by Martin Borman is detailed. Borman was head of the party administration, Hitler's personal secretary, and the man who controlled the Nazi party's "slush funds," so secret that even the official party treasurer did not know of their existence. Always the realist, Borman began to transfer this treasure to Argentina as early as 1943. In an operation code named *Aktion Feuerland,* cases of foreign currency, gold, diamonds, and platinum were shipped via armed convoys across France to Spain. Near Cadiz, they were supposedly loaded onto German U-boats for the long haul across the Atlantic to isolated Argentine beaches. The amount of treasure transferred must have been enormous; shipments continued on a regular basis for about two years, until the end of the war.

Once in Argentina, a small group of German agents acted as "trustees," depositing the funds in several banks under the name of a Señorita Eva Duarte. Knowledgeable readers will recognize the name; at the time, Señorita Duarte was the mistress of Colonel Juan Perón, a middle-aged Army officer with political ambitions. Later, in 1945, she married Perón, and, in 1946, became "First Lady" when her new husband was elected president of Argentina. No one now knows for certain the value of the Nazi assets that passed through Evita Perón's control, but this money was undoubtedly the fuel behind the Peróns' rise to political power. In his book, Ladislas Farago reports on allegations that 75 percent of the Nazi money was kept by Juan and Evita Perón. In 1947, Mrs. Perón went on a "good will" tour of Europe; reportedly, according to documents discovered in Argentina after Perón's fall from power, she took $800 million in gold with her, for deposit in Swiss numbered accounts. Presumably, it was part of these funds that her husband tried unsuccessfully to claim after her death in 1952. It must be noted, however, that supposedly the amount in dispute was only about

$15 million; apparently the rest was either spent, converted from gold to currency and transferred back to Argentina, given back to the Nazis, or reclaimed without fuss by Juan Perón when he was exiled from Argentina in 1955.

In any case, let's get back to our story of American pressure on the Swiss. After Franklin Roosevelt's death in April 1945, the power of the New Deal in Washington began to wane. When the new president, Harry S. Truman, replaced Roosevelt's secretary of the Treasury, Henry Morganthau, Jr., with his own appointee, prospects for a settlement with the Swiss brightened. As Roosevelt's cabinet member, Morganthau had been one of the prime movers behind the "Morganthau Plan." Fortunately for the Germans, this plan was never implemented by the Allies; it called for reducing postwar Germany to an agricultural state by destroying German industrial and financial power.

Truman's officials were more pragmatic than the New Dealers they replaced; they had less fervor for an antitrust, cartel-busting approach to German business. Nevertheless, the U.S. Treasury Department still waged a crusade against Swiss bank secrecy. Unfortunately for the Swiss, Washington in 1945 and 1946 was in a better position to bring pressure against the Swiss government than it had been in 1941. American military administrators now controlled southern Germany and the parts of Austria that bordered Switzerland. The Confederation was an island in a sea of American power and influence.

Swiss bank secrecy had withstood the Nazis, but the Swiss were only partially able to resist American pressure. Swiss diplomats met in Washington with a team of American, British, and French negotiators. The sessions were conducted in secrecy, but ever since there have been rumors that the Americans threatened to cut off Swiss imports of food and fuel if the Swiss did not accede to their demands. Switzerland resisted gamely, but the Americans still held the frozen assets in New York and controlled the critical land routes into the Confederation. In the end, a compromise was reached, one that still kept Swiss banks safe from foreign inspectors but relinquished German assets in Switzerland to the Allies.

All German property in Switzerland was to be identified and seized, but only by the Swiss themselves. The Allies and the Swiss were to divide the proceeds of the seizure, the Allies agreeing to use their share to help pay for rehabilitation efforts in Europe, and not for reparations as originally intended. This compromise, called the "Washington Agreement," did not completely satisfy the Swiss, but they were in no position to argue any further. Finally, with the U.S. State Department pressuring the Treasury to settle the matter, the blacklist was lifted and the frozen Swiss assets released.

The Swiss have always held that the Allied seizure of German private property was ethically wrong, especially since most private German assets in Switzerland had been sent there to keep them out of the Nazis' hands. They felt a moral obligation to those Germans who lost property because of Switzerland's forced cooperation with the Allies. For this reason, the Swiss share of the proceeds of confiscation was used to quietly reimburse private German depositors and the former German owners of property in Switzerland. Swiss bankers pride themselves that eventually all their German customers were paid for the assets the Swiss had given up under American pressure. This repayment did much to restore European confidence in the Swiss banking system; the Germans again quickly became perhaps the heaviest foreign users of Swiss accounts.

Waivers of Secrecy

Surprisingly, Swiss bankers today exhibit less antagonism toward the United States than might be expected. Understandably, they remain cautious about involvement with the American Treasury, and, as a result, quite a few banks seem reluctant to accept Americans as customers.

One of the ways that some Swiss banks use to discourage American depositors is by requiring a "waiver of secrecy" from them. This waiver usually includes a statement that the customer will satisfy his obligations to the U.S. Treasury on his "own initiative." It also authorizes the bank to give the U.S. tax authorities any information they may request. Some waivers are very loosely worded, permitting account details to be given to just about anyone. One bank's release statement allows it to pass data to the IRS or "to any other U.S. government agency or any other U.S. public institution or agency if . . . requested by them."

There seems to be some disagreement among Swiss bankers as to the propriety of requiring such authorizations. Some take the position that no "true" Swiss bank should ever ask for such a waiver, since it denies the customer the benefits of bank secrecy.

Many, but certainly not all, of the American banks operating in Switzerland require signed waivers from U.S. residents. It is understandable why they do; although the branches operate under Swiss law, their home offices are very vulnerable to U.S. government pressures.

There is no real reason to sign this sort of waiver, however. Most banks do not ask for them; those that require waivers offer no special advantages over those that do not. In fact, demanding waivers of secrecy in favor of the U.S. Internal Revenue Service seems to be a special form of discrimination practiced only against Americans.

Holding Up Your End

Perhaps the banks that do require waivers are not just discriminating against Americans. Maybe they just consider us too unsophisticated to appreciate true banking secrecy.

In the aftermath of Watergate, there is ample evidence to support this view; we do not seem to know how to keep a secret. The newspapers of the world have carried many reports of American politicians, spies, and businessmen testifying before grand juries and investigating commissions. Not only have the details of discreet political payoffs and secret business arrangements been exposed, but the affairs of our intelligence community have been dragged out into the open and raked over. Regardless of how much this delights newspaper editors, reformers, and our enemies, we must seem like a nation of blabbermouths to the Swiss.

One recent example of this sort of thing is the Northrop bribe investigation. The Northrop Corporation is an American aircraft manufacturer that has been successful largely because of its ability to sell military aircraft overseas. Northrop, in 1971, apparently set up a small Swiss company, the Economic and Development Corporation, or EDC. This Swiss organization was then paid a commission of 1½ percent on all international sales of Northrop's F-5 fighter-bomber. In turn, EDC "promoted" the sale of the plane with "the right people in the right places." Allegedly, EDC was used as a conduit for bribes to key foreign officials involved in aircraft procurement.

In hearings before a Senate subcommittee, a high Northrop official apologized publicly to Saudi Arabia for bribing Saudi air force generals with $450,000. The investigating subcommittee made public over 500 pages of Northrop documents relating to its involvement with EDC. These revelations prompted Senator Charles Percy to call for the disclosure "of all dummy corporations created by multinationals for special financial or tax purposes.''

Meanwhile, back in Switzerland, EDC was silent. Its officers, almost certainly Swiss bank officers or their appointees, were left trying to maintain bank secrecy. The fact that Northrop had publicly testified about its deal with EDC did not release the Swiss from their obligations under the banking law.

As a by-product of Nixon's fall from grace, investigations into violations of the federal campaign contributions law turned up another example of how not to use a Swiss bank account. The giant Minnesota Mining and Manufacturing Company (3M) was exposed for making illegal corporate contributions to state and federal politicians. Rather than face a trial, 3M and several of its corporate officers admitted their guilt.

In six years, from 1963 to 1969, 3M allegedly transferred almost $500,000 to a slush fund operated through two or more Swiss bank accounts. Phony insurance premium charges were reportedly paid from a 3M Swiss account to another Swiss account. Large fees were also paid to a Swiss lawyer for legal services that supposedly were never performed. The laundered money, now off 3M's corporate books, was then withdrawn from the Swiss bank in cash and brought back to the United States. Kept in a headquarters safe, the money was apparently used to make unlawful political contributions. The company's initial mistake was to contribute $30,000 to Nixon's reelection campaign fund in 1972; it was this donation that presumably triggered the investigation.

The firm's arrangements worked well and were secure until January 1975. Early in that month, Richard Allyn, a Minnesota assistant attorney general, served a search warrant on 3M's board chairman, Harry Heltzer. The search party soon found what it wanted, several file folders labeled ''Political Contributions'' and a ledger detailing the transactions of the slush fund.

Grand jury indictments soon followed. Because those indicted pleaded guilty, there was no publicity-generating trial. There was little national press coverage until *The New York Times* published a comprehensive story on the scandal, by Michael C. Jensen, in March 1975. This writer is indebted to the *Times* and to Mr. Jensen for details of this affair.

These two case histories are enough to illustrate an essential lesson of banking secrecy. In both the Northrop and the 3M cases, secrecy was broken on this end. The Swiss upheld the secrecy arrangements in their usual professional manner. Because of the tax and political aspects of both cases, it can be predicted that the Swiss will not cooperate with American investigators. But in both affairs, there is no real need for more information from the Swiss; 3M's and Northrop's corporate files provided more than enough evidence. Their urge to document, record, and keep books is reminiscent of Nixon and his tapes, which led to his downfall.

Most readers of this book will undoubtedly be interested in bank secrecy only as a protection against the future. Perhaps a tiny minority might be contemplating some grander scheme, with its manipulations hidden behind the screen of secrecy. Regardless of intent, anyone who expects to use Swiss bank secrecy successfully must maintain his own security arrangements.

A Swiss account is not secret if the owner brags about it to his acquaintances. If a divorce is a possibility, or a spouse simply talkative, wisdom suggests that he or she not be told that a Swiss account even exists. If taxes are evaded, prudence prohibits letting one's accountant know; the IRS pays informers well for information on tax evaders. Above all, if a Swiss account is maintained as a secret account, common sense rules out accumulating a file of letters and statements from a Swiss bank; records provide evidence, and evidence convicts.

A Side Note

Banking secrecy cannot be simply disregarded, as unpatriotic or un-American, even by those readers who see a Swiss account as primarily protection against inflation. If a hard-currency hedge is successful, if gains are made that offset the declining value of the dollar, the "profit" is subject to American taxes. It is uncertain whether the IRS will attempt to tax such foreign exchange "profits" at regular rates as ordinary income or will allow taxpayers to classify them as "capital gains" if the currency is held for more than six months.

Since such problems have yet to be decided in court, this remains a very gray area. It is ironic, though, that many Americans, otherwise law abiding, will be tempted to maintain secret accounts to achieve their hedge goals without a tax handicap.

The Future of Secrecy

For Americans, the future will probably bring increased pressure against their use of Swiss bank secrecy. Even now it is illegal to maintain a *secret* account, for all foreign bank accounts must be declared to Internal Revenue at tax return time. The future dangers to secrecy lie in the predictions made in chapter 3: that U.S. residents may be required to give the government a blanket "waiver of secrecy," that additional transfer restrictions might be imposed, or that all foreign accounts may be made illegal for private parties.

Recent probing of the Central Intelligence Agency's activities brought to light an extensive mail monitoring operation. Foreign mail was checked, addresses noted, and letters sometimes opened and photographed. The use of secrecy would be threatened by a similar operation directed at mail to and from Switzerland. Even without opening the letters, return addresses would provide investigative leads. American account holders would be forced to seek other ways to communicate with their Swiss banks.

The United States for years has pushed for arrangements with the Swiss for access to their bank records. In December 1974, the Swiss Nationalrat ratified a treaty which, if approved by both the U.S. and Swiss upper houses, would provide better procedures for disclosure in criminal cases. Although U.S. officials can be expected to publicize this pact far out of proportion to its real effect, it is an opening wedge. Over the long term, perhaps twenty years, support could develop for greater cooperation.

Although Americans may find it more difficult to utilize, banking secrecy will remain the law in Switzerland. Both the Swiss voters and the Swiss bankers would have it no other way. No matter what happens elsewhere, the Swiss treasure their financial privacy, and would defeat any attempt to impose restrictions upon them. Swiss banks depend on secrecy to draw a certain portion of their foreign trade, even though secrecy was not planned with that in mind. The Swiss banking system has grown too large to exist solely on the trade of Swiss residents; it can only be hoped that Swiss bankers value their American business enough to resist future moves by the U.S. government.

8

Swiss Regulations Affecting Americans

REGARDLESS OF THE REASONS Americans may have for maintaining Swiss franc accounts, two Swiss regulations will complicate their banking affairs. Neither ruling was enacted to restrict personal accounts, but they are a factor that must be considered.

Limitations on Interest

Swiss banks are allowed to pay interest only on the first 50,000 Swiss francs held in an account by foreign depositors. An additional 50,000 francs may be accepted on an interest-free basis. On any balance over SFr 100,000, however, the banks must collect a "negative-interest" tax of 10 percent a quarter (40 percent annually) for the benefit of the Swiss government.

Basically, under the provisions now in effect, Swiss banks are not allowed to pay any interest at all on Swiss franc accounts held by nonresidents. However, the first 50,000 francs in savings accounts or savings books, and in deposit or investment accounts, are exempt from these restrictions. A nonresident is allowed only one Swiss franc interest-earning account.

The negative-interest charge is collected monthly, a prorated one-third of the 10 percent quarterly charge. The tax computation is based on the average daily balance for the month. A temporary surge in the amount of francs in an account does not necessarily create a tax liability; if the daily average balance for the entire month is less than SFr 100,000, no tax is deducted for that month.

Foreigners with Swiss franc accounts that were established before October 1974 are fortunate; they can maintain higher balances without being penalized by the interest limitations or the negative-interest tax. The current regulations were imposed on November 20, 1974, retroactive to October 31, 1974; if an account was already in existence on that date, the balance as of October 31 is exempt from these restrictions. Interest limitations and negative-interest charges are based only on increases over the October 31 account balance. For instance, if the balance of a previously established account were SFr 200,000 on October 31, 1974, interest could now be paid on all balances up to SFr 250,000 (SFr 200,000 + SFr 50,000). Negative-interest tax would not be deducted until the average balance in this account exceeded SFr 300,000 (SFr 200,000 + SFr 100,000).

These restrictions and charges were imposed by the Swiss Bundesrat, the Federal Council, to discourage the inflow of foreign money to be exchanged for Swiss francs. Switzerland is a small country and does not want its money to replace the dollar as the primary international currency. Similar measures have been in effect, almost continually, since 1971. During the monetary crisis of that year, foreign money poured into Switzerland, seeking the safety of the Swiss franc. The Swiss government, in an effort to stem or at least slow the flood, put certain emergency regulations into effect. A limit of SFr 50,000 for interest purposes was imposed; for a while, from July 1972 to

September 1973, there was also a negative-interest tax of 2 percent a quarter.

The 1971 interest ceiling for foreigners remained in effect until October 21, 1974. Then, in an apparent miscalculation, the Federal Council allowed Swiss banks to again pay interest to nonresident foreigners on the same basis as to the Swiss themselves. The result was another inpouring of foreign money, and a tremendous surge in the demand for Swiss francs. As dollars and other weak currencies were sold for Swiss francs, the exchange value of the franc increased rapidly. In one day alone, on November 14, 1974, the Swiss franc rose by 2.9 percent against the dollar.

This state of affairs lasted only one month, during which there was steady upward pressure on the franc. To protect the franc, in late November, the Federal Council reimposed the interest limitations and added a quarterly 3 percent negative tax. They acted because exports and tourism are two main props of Switzerland's delicately balanced economy. As the foreign exchange value of the Swiss franc rises, Swiss goods cost more and become less competitive on the world market. The tourist industry also suffers as fewer foreign visitors can afford to vacation in Switzerland.

Despite the reimposition of interest limitations, and the addition of a 3 percent negative tax, foreign money continued to flow into Swiss franc accounts. Apparently, there were non-Swiss, with large amounts of money, who were quite willing to pay an annual 12 percent penalty for the privilege of keeping their liquid assets in Swiss francs.

Consequently, the Swiss Federal Council increased the negative-interest penalty to 10 percent quarterly, or 40 percent annually, effective January 27, 1975. This drastically higher rate achieved the desired effect, to stop larger chunks of the weaker currencies from being converted into Swiss franc deposits. As of this writing, the negative-interest tax remains at this level.

Three Loopholes

Three great loopholes exist in the interest limitation regulations, however. The first is deliberate. The regulations are aimed at large depositors, primarily multinational corporations and institutions, who control a huge international pool of liquid capital. A $50 million lump of Arab oil money, moving into Swiss francs, is the equivalent of 10,000 individual accounts for $5,000 each. The Swiss would rather have the 10,000 smaller accounts; they are a more stable type of deposit, considerably easier to reinvest, and far less likely to be withdrawn as a lump sum at a later date. If the amount you wish to tuck away, at interest, in Switzerland is less than 50,000 Swiss francs, or about $20,000, there is no problem at all.

Furthermore, joint accounts of up to SFr 100,000 can also be maintained under the basic exemption; or a husband and wife can each open a separate account for the same effect. Current accounts, the equivalent of checking accounts, earn no interest but are exempt from negative-interest tax up to SFr 100,000.

Loophole No. 2 is inherent in the Swiss banking system. Since each foreign depositor is allowed only one interest-bearing account, banks are now required to ask new depositors if they have another exempt account anywhere in Switzerland. Swiss bank secrecy, however, prevents banks from exchanging information on depositors with other banks or with the Swiss government. There is nothing, therefore, to prevent an American overseas depositor from having several interest-bearing accounts, each under SFr 50,000 and each in a separate bank. The only problem is keeping track of the different accounts and not confusing the paperwork in any way.

The third gap in the regulations is that the restrictions on account size apply only to Swiss franc accounts. Unlimited sums may be kept on deposit in other currencies. Almost all Swiss banks offer current accounts, from which withdrawals can be made at any time; these may be denominated in U.S. dollars, Dutch guilders, Canadian dollars, or just about any other major convertible currency. A few banks offer interest-earning accounts in such currencies as the West German deutsche mark. Swiss banks have also devised a system of placing deposits in other currencies, outside of Switzerland, where the money earns interest that is not subject to the Swiss federal tax.

Swiss Withholding Tax

A major source of revenue for the Swiss government is the Federal Anticipatory Tax. This is a withholding tax of 30 percent, collected on interest income and on dividends from bonds and stocks. Whenever a Swiss bank credits earned interest to an account, 30 percent of the interest is deducted automatically and paid directly to the Swiss federal authorities.

This tax withholding at the source applies to Swiss account holders as well as to nonresident depositors; a Swiss taxpayer can claim credit for the interest deduction when he pays his cantonal taxes. To avoid the problems of dual taxation, an income tax convention was signed between the United States and Switzerland on May 24, 1951; this agreement set up the necessary procedures for Americans to claim a partial refund on taxes held out by the Swiss. An American taxpayer, if he so chooses, can obtain a refund of five-sixths (83.3 percent) of the amount withheld, directly from the Swiss Federal Tax Administration.

To obtain a refund, it is necessary to complete Form R–82, "Claim to Refund of Swiss tax." Copies of this form are obtainable from the Administrative Office of International Relations, Internal Revenue Service, Washington, D.C. 20225. Both sides of the R–82 form are shown in illustrations 8–1 and 8–2.

Since the Swiss banks, maintaining secrecy all the way, collect and forward the withholding tax without identifying the ac-

For claimant:

RETAIN THIS COPY for your file while claim is pending. Do not forward it with original and duplicate to Switzerland.

R 82   Claim to refund of Swiss tax

withheld at source on dividends and interest derived from sources within Switzerland

---

Form for use by: (a) Individuals resident in the United States (other than Swiss citizens who are not also citizens of the United States) (b) United States corporations (c) other United States entities.

Filing of claim: This form, duly completed and signed before a notary public of the United States, must be sent (duplicate unseparated) to the Federal Tax Administration of Switzerland, Bundesgasse 32, CH - 3003 Berne, Switzerland. It must be accompanied by suitable evidence of deduction of Swiss tax withheld at source, such as certificates of deduction, signed bank vouchers or credit slips, etc.; these documents (certificates of deduction excepted) will be returned to the claimant. If the claimant, at the time of claiming, is outside the United States, the declaration may be made before a United States consular officer.

Time of filing: This form may be filed on or after July 1 or January 1 next following upon the date payable of the income, but **not later than** December 31 of the **third** year following upon the calendar year in which the income became payable.

I. Claimant

Name in full: ....
(Block letters)

Full residential address: ....

II. Questions to be answered by the claimant

On the date(s) set out in column 5 on the back hereof:

1. were you beneficially entitled to the income specified on the back hereof? ....

2. were you engaged in trade or business in Switzerland through a permanent establishment situated therein? ....

3. a) were you an individual resident in the United States? ....   b) were you an individual resident in Switzerland? ....

   c) were you a citizen of the United States? ....   d) were you a citizen of Switzerland? ....

4. were you a United States corporation? .... (indicate State of incorporation) ....

5. were you a United States entity (other than a corporation)? .... (give full details of claimant and of all persons concerned, including their residence, wherever situated, and their proportionate shares under observations on the back hereof)

III. Further requirements

6. Claimant's last United States income tax return, relating to the year .... was filed with the District Director of Internal Revenue at

   ....

   Claimant's Taxpayer Identifying Number ....

7. The claimant has not filed or caused to be filed any other claim for refund of Swiss tax in respect of items of income listed on the back hereof and has no knowledge of any other person or persons having claimed or caused to be claimed a refund of Swiss tax in respect of such income

8. The claimant will furnish additional information and/or documentary evidence if called upon to do so by the Federal Tax Administration of Switzerland

IV. Claim

9. The claimant therefore claims refund of Swiss tax amounting to Swiss Fr. .... as set out on the back hereof which amount

   is to be remitted to him with Check on Berne or to be paid for his account to ....

   ....

V. Declaration

I/We hereby solemnly declare, under the penalties of perjury, that the statements made by me/us in the present claim, including the data listed on the reverse side hereof, are correct and true to the best of my/our knowledge and belief.

....
Signature of claimant or declarant(s)

If signed by persons other than the claimant, their full names, residential addresses and capacity must be added hereafter:

....

....

Declared at ....

   this .... day of .... 19...........

before me ....   (Seal)
(Signature and title of notary public or consular officer)

Address ....

14112

Illustration 8–1: IRS Form R-82 (front)

Back of Form R 82

SCHEDULE of income taxed at source, in respect of which refund of Swiss tax is claimed

Specification of income entitled to tax refund at the rate of
25 %: Interest on Swiss bonds, bank deposits and certain long-term loans.
In column 6 also list interest on bank deposits on which 27 % has been deducted and refund of 22 % is made.
15 %: Dividends from Swiss corporations and similar income

In column 2, state exacte date of acquisition, if acquired within twelve months prior to date payable shown in column 5.
If acquired earlier, just state "prior to 19 . . .".

Capital investment			Income taxed at source (enter **gross** amounts)			
Description of securities (stock in Swiss corporations, bonds, etc.), bank deposits, loans, etc. Name of debtor	Date of acquisi- tion	Number of shares; the others total par value Fr.	Rate of dividend, interest %	Date payable of dividend, interest etc. (day, month, year)	Interest Fr.	Dividends Fr.
1	2	3	4	5	6	7

Observations
(Use separate sheets in duplicate, if necessary)

Enclosures:

Total gross amounts of income taxed   Fr. .... Fr. ....

Claim for refund

25 % on total of col. 6 Fr. ....

15 % on total of col. 7 Fr. ....

Total claim   Fr. ....

For official use only

Fr. .... Fr. ....

Fr. .... to be refunded

Refund made ....

Check No. ....

Duplicate sent to O. I. O. ....

GPO 869-573   R 82

Illustration 8–2: IRS Form R-82 (back)

count holders, it is necessary to provide the Swiss tax authorities with some details. Form R–82 asks for the name of the depositor's Swiss bank, the account number, and details on the amount of interest earned and the tax collected. The claimant must compute the amount of refund due, and specify whether the refund is to be sent to him by check or paid directly back into his Swiss account.

Proof that the tax was deducted, generally a copy of an account statement from your bank, should accompany the claim, which must be signed before a notary public. The completed refund request is sent to: Federal Tax Administration of Switzerland, Bundesgasse 32, CH-3003 Bern, Switzerland.

Whether or not an American depositor should file a claim for a tax refund depends on several considerations. The amount of the refund will equal 25 percent of the total interest earned on the deposit, which is certainly significant. Six percent interest becomes only 4.2 percent, and 5 percent only 3.5 percent, if a refund is not claimed.

A taxpayer who did not disclose ownership of a foreign account on his U.S. tax return would probably decide not to ask for a refund. Form R–82 is an American IRS form; a copy will undoubtedly be checked against the individual's U.S. tax returns. If there is a discrepancy, the ensuing hassle with Internal Revenue would tend to make any refund not worth the effort.

An American with several Swiss franc interest-bearing accounts also finds himself in an interesting dilemma. The prime reason for opening separate accounts in different banks is to place more than the allowed 50,000 francs at interest. The more money on deposit in Swiss francs, the more interest earned, the more tax withheld. However, to file a claim for a refund on more than one account is to call the attention of the Swiss tax authorities to the fact that the depositor possesses multiple accounts. This individual will probably also decide not to apply for a refund and just to settle for a reduced interest rate.

A Last Comment

Regulations just naturally breed paperwork and loopholes and modifications. Sooner or later, if pressure on the Swiss franc slackens, the reader can expect the negative-interest rulings to be eased. At some future date, however, if the influx of foreign funds became unmanageable, the Swiss government might conceivably be forced to ban the opening of new Swiss franc accounts by foreigners. Regardless of what the Swiss authorities might do, it is unlikely that they will apply harsher terms to already existing accounts; and this is just another reason why an American should open a Swiss account while he is still able to.

9
Types of Swiss Bank Accounts

SWISS BANKS OFFER a wide variety of accounts. To select an account for his purposes, a potential depositor should understand the basic differences between the various kinds of available accounts.

Many of the account types offered by Swiss banks resemble their American counterparts. The major difference is that Swiss banks are universal banks. Commercial banks and savings banks both offer checking-type accounts as well as savings-type accounts.

Two Basic Categories

Depositors' accounts in any bank, in any of the world's banking systems, are divided into two broad categories: demand deposits and time deposits.

Demand deposits are those which may be withdrawn from the bank by the customer at any time, without prior notification.

Money on deposit in demand accounts, since it can be removed from the bank suddenly, provides little support for a bank's long-term loans.

Time deposits are those which are committed to the bank for a longer period of time, by means of withdrawal restrictions. The money that can be taken from these accounts is limited to certain amounts during a given time period. Since these deposits are more predictable, they form the basis of a bank's loan-making ability.

Current Accounts

Current accounts are the most common type of Swiss demand deposit. This type of account is called *Kontokorrent* in German. Sometimes, a Swiss bank will refer to a current account as "at sight," or as a "sight deposit," after the British usage.

Current accounts are very much like American checking accounts, although a checkbook is not usually issued. These are all-purpose accounts, used to hold funds temporarily. The funds in a current account remain available for use at any time, without restriction.

When making investments through a Swiss bank, a current account is often used as a base account. For example, a depositor dealing in securities must have a current account. The cost of the stock purchased is deducted from his current account; proceeds from a sale of stock are automatically deposited back into the account.

Sometimes a bank customer will have two or more current accounts, denominated in different currencies. An individual's investment program might involve buying short-term certificates of deposit, denominated in U.S. dollars, and stocks listed on the Zurich stock exchange, priced in Swiss francs. Such an investor would probably require two current accounts, one in dollars, the other in francs.

Checkbooks are not normally issued for current accounts, unless they are specially requested. Withdrawals can be made by a letter of instruction to the bank. If so instructed, the bank will send a remittance to the depositor, or to anyone else, anywhere in the world, that he may designate. However, if withdrawal instructions are sent by Telex or by cable, most Swiss banks will only remit a draft to the customer's home address of record, unless specific arrangements are made beforehand.

A checkbook might be useful to an individual who traveled a great deal. With a passport for identification and a letter of introduction from his Swiss banker, he could cash checks at almost any bank in the world. Moreover, the checks could be written in any convertible currency, simply by crossing out the denomination imprinted on the check and writing in the desired currency. In France, a check could be written for French francs; in Hong Kong, for Hong Kong dollars; or, in Israel, for Israeli pounds.

It is not recommended that a Swiss checking account be used to pay routine bills in the United States. The American check clearing system relies on magnetic numbers imprinted on all checks. A check drawn on a Swiss bank would cause all sorts of confusion in a typical American bank. Besides, for obvious reasons, it is not a good idea to flaunt ownership of a Swiss account.

As you have learned, the Swiss themselves generally rely on the efficient postal giro system to pay their small bills. As an inducement to use bank checking accounts, a nominal rate of interest is paid on current accounts. Sometimes, when you inquire about accounts from Swiss banks that do not have many foreign depositors, they will send you literature intended for Swiss residents. For example, I have a brochure, in German, from a cantonal bank. It offers $1^1/_2$ percent interest on Kontokorrent deposits. Unfortunately, though, Swiss federal regulations have not allowed Swiss banks to pay interest on current accounts maintained by foreigners since 1971.

There are sometimes small charges made for servicing current accounts. Some banks will levy a small percentage, based on the amount of activity, the number of withdrawals during a given period. Most banks will also charge the account for such incidentals as foreign postage, the cost of bank drafts or cables, etc.

Time Deposits

In this category fall the accounts that are similar to savings accounts in the United States. They should not be confused with the "certificates of deposit," or CDs, currently being pushed by American banks. Swiss CDs are discussed later in this chapter. The CDs issued by Swiss banks are sometimes called "time deposits" in English. As used here, the phrase "time deposits" refers only to the general classification of accounts that are not "current accounts."

Interest rates paid and the withdrawal restrictions that apply are the main differences between the several types of accounts in this category. Higher interest rates are paid on those accounts where withdrawals are more limited.

Account terminology will vary slightly from bank to bank. In their English correspondence and literature, the banks will often translate the account names differently. The accounts, however, are essentially the same from bank to bank.

The most common types of time deposits are explained below. Not all banks offer all the accounts described. Interest rates and other details given here are only representative of what can be expected. For the specifics, there is no substitute for information from a particular bank.

Deposit Accounts

Einlagekonto or *Depositenkonto* are the German translations of "deposit account." Some banks call this account a "private account." Regardless of name, it typically pays 3¹/₂ percent per annum. Generally, withdrawals can be made up to SFr 10,000 monthly, without notice. Three months' advance notice is required for larger withdrawals.

Many banks allow depositors to use deposit accounts as the base accounts for their investment funds. They can buy gold, or stocks, or make other investments from this type of account. When such investments are made through the bank, the normal withdrawal restrictions usually do not apply.

Savings Accounts

Savings accounts, or *Sparkontos,* pay more interest but have tighter limitations on withdrawals. This type of account might pay 5 percent interest, with the depositor able to withdraw only SFr 5,000 freely within a thirty-day period. Advance notice required for larger withdrawals might run six months.

In the United States some banks still use savings books to record deposits, withdrawals, and interest. Other banks provide periodic statements rather than passbooks. In Switzerland, too, both systems are used, depending on the bank.

Banks with many foreign depositors often issue deposit memorandums, with occasional statements, for the various types of savings accounts. Banks with a largely local clientele sometimes

Art der Anlage	Derzeitige Bedingungen und Verfügungsmöglichkeiten	Type de placement	Conditions actuelles et possibilités de prélèvement	Type of Investment	Present conditions and possibilities of withdrawal
Kontokorrent Schweizer Franken: Fremdwährung:		**Compte courant** Francs suisses: Monnaie étrangère:		**Current account** Swiss francs: Foreign currency:	
Einlagekonto (Schweizer Franken)	% p.a.: innerhalb von 30 Tagen bis zu Fr. 10 000.– frei verfügbar, höhere Beträge nach dreimonatiger Kündigung.	**Compte de dépôts** (francs suisses)	% p.a.: prélèvement libre jusqu'à Fr. 10 000.– par période de 30 jours; préavis de 3 mois pour tout prélèvement supérieur.	**Deposit account** (Swiss francs)	3½ % p.a.: up to Fr. 10 000.– freely available within any 30-day period; advance notice of 3 months for larger sums.
Sparkonto (Schweizer Franken)	% p.a.: innerhalb von 30 Tagen bis zu Fr. 5000.– frei verfügbar, höhere Beträge nach sechsmonatiger Kündigung.	**Compte d'épargne** (francs suisses)	% p.a.: prélèvement libre jusqu'à Fr. 5000.– par période de 30 jours; préavis de 6 mois pour tout prélèvement supérieur.	**Savings account** (Swiss francs)	5 % p.a.: up to Fr. 5000.– freely available within any 30-day period; advance notice of 6 months for larger sums.
Anlagesparkonto (Schweizer Franken)	% p.a. bis Fr. 10 000.– % p.a. über Fr. 10 000.– innerhalb eines Jahres bis zu Fr. 5000.– frei verfügbar, höhere Beträge nach sechsmonatiger Kündigung	**Compte d'épargne-placement** (francs suisses)	% p.a. jusqu'à Fr. 10 000.– % p.a. sup. à Fr. 10 000.– prélèvement libre jusqu'à Fr. 5000.– par période d'un an; préavis de 6 mois pour tout prélèvement supérieur.	**Investment savings account** (Swiss francs)	6 % p.a. up to Fr. 10 000.– % p.a. over Fr. 10 000.– up to Fr. 5000.– freely available within a period of one year; advance notice of 6 months for larger sums.
Festgeldkonto (Schweizer Franken Minimum Fr. 50 000.–)	% p.a. je nach Laufzeit. Anlagen von 3 bis 12 Monaten.	**Compte à terme fixe** (francs suisses minimum Fr. 50 000.–)	% p.a. selon la durée du placement allant de 3 à 12 mois.	**Fixed term deposits** (Swiss francs, minimum Fr. 50 000.–)	6 % p.a. – % p.a. according to duration, deposits being possible from 3 to 12 months.
Festgeldkonto (fremde Währungen, vorwiegend in US-Dollars)	Die Zinssätze richten sich nach den jeweiligen Marktbedingungen. Anlagen von 3, 6 oder 12 Monaten.	**Compte à terme fixe** (monnaies étrangères, notamment en dollars USA)	Taux d'intérêt selon les conditions du marché. Dépôts de 3, 6 ou 12 mois.	**Fixed term deposits** (foreign currencies, mainly US-Dollars)	Interest rates in accordance with prevailing market conditions. Deposits of 3, 6 or 12 months.
Kassenobligationen unserer Bank	% p.a. für feste Laufzeiten von Jahren. % p.a. für feste Laufzeiten von Jahren. % p.a. für feste Laufzeiten von Jahren. Ausgabepreis: 100 % zuzüglich 0,6 % p.a. halber eidg. Titelstempel.	**Obligations de caisse** de notre Banque	% p.a. d'une durée ferme de ans. % p.a. d'une durée ferme de ans. % p.a. d'une durée ferme de ans. Prix d'émission: 100 % plus 0,6 % p.a. moitié du timbre fédéral sur titres.	**Cash Bonds** of our Bank	6½ % p.a. for fixed durations of 3-4 years. 7 % p.a. for fixed durations of 5-8 years. % p.a. for fixed durations of years. Issue price: 100 % plus 0.6 % p.a. ~~half of federal stamp duty on securities~~ 1%oo turn over tax
	Die auf diesen Anlagen entrichteten Zinsen unterliegen der eidg. Verrechnungssteuer von 30 % ungeachtet der Staatszugehörigkeit und des Wohnortes des Kunden. Aenderungen der Bedingungen bleiben vorbehalten.		L'intérêt provenant de ces placements est assujetti à l'impôt anticipé suisse de 30 %, sans égard au domicile ou à la nationalité du client. Lesdites conditions sont données sous les réserves d'usage.		Interest on these investments is subject to 30 % Swiss withholding tax, regardless of the client's domicile or nationality. The above conditions are given under the usual reserves.
Obligationen und Aktien	Auf Wunsch vermitteln wir gerne nähere Angaben.	**Obligations et actions**	Renseignements détaillés sont communiqués sur demande.	**Bonds and shares**	Detailed information is supplied on request.

Illustration 9–1: Multilingual account descriptions from a large bank

use passbooks to record account activity. But, no matter; banks using savings books will hold the passbooks in safekeeping in their vaults for foreign depositors. This prevents loss in the mail and allows the bank to post accrued interest easily. If necessary, the passbook could be sent to you by registered mail. Or, if you were in Switzerland, you could obtain the booklet simply by identifying yourself.

In its English correspondence, a Swiss bank will usually identify a passbook-style account as a "savings book" account. In German, *Sparkonto* means a savings account, and *Sparheft* generally indicates a savings book is involved.

Investment Savings Accounts

If a depositor does not anticipate needing to draw upon the money in an account, he can earn higher interest rates with an investment savings account. Called *Anlagesparkonto* in German, this type of account would commonly earn 6 percent interest. However, only SFr 5,000 could be withdrawn without notice in a given year. Six months notice, again, would typically be required to obtain larger sums.

Youth Savings Accounts

Savings banks and cantonal banks offer a greater variety of savings accounts than the commercial-type banks. One special type of account is the *Jugendsparheft,* or youth savings book account. One bank quoted 6 percent interest, up to an account maximum of SFr 10,000, for this special type of account. Minimum deposit required was only SFr 10, with withdrawals limited to SFr 1,000 yearly. Higher amounts require six to twelve months notice.

Ersparniskasse in
am   platz
Gemeinnützige Stiftung
«Die Kleinbank mit der persönlichen Note»

Ab 1.Juli 1974 erhalten Sie mehr Zins:

7% **auf Kassenobligationen**
Laufzeit: 5, 6, 7 und 8 Jahre fest
Abschnitte zu Fr. 1000.—, Fr. 5000.— und Fr. 10 000.—

6½% **auf Kassenobligationen**
Laufzeit: 3 und 4 Jahre fest
Abschnitte zu Fr. 1000.—, Fr. 5000.— und Fr. 10 000.—

6½% **auf Jugendsparhefte**
für Personen unter 20 Jahren
zur Förderung des Sparsinns der Jugendlichen
mit einem Vorzugszins

6% **auf Alterssparhefte**
für Sparer über 60 Jahre
bis Fr. 5000.— pro Monat frei verfügbar

6% **auf Anlagehefte**
zur Anlage mittelfristiger Gelder
Minimaleinlage Fr. 1000.—

5% **auf Sparhefte**
monatliche Bezüge bis Fr. 5000.— ohne Kündigung

4% **auf Privat- oder Salärkonto**
bis Fr. 10 000.— pro Monat frei verfügbar

Illustration 9–2: German-language flyer from a savings bank, showing interest rates

As the name implies, these accounts are designed to encourage younger savers. Age limits vary a bit from bank to bank, but twenty years of age is the typical upper limit. Such an account might be the ideal way to introduce a youngster to Swiss banks and to the concept of international investment in general.

Certificates of Deposit

As a deposit form, certificates of deposit, or CDs, are much the same the world over. A depositor's money is accepted by the bank for a definite time period. The bank pays a higher rate of interest because it knows it will have the money available, and therefore lendable, until a certain date. At the end of the agreed upon period, principal plus earned interest are returned to the depositor. Often arrangements are made to have the money redeposited automatically in a new certificate.

Generally, the Swiss usage in English for CDs is "fixed time deposit" or "fixed term deposit." In German, they are *Festgeld*, or *Festgeldkontos*. *Fest* means fixed or solid, *geld* is money.

Under the emergency regulations of 1971, Swiss banks are not permitted to accept Swiss franc fixed term deposits from foreigners. Overseas depositors may, though, invest in fixed term deposits in other currencies. Some banks offer these certificates denominated in dollars. Direct time deposits with Swiss banks, however, are liable for the 30 percent Swiss anticipatory tax, or withholding tax, on the interest earned.

Swiss banks are nothing if not accommodating. To help their foreign clients evade this Swiss tax, Swiss bankers offer fixed term certificates of deposit issues and guaranteed by other European or American banks. A depositor's money is placed, through the Swiss bank but at the depositor's own risk, with another bank outside of Switzerland. Since the interest earned on these CDs is technically earned outside of Switzerland, withholding taxes do not apply. This type of deposit is most commonly available in dollars, English pounds sterling, German marks, or Dutch guilders. Terms are usually only three, six, or nine months.

Such deposits are carried in the name of the Swiss bank. In other words, the records of the Dutch or German bank issuing the CD show only the name of the Swiss bank arranging the deposit. The account holder's name appears only in the Swiss bank's own records. In such ways is bank secrecy preserved.

These fixed term deposits are always made in round figures, in units of US$1,000 or DM1,000, etc. Minimum amounts for fixed term deposits vary widely, from US$1,000 upwards, depending on the practices of the banks involved. A little comparison shopping is necessary, however, to find certificates issued in the smaller amounts.

Interest rates vary daily, according to the market for such money and the currency involved. Rates in early August 1974 reached a peak of about: Dollar—10 to 10$^{1}/_{2}$ percent; Sterling—12 to 13 percent; Guilder—7$^{1}/_{2}$ to 8 percent; and Deutsche Mark—7$^{1}/_{2}$ to 8 percent. Since then, the interest has dropped somewhat.

Since these are indirect deposits, through the Swiss bank rather than with the Swiss bank, the interest is paid in full to the depositor when the term deposit matures. For its services in arranging the certificates, the bank collects a service charge, determined by the amount and currency of the deposit. Again, you must ask a particular bank for its fee schedule. Average charges run $^{1}/_{16}$ to $^{1}/_{4}$ of 1 percent of face value, with a flat minimum per transaction.

Festgeld deposits, or fixed term deposits, are practical for moderate sums between about US$5,000 and US$30,000. For larger amounts, there is an even faster track, paying somewhat higher interest rates.

Fiduciary Eurocurrency Deposits

Swiss banks will place a depositor's money in the Eurocurrency market under conditions similar to the interbank certificates just described. The major difference is that larger sums are required, and the interest rates are higher.

Some banks, such as the private banks and the Swiss affiliates of the London merchant banks, specialize in Eurocurrency placements. Again, the bank acts as agent, but funds are placed at the depositor's risk. Swiss withholding taxes do not apply.

Terms are short, one month to six months, with some one year deposits. Minimums depend on the currency: US$50,000; £10,000; 100,000 deutsche marks, guilders, or French francs.

Typical interest rates quoted in February 1975 were: Dollar—$6^5/_8$ to $7^{11}/_{16}$ percent; deutsche mark—$5^3/_4$ to $6^5/_8$ percent; sterling—$12^7/_8$ to $13^1/_4$ percent; and French franc—$10^3/_4$ to 12 percent.

The February quotes above were somewhat lower than they were in mid-1974. In August 1974 the rates were about: Dollar—$12^{15}/_{16}$ to $13^5/_{16}$ percent; deutsche mark—$8^1/_8$ to $9^5/_8$ percent; French franc—$17^3/_4$ to $18^1/_8$ percent. These Eurocurrency rates fluctuate slowly over a wide range, depending on the demand for this sort of money.

Again, the precise rates vary daily. The banks that handle these deposits will gladly quote you current rates. By the time their quotes arrive in the mail, however, they will be out of date. Unless you are dealing in such sums that you are in contact with your Swiss bank by Telex, you will have to rely on them to place your money at the going rate.

You will notice that the less stable the currency, the more chance of devaluation, the higher the interest rates. A depositor gets paid for his risks.

It should be obvious, but a warning anyway! Fiduciary deposits are the big time. Multinational corporations, Arab finance ministers, and Zurich private bankers are active in this market. Any American private depositor moving into this type of investment should understand foreign currency fluctuations, and the nature of the Eurocurrency market. (For an elementary explanation, see chapter 13.) Subscribing to at least one or two advisory services would be a very good idea. There won't be one damp eye for you if you get caught in an overextended market or a currency devaluation.

Bank Bonds

Many Swiss banks offer their own bonds directly to the public. These bonds are denominated in Swiss francs, and generally are sold in multiples of SFr 1,000. In German, they are called *Kassenobligationen,* or "cash obligations."

Two or three classes of Kassenobligationen are usually offered, differing in the interest paid by the bank. Terms commonly run from three to eight years. Interest varies from about $6^{1}/_{2}$ percent to $7^{3}/_{4}$ percent, with the higher rates on the longer term bonds.

To invest in these bank bonds, your money should not be needed for the term of the bond. The principal will not be available until maturity. Interest on these bonds, since they are denominated in Swiss francs, is also subject to the 30 percent Swiss withholding tax.

Other Accounts

Banking is a very competitive business in Switzerland. Naturally, some banks have devised special accounts to attract more customers. Banks without special literature for overseas depositors will sometimes send their regular brochures, describing all their services in French or German.

Some of these special services, such as salary accounts, are useful only to those depositors living and working in Switzerland. Called *Salärkontos* or *Gehaltskontos,* salary accounts are special arrangements by which employers deposit their employees' pay directly into their bank accounts. In some cases, cash withdrawals can be made from automatic machines, occasionally located right on the employer's premises.

Another type of special account, however, might be of interest to Americans over the age of sixty or sixty-five. They are the older depositor's answer to youth savings accounts. Called *Alterssparhefte* in German, these accounts are what an American bank might call a "senior citizens savings book." Either higher interest or lower withdrawal restrictions are featured. As an example, an Alterssparheft paying 6 percent interest, comparable to a regular investment savings account, would allow withdrawals up to SFr 5,000 monthly without prior notice. The comparable investment savings account in the same bank would allow free withdrawal of only SFr 5,000 annually.

Reference List of Account Names

German account names were given in the type descriptions of this chapter. Since the English translations vary from bank to bank, the German titles can serve as a reference point. If you are unsure of exactly what type of account is being described, or what type of account to ask for, the German account name can always be used to clear things up.

Here is a list of common account names in English, German, French, and Italian.

English	German	French	Italian
Current account Checking account Sight deposit	Kontokorrent Girokonto *	Compte courant	Conto corrente
Deposit account Private account	Einlagekonto Depositenkonto	Compte de dépôts	Conto di deposito
Savings account Savings book	Sparkonto Sparheft	Compte d'épargne	Conto di risparmio
Investment savings account Term savings account	Anlagesparkonto	Compte d'épargne-placement	Conto di risparmio-investimento
Certificate of deposit Fixed term deposit Fixed time deposit	Festgeld Festgeldkonto	Compte à terme fixe	Conto vincolato
Bank bonds Cash obligations Cash bonds	Kassenobliga-tionen Kassenscheine *	Obligations de caisse	Obbligazioni di cassa

* used only occasionally

10

How to Open Your Account

BY NOW, YOU SHOULD BE IMPATIENT to get to the heart of the matter, the actual procedure for opening a personal Swiss bank account. You have probably made some preliminary decisions as to the types of accounts that interest you the most.

This chapter covers the mechanics. It will take you step by step through the details, from the initial contact to the transfer of funds. It will also explain the account opening forms commonly used by Swiss banks.

Choosing an Account Type

The amount of money that a potential depositor has available for deposit is the most important factor in choosing a bank and determining the type of account to be opened. Obviously, an individual with $50,000 or $100,000 in liquid capital has a wide choice of possibilities. The options for someone with only $200 are naturally more limited. However, both can find a safe home for their money in Switzerland.

Anyone considering placing more than $20,000 in a Swiss bank must weigh the interest limitation and negative interest factors. As noted previously, Swiss banks may not now pay interest on Swiss franc deposits over SFr 50,000, roughly $20,000. In addition, they must charge a forbidding 10 percent quarterly tax on all balances over SFr 100,000, or about $40,000.

These factors merit consideration, but where there is a will there is a way. Basically, larger amounts could be placed as a lump sum or as several separate deposits.

As a lump sum, one solution would be to open an account in one of the hard currencies other than the Swiss franc. There is no negative tax on German deutsche mark or Dutch guilder accounts, although interest-bearing accounts in these currencies are not offered by many Swiss banks. Alternatively, the money could be placed in an investment management account (see chapter 14) in any of the private or other banks specializing in such services. Your Swiss banker would then handle the placing of the money to achieve your investment goals while staying clear of the interest and tax restrictions.

A combination of several accounts could be handled in many ways, depending on the investment goals and the amount of risk felt acceptable. If getting out of dollars and into a hard currency were the prime consideration, one strategy would be just to tuck the money into several interest-bearing Swiss franc accounts, each in a different bank. Each account would of course be limited to the maximum of 50,000 Swiss francs. Bank secrecy would nullify the ruling restricting each foreign depositor to only one interest-earning Swiss franc account. A little extra paperwork would be involved in keeping track of the different accounts, but there would be the added advantage of diversification, with the money in different banks.

As is always the case, the more money available, the more options that can be exercised at the same time. An investor might decide to keep part of his resources in conservative, savings-type accounts, earning interest while waiting for better days; and, on the remainder, to accept slightly higher risk to earn a higher return. Such a combination might include: (1) interest-earning deposit or savings accounts in Swiss francs, in one or more banks; (2) a current account in another hard currency used to make high-yield, short-term Eurocurrency deposits. Arrangements could be made with the bank to "roll" the Eurocurrency deposits, placing new ones as earlier deposits matured and were paid back into the base account. The current account should probably be in deutsche marks or guilders to avoid occasional high balances in Swiss francs that are liable for the 10 percent negative interest tax.

An average depositor with more limited resources has only a slightly smaller choice of banks and account types. Most banks offer accounts tailored to the depositor with a $2,000 to $5,000 stake. The investor can choose from a variety of offerings, including bonds available in SFr 1,000 units. The most common choice here, however, will probably be a savings-type account, offering safety, a decent yield, and simplicity.

Withdrawal restrictions on an account demand careful consideration against your plans and future needs. The smaller the sum that can be withdrawn without notice, and the longer the acceptable notice required to take out larger sums, the higher the interest rate will be. Future needs should be balanced against the natural desire to earn a higher rate of interest.

An important note: withdrawal restrictions are taken very seriously by Swiss bankers. Their approach is conservative. They do not make loans based on deposits that can be withdrawn without notice. American banks will allow you to pull out money that is committed on time deposits, adjusting the interest rate downward, and perhaps penalizing you a few months' interest. Not so with Swiss banks. If you deposit your money, and agree to limit withdrawals to a certain amount within a given time period in order to earn a higher rate of interest, that is the way it will be. Keep the restrictions in mind when you pick an account type.

An individual with a small amount of capital, say only $100 to $1000, can still take advantage of a Swiss bank account. Without question, the options in this case are limited to a deposit, savings, or investment savings account in a bank that requires a low minimum deposit.

The smaller size of the account works to the depositor's advantage here. It is possible to choose a bank with a low minimum requirement, and to put the money into the highest yielding type of deposit account. If the amount of capital deposited is less than the basic withdrawal restriction, the withdrawal restriction can be ignored as a consideration. For example, a 6 percent account might allow withdrawals to SFr 10,000 (or about $4,000) per year. As long as the total amount on deposit were less than SFr 10,000, in an emergency the total amount on deposit could be removed without notice.

In all probability, someone starting an account with a small amount, as a savings reserve, would plan to add to it regularly. As the account grew in size, the withdrawal restrictions would again require consideration.

By Mail or in Person?

The most common misconception about Swiss bank accounts is that it is necessary to go to Switzerland to open one. If you were to confide to a close friend that you had a Swiss account, his most likely reaction would be to ask, "When were you in Switzerland?"

Sometimes it is advisable to personally visit a Swiss bank to open an account. These special situations are discussed toward the end of this chapter. Almost always, however, it is more practical for an American to handle the whole procedure by mail. It is also less expensive, quicker, and less involved.

Picking Some Possible Banks

At this stage, the listing of banks included in this book becomes important. Chapter 12 is devoted to a listing of Swiss banks that accept deposits from nonresidents. Their correct names and addresses are given, together with a summary of the types of accounts and interest rates offered.

Please note that the information on interest rates is offered only as a guideline. The listed rates were correct when the survey of banks was completed; with time, however, the rates may vary, depending on many factors, most of them unpredictable. The only way to determine the actual rates a bank is now paying is to write and ask. But rates on savings-type accounts are not likely to fluctuate very much. For the near term, the information given will presumably remain reasonably correct.

The first step, then, is to refer to the listing of banks. Bearing in mind the types of accounts you are considering and the amount of money you desire to deposit, check carefully over the listings. Note the names and addresses of about six banks that interest you.

Initial Contact

At this point, you have two alternatives. You can either send an initial deposit directly to a selected bank, and complete the necessary paperwork later, or you can write to the banks for information and forms.

The first alternative, transferring your initial deposit on the first contact, is covered a little further on in this chapter.

Presumably, most readers will prefer the second option, writing for up-to-date information. Opening a Swiss bank account is a new experience. Comparing the materials sent by the different banks gives an opportunity to select a bank, and an account type, at leisure.

To each of the banks on your preliminary list, you should send a short letter requesting information on the types of accounts offered and their current interest rates. You should specifically ask for forms to open an account. Swiss bankers tend to think literally, to take requests verbatim. If you ask for information, they'll send information. If you ask for forms, they'll generally send forms.

In answering queries from prospective customers, the banks follow different procedures. Some banks with a large overseas trade will routinely send a complete information packet. Other banks, more accustomed to walk-in customers than to mail depositors, will answer with a letter of information, explaining that they will send the necessary forms for completion after the initial deposit is received.

The following is a suggested form of initial contact letter, requesting information and forms.

123 Main Street
Anywhere, Missouri 20220 USA
15 April 197–

Bank Hofmann, AG.
Talstrasse 27
8001 Zurich, Switzerland

Gentlemen:

Would you please send me details on the types of accounts offered by your bank?

Information on current interest rates, and the forms necessary to open an account are also requested.

Sincerely yours,
Richard M. Doe

If you are interested in services other than current or savings-type accounts, you should ask for data on these services in your first letter. It will save unnecessary extra correspondence. Sample third paragraphs follow:

I am particularly interested in time deposits in Eurocurrencies. Information on this service would also be appreciated.

I am particularly interested in investing in precious metals and gold coins. Information on this type of investment would also be greatly appreciated.

I am particularly interested in the purchase of securities. Information on this service, if offered through your bank, would also be greatly appreciated.

The use of red-and-blue-trimmed airmail envelopes is suggested. A letter sent airmail, in a plain envelope, stands a good chance of being misdirected and sent by surface (boat) mail. Airmail postage from the United States to Switzerland, at this writing, is 31 cents per $1/2$ oz. There is also a special 22-cent "Aerogramme" letter, that requires no envelope, available at the post office. No enclosures are permitted in Aerogrammes, so these forms may be used to write for information, but not to transmit funds.

The Banks Reply

About two weeks after sending off your query letters to Switzerland, you will receive the banks' replies. Swiss banks, for reasons of secrecy and economy, generally use plain airmail envelopes. At the most, a box number is given as a return address. Sometimes, a bank employee's home address is handwritten as the return address.

Contents of the plain envelope will vary. Almost always there will be a letter, on the bank's stationery, describing the various types of accounts recommended or available to foreign depositors. The larger banks, with a large volume of inquiries, will often use a form letter, typing in your name and address. Many times, these banks will send a complete information packet, with account descriptions and application forms in English.

Private banks, and those dealing on a more limited basis with English-speaking outlanders, will sometimes send a specially composed letter describing their services. Some banks will send a copy of their latest annual report, multilanguage brochures explaining their services, or detailed information on their specialties.

Quite often, in dealing with banks that have few if any dealings with Americans, you will receive a letter written in an English that seems strange and stilted. Misspellings abound. Bear in mind that your inquiry was probably answered by a Swiss who learned his English in school, and doesn't use it enough to achieve written fluency. No matter, you'll be able to understand it. Numbers are the same in all languages. And, after all, how many American banks could even answer a letter in German or in French?

Some banks will describe their services, and explain that they will send the appropriate forms for completion after the initial deposit. Opening an account here is very much like sending a deposit without inquiring first, except that your information is up to date and the bank is expecting your money. These situations are covered a little later on.

Regardless of how elaborate or simple the reply, the banks will need basically the same information on each depositor. They may provide a long form, with all the information requested on one sheet, or several separate cards to collect the data. A form package generally consists of an application form or signature card, a designation of a power of attorney, an ac-

REQUEST FOR THE OPENING OF AN ACCOUNT

* see list of Branches overleaf

The undersigned

Family name	First name(s)	Date of birth
Mr. Mrs. Miss		

Place of residence	Country	Street and number

Nationality	Occupation	Reference

wishes to become a client of   Bank.

ACCOUNTS DESIRED*

☐ **Current account**

    ☐ in Swiss francs

    ☐ in US dollars

    ☐ in _____

☐ **Private account** in Swiss francs

☐ **Savings book** in Swiss francs   } opened in one name only

☐ **Investment books** in Swiss francs

ACCOUNT HOLDER(S)

☐ account to be conducted in the applicant's sole name

☐ account to be conducted in the joint names of

_____ and/or

_____ (not more than two persons)

POWER OF ATTORNEY

☐ none

☐ to be conferred upon the following person(s), valid also after the death of the principal(s)

1. _____

2. _____

   Family name   First name(s)   Place of residence   Date of birth

CORRESPONDENCE

to be established in ☐ English ☐ German ☐ French ☐ Italian

☐ to be forwarded regularly to the following address

Please, only 4 lines
with 24 characters
each!

☐ to be retained with the Bank and to be forwarded to the address of the account holder(s) upon special request only.

The Bank's Terms of accounts and the General Conditions have duly been noted.

Date: _____ Signature: _____

☒ please mark if applicable

Illustration 10–1: Account application form from a large bank

Correspondence to be addressed as follows:

Holder (s):

Domicile and address:

to BANQUE

Ref.:

I / we have taken note of the **conditions printed on the reverse** hereof governing my / our relationships with Banque I / we shall sign individually / jointly as follows:

Family Name	Christian Name(s)	Mr. / Mrs. / Miss	Nationality	Signature
1)				
2)				

I / we have granted power of attorney with right of representation, **in accordance with the conditions overleaf,** with individual / joint signature to the following:

Family Name	Christian Name(s)	Mr. / Mrs. / Miss	Nationality	Signature
3)				
4)				

Observations (Date of birth of the minor, etc.):

Place and date:
Signature of Holder(s):

8. 71 1000

Illustration 10–2: Signature card with power of attorney designation

knowledgment of general conditions, and a signature verification form. (See illustrations 10–1, 10–2, and 10–3.)

Signature Cards

Personal accounts may generally be carried in one of three forms. A single name account is an account in one name only. Joint accounts are carried in two names, but only one signature is required to instruct the bank. Another type of joint account

172

Nous confirmons par la présente l'authenticité du spécimen de signature ci-après:
We confirm herewith the authenticity of the signature specimen executed below:

Nom:
Name:

Prénom:
First Name:

Nationalite:
Nationality:

Date de naissance:
Date of Birth:

Spécimen:
Spécimen:

Lieu et date:
Place and Date:

Timbre et signature valide:
Stamp and legal signature:

4.74

Illustration 10–3: Typical signature verification form used by many banks

requires a collective signature, with two people signing together to effect a withdrawal or other bank action.

On the application form or signature card, you will be required to designate one of the above types of account. Space is always provided for a specimen of each signature. Signature in German is *Unterschrift; Unterschriftsprobe* means specimen signature. *Einzelunterschrift* indicates single signature, and *Kollektivunterschrift* is simply a collective signature. The bank will also want to know your home address, the address to which mail is to be sent, and often your language preference for correspondence.

In Europe, most countries provide their citizens with identity cards which carry a number. European countries are about the size of American states. Since most middle class Europeans cross national borders as frequently as we cross state lines, they generally also have passports. Many Swiss banks, accustomed to providing accounts for Europeans, ask for a passport number or an identity card number as routinely as American banks ask for a social security number. If you have a passport, by all means provide the bank with the number. If not, you may safely ignore this question. If you feel that you might want to visit your bank someday, it might be desirable to apply for a passport now. (Information is included in chapter 15 on obtaining a U.S. passport.) When a passport is issued, you can notify the bank of your passport number. But don't delay opening an account just because you don't have a current passport.

Power of Attorney Designation

Since no one lives forever, Swiss banks want to know who your beneficiary is. However, under Swiss law the banks are not allowed to accept instructions naming a beneficiary, nor instructions such as a will that becomes valid only after the account holder's death. Instead, they will routinely ask you to open a joint account with the right of survivorship, or to grant a power of attorney.

Unlike Anglo-Saxon law, under Swiss law a power of attorney remains effective after the death of the principal. Under article 35 of the Swiss Code of Obligations, a power of attorney "shall not cease by reason of loss of principal's capacity to act nor by his death, but shall continue to remain in force." In the United States, when designating an attorney-in-fact, you are naming someone to act in your stead, giving them the power to act for you in your absence. In Switzerland, you are doing the same, but you are also naming your beneficiary, at least as far as a particular bank account is concerned.

Granting a power of attorney has basically the same effect as establishing a joint account. Under Swiss law, in case of the death of a holder of a joint account, the surviving account holder still controls the account. An attorney-in-fact also retains full power over an account in case of the death of an account holder. Both a joint holder, where one signature is sufficient, and an attorney-in-fact also have full power over the account during the lifetime of the primary account holder.

When granting a power of attorney, several attorneys-in-fact may be appointed at the same time. It can be specified that the individual signature of any one holder of a power of attorney is sufficient. Or, alternatively, you may require that two signatures are necessary to instruct the bank to act, by designating joint powers of attorney.

Power of attorney designations remain in effect until revoked by notifying the bank in writing. On the bank's forms, a sample of the specified individual's signature is needed; you cannot designate a person to act for you without providing their signature on the card. Additionally, some identifying data, such as an address, date of birth, nationality, and passport number are usually necessary for each designated attorney-in-fact.

If you are worried about granting a power of attorney to someone, perhaps because you fear that in a future dispute or misunderstanding they might use their signature power to empty the account, there is a simple solution. At the time you provide their specimen signature to the bank, it is not necessary to let the designated person know the name of your bank, its address, or your account number. This information can be sealed in an envelope and left in the care of a third party, perhaps your lawyer or accountant, to be delivered when certain circumstances, such as your demise, occur. Just be sure that if you follow this course of action some provision is made to provide the appointed attorney-in-fact with the necessary information at the time he will need it to act for you.

Signature Verification Forms

Since the Swiss banks are dealing with their mail depositors at long distance, most of them will require a verification of a new depositor's signature. Despite bank secrecy, the banks want to know whom they are dealing with.

The rules for signature verification are not clear-cut. Each bank has slightly different requirements. Unlike powers of attorney, where the rules of the game are spelled out by Swiss civil law, the banks make their own policy on signatures.

Generally, they require that your signature be witnessed, on the signature card or on a special form, by some sort of official. As one bank puts it, ". . . we ask you to have your signature . . . legalized by a Swiss consulate, your bankers, or by a notary public."

If you live in or near a city served by a Swiss consulate, your signature verification problems are solved. The official verification form costs a few dollars but it should impress your Swiss bank. (A list of Swiss consulates in the United States is provided as part of chapter 15.)

A sample of a special signature verification form provided by a Swiss bank is illustrated in this chapter. Other banks provide no special verification card but ask that the specimen signature on the bank signature card be officially witnessed. If you wish to be discreet, you can have your signature verified on a "neutral" form, one that gives no indication that it is intended for a Swiss bank. Sometimes the Swiss bank provides a suitable form. If not, here is an example of a satisfactory substitute, which you can type up and fill in.

To Whom it May Concern:

Signature verification of:

_____

First Name   Last Name

Date of birth: _____

_____

Specimen Signature

This is to certify that I have witnessed the above signature, which was signed in my presence, and after an examination of the personal identification of the above individual, certify the authenticity of this signature.

_____

Signed

_____

Title

Place: _____
Date: _____

Swiss banks place great faith in other bankers. A signature verification by another bank is generally acceptable to the Swiss banks. Some banks will specify that the American bank should be one with a Swiss correspondent, but this includes most larger banks. The only problem here is that most Swiss banks do not seem to understand that an American does not really want to hassle with his bank about providing a signature verification for a Swiss bank. It's sort of like asking your current doctor to refer you to another physician because you feel the first doctor is a bit of a quack. Personally, I'd have an American bank verify my signature only as a last resort, and then only on a "neutral" form.

Notary publics are acceptable to many Swiss banks, but, unfortunately, not to all. Schweizerische Bankgesellschaft, the Union Bank of Switzerland, goes so far as to stamp its signature verification slip with: "Notary Public not accepted." If a bank does not clearly state to the contrary, a notary's verification would be an excellent choice.

Signature verifications are a nuisance, but the Swiss banks want a piece of paper to show that they've made an effort to check a foreign depositor's identity.

A few banks take a more practical approach and require no verification paper. They accept your specimen signature at face value, without "official" witnesses. According to the terms of one bank, "The Bank undertakes to check the authenticity of any signature but is not bound to make any further control on their legality. The Bank is not responsible for any damage resulting from undetected forgeries." In other words, the bank will check the signature on an instruction against the specimen, and if they match, will presume that everything is okay. Shame on you if you let someone else know where your account is and what your special signature is at that bank.

General Conditions

Somewhere in the material sent you by the Swiss bank will usually be a statement of the bank's general business conditions, the working rules of the banking relationship. The conditions cover signatures, powers of attorney, notifications to clients, statements, overdrafts, etc. You should read them carefully, and understand them. Generally, when signing the signature card, you are affirming that you have received a copy of the "general business conditions," and have read and accepted them. Some banks go a bit further, and send you two copies of the conditions. You are asked to sign one copy and send it back to the bank.

American banks follow a similar practice. Have you ever read the fine print on the back of the signature card at an American bank?

Opening an Account Without Forms

Some readers might prefer to open a Swiss account without waiting for a bank to send them an information packet and forms. Perhaps they might wish to get some bonus money safely tucked away, before they are tempted to spend it. Perhaps currency transfer restrictions are in the offing, and it's now or probably never. Whatever the reason, it's a simple procedure.

Some Swiss banks, when they receive money from an overseas depositor on the first contact, hold the deposit in a special escrow-type account. When the proper paperwork is completed and returned to the bank, they then open a regular account and assign an account number. Other banks, especially if they receive adequate information with the deposit, will immediately assign an account number and open a regular account.

Each bank follows its own internal working procedures in handling accounts opened in this way. The key element is information; the banks naturally hesitate to officially open an account until they are certain as to exactly what type of account you prefer. It is obvious that in your letter transmitting the deposit you should clearly state what type of account you want, and what currency you wish it to be denominated in.

You can refer to chapter 12, the listing of Swiss banks, to select an appropriate bank. Since this listing provides information on the account types, and minimum deposit requirements, you are not operating in the blind. Again, you are cautioned to bear in mind that interest rates may have changed between the time this listing was prepared and the date you make use of it. A $4^1/_2$ percent deposit account may now pay 5 percent, or only 4 percent.

Here is a sample of the sort of letter you should use in this situation.

123 Main Street
Anywhere, Missouri 20500 USA
15 July 197–

Migros Bank
Seidengasse 12
8023 Zurich, Switzerland

Gentlemen:

You are being sent this letter to request that you open an account in my name.

Enclosed you will find two bank money orders (giros), each for US$1,000, totaling US$2,000, as an initial deposit.

It is requested that you open a Swiss franc deposit account (Depositenkonto) in the name of Richard Doe. I intend to designate my wife, Mary Doe, as attorney-in-fact with powers over this account.

Will you please inform me what your current interest rate is on this type of account?

It is also requested that you send me the necessary bank forms such as signature card and signature verification form for completion. They will be returned to you promptly so that your records will be complete.

Thank you for your courtesy. I await your reply.

Sincerely yours,
Richard Doe

Transferring Funds

Your money can be transferred to Switzerland in one of several ways:

(1) Using your personal check, by mail.

(2) Using money orders, by mail.

(3) Through the foreign department of almost any large bank. The bank will arrange the transfer directly to the Swiss bank of your choice.

(4) In person, by flying to Switzerland. Cash, letters of credit, cashier's checks, bank drafts, or other forms of negotiable instruments can be used to physically handle the transfer of assets.

By Personal Check

Using your own personal check is perhaps the simplest and most direct way to transfer funds. Even though your local department store won't take your check without demanding all sorts of identification, and perhaps photographing you in the process, any Swiss bank will accept it. On your first deposit, your account will probably not be credited until your check has cleared. The check will be routinely returned to you through your American bank with your regular monthly statement. A drawback, however, is that the check, in clearing, will go through many hands, including the Federal Reserve System. Your bank, if it's interested, will know that you have a Swiss account. American banks are required to keep a record of all out-of-U.S. transfers, including checks, of over $5,000. American banks also maintain a microfilm record of all checks drawn on their depositors' accounts, available, naturally, for government inspection.

Money Orders

Money orders are perhaps the best way to transfer funds. Very discreet, too. Every bank sells money orders. So do drug stores and neighborhood convenience grocery stores.

Unless they are marked to the contrary, bank money orders are good the world over. A major use of money orders of all types is to remit small sums overseas, to dependent relatives, for example. Many tellers, however, will inform you that the money orders issued by their bank are good only in this country. As a matter of policy, some banks would prefer that you use their foreign exchange departments, where they can charge higher fees than the 25 cents or 40 cents commonly charged for personal money orders.

Limits on the amount that money orders can be bought for vary. In my city, bank money orders are commonly valid up to $1,000. Money orders from commercial companies, such as American Express or Travelers Express, can usually be bought only in smaller denominations. Their common limits are $200 and $250.

Regardless, the amounts of money that can be transferred by money order are astounding. Buying four to sixteen money orders a day requires only an hour or so, and some extra diligence. Two or three small denomination money orders can be purchased at one outlet without much fuss.

Transferring $4,000 per day regularly for thirty days will put $120,000 in a Swiss account. Several money orders can be mailed in one envelope. Four thousand dollars a day is well under the legal limit of $5,000, at which point you are required to fill out forms. Since, for all practical purposes, compliance with the legal limit of $5,000 per day is voluntary, I'm sure that many people will just ignore it, and send off as much as they like.

Although large amounts can be transferred to Switzerland

using multiple money orders, money orders leave a trace, too. They eventually come back to the issuing company.

On their face, money orders commonly carry some such restriction as, "This personal money order is sold upon the following conditions: (1) The purchaser sign, in ink, his/her name and address after filling in a date and the name of the payee . . ." If the individual money order user did not want to leave a record of transfers abroad, he could adopt a practice of the Swiss bankers. He could sign the money order, but in an illegible scrawl. The required address could be simply his town and state.

Of course, when using money orders to transfer funds, it is important to type or clearly print in the name of the recipient bank. Whether or not the bank can read the sender's signature is unimportant. Since American-style deposit slips are not used, each mail deposit, on either a new or an established account, must be accompanied by a note telling the bank the name of the account to which the money is to be credited. The amount of the deposit, and, if the account is already established, the account number, should also be mentioned.

If a currency transfer restriction crunch ever comes, I can imagine the problems the Treasury will have digging through the records of money order companies. If many people adopted the practice of signing Swiss-style, the government would need battalions of agents to check the records.

Some further notes on money orders. When the money is withdrawn from a bank account and then used to immediately purchase a bank money order, many banks will routinely note the number of the customer's account on the bank's copy of the money order. A few banks still insist, when selling money orders, on typing in the name of the recipient. Obviously, if privacy is important, people who do not wish to be cross-referenced will purchase their money orders elsewhere.

And a final note. Money orders are also sold by U.S. post offices. Anyone using a postal money order to transfer money to a Swiss bank is automatically providing the federal government with a full record of the transaction. Money orders are available from so many other sources that a postal money order would be an absolute last and worst choice.

Through an American Bank

Any U.S. bank with a foreign exchange department can handle the entire transaction, paperwork and all. They can also sell you a draft made out to a Swiss bank, which you can then airmail to Switzerland, or have the bank transmit it for you. Many American banks will try to talk you out of opening a Swiss account, however. Asking an American bank to help you open a Swiss account is something like going to a Ford dealer and trying to buy a new Mercedes Benz. Both the car dealer and the bank will try to sell you their own merchandise. No one likes to give business to a competitor.

Another objection, and the primary one in my opinion, to transferring money or opening a Swiss account through a U.S. bank is the lack of privacy. While it is not now illegal to have a foreign bank account, in the intermediate to long term, it could very well become so. If things get desperate, and the U.S. government institutes severe exchange limitations, I can imagine platoons of Treasury agents combing bank records looking for the names of people who have transferred assets to Switzerland. If you use a bank foreign exchange department, you'll be on record.

U.S. branches of Swiss banks fall into the same category as American banks. A New York, Chicago, or Los Angeles office of a big Swiss bank necessarily operates under U.S. banking laws. While they can give you good advice, and perhaps verify a signature, they must maintain records that are accessible to Internal Revenue and Treasury agents.

Flying Money to Switzerland

Transferring your funds in person, especially in the form of cash, is not recommended. Couriers, flying the Atlantic with black attaché cases filled with small-denomination bills, are a staple of escape fiction. In real life, the process is a bit more cumbersome. Since antihijacking measures have become routine at our airports, hand luggage will be searched. While it is not yet illegal to transfer money out of the United States, you are asked to declare any amount over $5,000 that you take out. Imagine the embarrassment of being found with $50,000 in good old greenbacks in your briefcase. How do you explain it? At the very least, expect your name and address to be noted by some sort of bureaucrat and then forwarded to Internal Revenue for investigation.

Anyone clever enough to acquire large sums of unrecorded cash should be devious enough to find other ways to transfer it to Switzerland. Anyone who has accumulated this much money legally will want to avoid the suspicion of any hanky-panky.

It is reasonable, however, to take smaller sums, enough to open an account, to Switzerland in person. A thousand or two thousand dollars, in money orders, tucked in with your airline ticket is okay. That much in additional travelers checks is risk-free, too. This money could be used as an initial deposit to open an account. Additional deposits could then be made by mail.

The only valid reason I would consider for going to Switzerland to open an account would be to personally discuss investment plans with a Swiss banker. Indeed, as one prestigious private bank puts it, ". . . the most important thing is to know exactly your objectives and we would really appreciate if we can discuss about them during one of your next trip to Switzerland."

Special Considerations for Big Money

For those readers who have substantial funds that they desire to deposit, and who wish to avail themselves of the good offices of a Swiss private banker, a different approach is involved. Many private bankers answer routine queries with a noncommittal letter, or with an institutional brochure describing their firm in general terms. Few will give specific interest rates by mail. Their answer will be something like this, "Please indicate your wishes about the transactions you intend to handle with us and we shall offer the appropriate conditions." Most will also ask you how you heard about their bank, or who recommended their services.

If the sum involved is over $100,000, a trip to Switzerland should be considered, though it is not absolutely necessary. The cost of a trip to Zurich or Geneva, including a few days vacation in the process, is only $1,000 to $1,500. This is a small price to pay for meeting your banker face to face. The extra service that you will receive as a result of the trip makes it a good investment, too. You'll sleep better with your money in the hands of someone you have met personally.

For serious money, serious enough for a trip to Switzerland, a different initial letter is advised. You should make a selection of bankers from the list in chapter 12, and send each a letter in the following vein.

Gentlemen:

You are being sent this letter in search of information on investment opportunities.

Recently, I liquidated some of my U.S. investments. I now have approximately US$240,000 that I would like to place in a Swiss bank. My primary goal is security of capital. (or income from investments, or capital appreciation, as appropriate.)

I plan to be in Switzerland next month, the week of September 7, 197—.

Would it be possible to arrange an appointment with an officer of your bank to discuss appropriate investments?

Your firm's name and address was obtained from a listing in the English-language book *How to Open a Swiss Bank Account*.

Sincerely yours,
John Doe

For anyone capable of accumulating capital of these dimensions, the general information offered in this book should be enough to allow you to competently handle your own negotiations.

If you follow this course of action, and plan a mini-vacation to Switzerland to discuss investment plans personally with a Swiss banker, it would only be prudent to talk with more than one bank before making a final decision. Appointments should probably be made with two or three banks. It would be more convenient if the banks were all in one city, either Geneva or Zurich. However, if enough time were allowed you could handle discussions in both cities easily enough. Distances in Switzerland are short, internal transportation excellent, and the scenery breathtaking.

Opening a Company Account

The formalities and procedures for opening an account in the name of a business are basically identical to those for a personal account. A signature card and signature verification forms must be completed. In addition, proof that the account is an authorized company account will be needed.

The following is a quote from the general business conditions of one of the Big Five: ". . . there must be submitted an extract of . . . a board resolution or other documents as enacted by your local law . . . in order to prove that the persons signing the card on the lower right-hand corner are entitled to represent the company and to confer authorities, as the case may be. Non-registered entities, such as single proprietorships, etc., have to submit legally signed articles of association or by-laws." Copies of these supporting documents must be certified by a bank or by a Swiss consulate in the same manner as a signature verification form.

In Summary

Opening a Swiss bank account is really a simple process. One needs only to decide how much money to deposit, select an account type, write a letter, transmit the money, and fill out some elementary forms. The biggest hurdle is a psychological one. To open a Swiss account of his own, an individual must first overcome his personal inertia. The rest is easy.

11

Communicating with Your Bank

MOST AMERICAN DEPOSITORS WILL BE ASTOUNDED at the ease with which they are able to open a Swiss account. Their pride in their new bank account may turn to bewilderment, however, when they receive their first statement from Switzerland.

Swiss banks that accept deposits from overseas usually have the capability of corresponding in English. This is not really surprising. English is an international language; Europeans often use it to conduct business when neither party knows the other's tongue. American depositors are fortunate that English is their native language. Imagine the frustration of trying to open a Swiss account using only a minor language, perhaps Burmese or Indonesian.

Like banks everywhere, Swiss banks give special attention to new accounts. The initial paperwork is handled by individuals competent in English; there is little difficulty at this stage.

Bank Forms

Once the account is opened, however, records are kept in the prevailing language of the local Swiss canton. In Zurich and most of central and northern Switzerland, German is used. French predominates in Geneva and the western areas along the border with France. Banks in Bern, the national capital, are likely to use either German or French. In the Italian-speaking cantons, German, surprisingly, seems to prevail among the banks with an American trade.

English translations of application forms and account information sheets are quite common. It is unusual, however, for English to be used on the routine forms, such as statements, that a depositor will receive periodically. The miscellaneous statement forms sent American customers are identical to those issued a bank's local Swiss depositors. Despite the fact that these routine forms are different from those commonly used by American banks, they are not all that difficult to understand. The forms illustrated in this chapter are typical of the paperwork used by many Swiss banks. If you can decipher them, you can figure out anything your bank might mail you.

Illustration 11–1 is an acknowledgment of receipt of a small deposit of US$100. Explanations and headings are in three languages: German, French, and English. This form is basically the same as a deposit slip; the bank completes it and sends it to you the day they receive your mail deposit.

Key letters have been over-printed on this illustration to point out possible confusion points.

a. "7.10.1974" is October 7, 1974. An American would write this date as 10-7-74 or 10/7/74. Swiss usage follows the general world practice of putting the day first, then the month and year. Foreigners think that Americans write their dates backwards.

b. This describes the form of the deposit. In reality, a bank

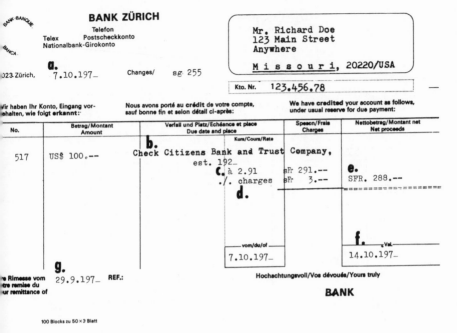

Illustration 11–1: Acknowledgment of receipt of a mail deposit

money order was sent, but it is described here as a "check."

c. The rate at which U.S. dollars were converted to Swiss francs, 2.91 SFr to a dollar, is shown here. One hundred dollars times 2.91 equals SFr 291. Again, exchange rates vary daily.

d. This is a flat fee for converting dollars to francs. The bank must use your dollars to buy Swiss francs.

e. Amount actually credited to the account. SFr 291 minus SFr 3 leaves a balance of SFr 288.

f. "Val." means *Valuta,* the date when the transaction becomes effective. The bank allowed one week for the check to clear.

g. Another date, this time a reference to the day the deposit was sent from the United States, and a good indication of the time lag involved when doing business by airmail.

The second form, illustration 11–2, is a *Tagesauszug,* roughly a "daily statement" in English. It basically repeats the data on the deposit acknowledgment slip, but originates in the bank

BANK

Postfach 8023 Zürich   Tel.   Postcheckkonto

BANK · BANQUE

BANCA

Herrn/Frau/Fräulein/Firma

RICHARD DOE
123 MAIN STREET
ANYWHERE
MISSOURI 20220   USA

Tagesauszug

| Kontobezeichnung | **a.** DEPOSITENKONTO | | | | | | |

| Konto-Nummer | 123 456 78 Abschluss | **b.** 3 1 1 2 7_   Auszug-Nr. | | | 1   Zürich, | 8 1 0 7 |

Text	Kapital Fr.			Wert	Zinsnummern		
	Soll	Haben			Soll	Haben	
a. Saldo / a. Zs.-Nrn. CHECK		2 8 8 0 0	1 4 1 0				**c.** 2 1
n. Saldo / n. Zs.-Nrn.		2 8 8 0 0					2 1

Francoposten: Fremde Währung
              Börsenkäufe- und Verkäufe
              Coupons
              Tratten und Rimessen
              Überträge und Storni

Auf Ihrem Konto nahmen wir heute obige Buchungen vor
Wir bitten Sie, den Auszug bei Empfang zu prüfen und uns
von etwaigen Unstimmigkeiten zu unterrichten.
Gutschriften über Checks und Wechsel erteilen wir unter
den banküblichen Vorbehalten.
                           S. E. & O

Illustration 11–2: A "daily statement," or *Tagesauszug*

bookkeeping department as the deposit is actually posted. This
form summarizes account activity on a given day. If there were
more than one deposit or withdrawal posted on the same day,
all would be listed. Note that it is in German only; the book-
keepers have dropped English and French.

Again, the over-printed letters indicate points of interest.

    a. This indicates the account is a *Depositenkonto,* or deposit ac-
       count. Some customers might have a current account, a *Kon-
       tokorrent,* too. The description serves to separate the paper-
       work on multiple accounts carried in the same name.

    b. *Abschluss* translates as "closing date." On December 31, a
       regular statement will be issued.

    c. This is the interest number, or *Zinsnummer,* which records the portion of the full annual interest this deposit will receive until the end of the interest period. This is indicated in a different way by various banks, and may not even appear on the forms sent to the depositor.

An *Abschlussbuchungen,* or closing statement, is shown in illustration 11–3. Most Swiss banks post interest only once or twice a year. This sample statement is in German and French only.

- a. *Abschluss per* means only "statement, as of." December 31, 1974 is the effective date.
- b. This statement was prepared early, on December 12, to beat the year-end rush.
- c. The balance before closing, *Saldo vor Abschluss,* is ·SFr 4,365. Europeans often use different methods of indicating thousands and decimals when writing numbers. Some banks might write this amount as 4'365.00, or even 4.365,00. Expect to find periods where you anticipate commas, and vice versa.
- d. Interest, or *Zins,* as a percentage. This account pays 5 percent or "5.000."
- e. Interest stated in Swiss francs. Since the total balance was not on deposit for the full year, the interest shown, SFr 163.69, is less than 5 percent of SFr 4,365.
- f. Whenever interest is posted to an account, the bank collects 30 percent anticipatory tax for the Swiss government. Thirty percent is shown as "30.000."
- g. Thirty percent of SFr 163.69, the interest, is SFr 49.10, the tax withheld.
- h. *Spesen,* which means expenses or charges, is a favorite word of Swiss banks. The SFr 3.10 deducted here is just a routine charge and includes foreign postage.
- i. This is the new balance, *Neuer Saldo,* including earned interest but minus tax and *Spesen.*
- k. *Wert* is another word for *Valuta,* the effective date. Again, "31.12" is December 31.

BANK

Herrn/Frau/Fräulein/Firma
M./Mme/Mlle/Maison

RICHARD DOE
123 MAIN STREET
ANYWHERE
MISSOURI 20220 USA

Postfach 8023 Zürich

BANK BANQUE

BANCA

Postcheckkonto

Auf Ihrem Konto haben wir folgende
Abschlussbuchungen vorgenommen:
Nous avons passé sur votre compte
les écritures de bouclement suivantes:

Kontobezeichnung
Nom du compte

DEPOSITENKONTO

Dieser Beleg ist aufzubewahren und Ihrem Antrag
auf Verrechnung oder ~~Rückerstattung~~ der Ver-
rechnungssteuer beizulegen

Konto-Nummer
No du compte 123 | 456 | 78 Abschluss per
Arrêté au 31 | 12 | 7_ Auszug
No de relevé Zürich,
Zürich, 12 | 12 | 7_

Text / Texte	Satz / Taux		Soll / Débit	Haben / Crédit
Saldo vor Abschluss/Solde précédent				4 365 0_
Soll-Zins/Int. débiteur	%	a/Nm.		
Haben-Zins/Int. créditeur	% 5 000	a/Nrn.		163 6_
Verr.-Steuer/Impôt anticipé	% 30 000	a/Fr.*	163 69	
Kreditkomm./Comm. de crédit	%	a/Fr.		
Zessionskomm./Com s/cessions	%	a/Fr.		
Debitumsatzkomm./Comm.s/mouv. déb.	%	a/Fr.		
Komm. auf Restumsatz/Comm. s/mouv. restant	%	a/Fr.	49 10	
Kreditorenumsatzkomm./Comm. s/mouv. créd.	%	a/Fr.		
Spesen/Frais			3 10	
Neuer Saldo / Nouveau solde	Wert / Valeur	31 12		4 476 4_

* = Verrechnungssteuerpflichtiger Betrag / Montant soumis à l'impôt anticipé

Ohne Ihre Nachricht innert den nächsten 4 Wochen nehmen wir Ihr
Einverständnis mit unserem Abschluss an. Für Debitoren-Konti
wollen Sie uns bitte den beigelegten Richtigbefund rechtsgültig
unterzeichnet zurücksenden.
Buchungen nach dem Abschlussdatum erscheinen in neuer Rechnung.

Sans vos nouvelles dans les 4 semaines concernant ce bouclement,
nous le considérons comme accepté. Quant aux comptes-débiteurs,
veuillez nous retourner le bien-trouvé ci-inclus dûment signé.
Les opérations effectuées après la date de clôture apparaîtront
sur le prochain relevé.

Illustration 11–3: A periodic closing statement, or *Abschlussbuchungen*

Each Swiss bank has its own style of forms. The ones you receive from your bank may differ in detail from the ones we have just analyzed, but the essential information will be the same. The forms illustrated are typical of those used for standard accounts.

Swiss banks offer many types of services other than current or savings-type accounts. If you become involved in buying or selling securities, gold, silver, or foreign currency futures, expect to be deluged with miscellaneous slips of paper. If you understand the basic account forms these will present no problem. The key phrases, such as balance, effective date, rate, commission, etc., are the same regardless of the type of transaction.

194

Deciphering the Exchange Rate

One of the minor complications of foreign exchange is that each country quotes the value of other currencies in terms of their own money. In its communications with its customers, a Swiss bank will note the pertinent exchange rate in terms of Swiss francs; for example, "2.49" or 2.49 francs to a U.S. dollar. An American, on the other hand, checking rates in his newspaper, will find the quotations given in dollars, ".4009" or US$0.4009 for a Swiss franc.

Do not be disheartened; converting one rate to another is only a matter of intermediate arithmetic. An exchange rate quoted in one currency is just a "reciprocal" of its equivalent in the other money. By way of explanation, please refer again to illustration 11–1, item "c"; the applicable rate noted on this deposit acknowledgment slip is "2.91," or 2.91 Swiss francs to a dollar. To convert, just divide 1 by 2.91; 1/2.91 or $1 \div 2.91$ equals .3436, the price in U.S. dollars of a single Swiss franc. To prove this to yourself, work the same problem in reverse, $1/.3436 = 1 \div .3436 = 2.91$ again.

Reciprocals can be found by doing the necessary long division manually. If available, an electronic calculator simplifies the process; many of the smaller pocket calculators even have a special reciprocal key, usually marked "1/x." If not, just follow the normal division procedures for your particular instrument. If you have a calculator and wish to practice a bit, it is suggested that you try converting a few of the rates shown in illustration 13–1 (chapter 13) to their equivalents in other currencies, and then back again to dollars.

Reference List of Common Terms

For convenience, here is a listing in German, English, and French of the banking terms most likely to appear on communications from your Swiss bank.

German	English	French
Konto	Account	Compte
Konto-Nummer	Account number	No. de compte
Ihr Konto	Your account	Votre compte
Währung	Currency	Monnaie
Betrag	Amount	Montant
Einlage	Deposit	Dépôt
Rückzug	Withdrawal	Retrait
Saldo	Balance	Solde
Nettobetrag	Net proceeds	Montant net
Saldo vor Abschluss	Prior balance	Solde précédent
Neuer Saldo	New balance	Nouveau solde
Zu Ihren Lasten	In our favor	En notre faveur
Zu Ihren Gunsten	In your favor	En votre faveur
Soll, Belastung	Debit	Débit
Haben	Credit	Crédit
Abschluss per	Status per (date)	Arrêté au
Wert, Valuta	Effective as of	Valeur
Kommission	Commission	Commission
Francoposten	Free of commission	Mouvement franco
Spesen	Charges	Frais
Porto	Postage	Port
Briefmarke	Postage stamp	Timbre-poste
Zins, Zinsen	Interest	Intérêts
Steuer	Tax	Impôt, Timbre
Verruchnungssteuer-pflichtiger	Subject to with-holding tax	Soumis à l'impôt anticipé
Kontoinhaber	Account holder	Titulaire de compte
Ort und Datum	Place and date	Lieu et date
Datum	Date	Date
Unterschrift	Signature	Signature
Tag	Day	Jour
Monat	Month	Mois
Jahr	Year	Année

German	English	French
Kauften	Bought	Acheté
Verkauft	Sold	Vendu
Kurs	Price, rate	Cours
Zahlung	Payment	Paiement
Check	Check	Cheque
Reisechecks	Travelers checks	Cheques de voyage
Akkreditive	Letter of credit	Crédit documentaire
Zahlungssufträge	Payment order	Ordre de payment
Tresorfäch	Safe deposit box	Coffre-fort
Vermögensverwaltung	Portfolio management	Gestion de fortunes
Kassenobligationen	Cash bonds	Bons de caisse
Wertschriften	Securities	Titres
Goldbarren	Gold bullion	L'ingot d'or
Buchhaltung	Bookkeeping	Comptabilité
Treuhändabteilung	Trust department	Département fiduciare

Although German banking terminology can seem overwhelming at first glance, it needn't be. The long, involved words are merely compounds, the equivalent of an English phrase. *Vermögensverwaltung* is typical. *Vermögen* means fortune, and *Verwaltung,* administration; the literal translation is thus "fortune administration," or what Americans would call "portfolio management."

Understanding the basic message is the important thing; analyzing the grammatical structure isn't necessary. The word lists in this chapter and in chapter 9 will give an idea of what a particular form is all about, and that's enough. The numbers are what count, and numbers are the same in Switzerland and in the United States.

Instructing Your Bank

Sooner or later, a depositor will want to send additional money to his bank or withdraw funds from his account. Since deposit and withdrawal slips are not used by overseas customers, it is necessary to instruct the bank by letter.

The important thing is to tell the bank clearly and concisely what you want them to do for you. Your letter should obviously include the essentials, such as the account number, the type of account, and the name in which the account is carried. Use a personal letterhead if possible; if not, be sure to include your return address and your name. The signature on the letter should be in the same form as your specimen signature on file with the bank.

Deposit instructions, transmitting funds to an established account, can be quite simple. Here is an example.

> 1600 Pennsylvania Avenue, N.W.
> Washington, D.C. 20500, USA
> 15 September 197–

Wirtschaftsbank Zürich
Postfach 3294
8023 Zurich, Switzerland

Gentlemen:
   Enclosed is a bank money order for US$4,000.
   Will you please deposit these funds to my credit in Swiss franc Depositenkonto No. 987–654?

> Yours truly,
> John Smith

Withdrawal instructions are almost as simple. When asking the bank to send you money, it is necessary to specify the currency desired, to whom the draft is to be payable, and where it is to be sent. In the following sample, the depositor is drawing funds for his own use.

123 Main Street
Anywhere, Missouri 20220 USA
12 January 197–

Basler Kantonalbank
Spiegelgasse 2
4001 Basel, Switzerland

Re: WITHDRAWAL REQUEST

Gentlemen:

Will you please withdraw from my Swiss franc savings account, Sparkonto No. 987–6543, francs equal to US$750?

Please send a check for this amount, in U.S. dollars, to me at my home address.

Yours truly,
John Doe

Withdrawals can be sent to anyone, anywhere, in any convertible currency. The next depositor's affairs are more complicated. He is using Dutch guilders from his Swiss account to buy dollars to send to Guatemala, where dollars are often preferred to the local currency. (Bank and return addresses are omitted in the remaining examples.)

Re: WITHDRAWAL REQUEST

Gentlemen:

Will you please withdraw from my Dutch guilder current account, Kontokorrent No. 12–4567, guilders equal to US$2,500?

Please send a check for this amount, in U.S. dollars, payable to Compania Alfaro, S.A., to the following:

Sr. Miguel Rivera Santos
8ª Avenida 13–55, Zona 17
Cuidad de Guatemala, Guatemala

Sincerely,
John D. Smith

Instructions to your bank can be as complex, or as personalized, as you desire. This lady is having funds sent to her from her Swiss account, while on an extended vacation abroad.

                              Re: WITHDRAWAL REQUEST
Gentlemen:

On the fifteenth of each month, for the next three (3) months, will you please withdraw from my Swiss franc Depositenkonto No. 987–654–32, Swiss francs equal to £400 sterling?

On September 15, on October 15, and again on November 1, 197–, please send a check, payable to me, for £400 sterling, to the following address:

> Ms. Mary Ellen Doe
> c/o Eden Plaza Hotel
> 68 Queensgate
> London SW7 5JT
> England.

Since I will be in England, please retain all correspondence and confirmations on this account temporarily at your bank. After December 10, 197–, the retained correspondence may be sent to me at my U.S. address.

                              Yours truly,
                              Mary Ellen Doe

The Time Element

Normally, using airmail to instruct your bank, it will take about two weeks to receive a withdrawal from a Swiss account. If need be, the process can be speeded up somewhat. Instructions can be cabled or Telexed to the bank. However, this type of withdrawal request does not arrive at the bank over the depositor's authorized signature. Consequently, most banks will only send payment directly to the depositor, at his address of record. If the need can be anticipated, arrangements can be made beforehand, by letter, permitting the bank to make payments to third parties or alternate addresses on cabled instructions. Arrangements can also be made to wire money directly to a depositor's account in another bank. Naturally, the other bank should be informed to expect the wired transfer.

There is always the possibility of using the telephone to communicate with your Swiss bank. This is not recommended, though, because of the language barrier. The probability of misunderstanding is too great. If personal contact had previously been established with an English-speaking bank officer, perhaps on a visit to Switzerland, the telephone could be used in special circumstances. For most account holders, this method remains impractical and unnecessary.

General Guidelines

To be happy with your Swiss bank, it is important to have a good relationship; this is essentially a matter of maintaining good communications. Both parties, the bank and the depositor, must understand each transaction. Confidence will grow if misunderstandings are avoided from the beginning.

The language barrier is the main hurdle to overcome. Although the letters exchanged by the depositor and the bank are written in English, it should always be remembered that the correspondents think in different languages. Correspondence from your Swiss banker will often seem a bit stiff and unnatural. The formal tone does not indicate a lack of interest or an unwillingness to be helpful; it is merely a carryover from the thought patterns of another language and from a different set of business customs.

An effort should be made to be careful and concise in your letters of instruction to your bank. Know exactly what you want the bank to do before you attempt to ask them to do it. Plan your letter to make sure all the necessary points are included. Whenever possible, use banking terminology, and avoid slang or abbreviations. Clarify the English description with the German or French word if misinterpretation seems possible. Example: "Will you please open an investment savings account

(Anlagesparkonto) in my name?'' Review your message for clearness and completeness before mailing it.

Each communication from Switzerland should be read carefully to determine exactly what the bank has done. Some of the forms you receive may have English headings, which makes it easier. If there is no English, use the samples and the word lists in this book to decipher the message.

Simpler banking arrangements, such as standard savings-type accounts, offer little possibility of confusion. Funds are deposited and eventually withdrawn. When venturing into more complicated transactions, though, a good rule is to *understand exactly what you are doing*.

If uncertain, ask questions before committing yourself. If, for instance, the purchase of Swiss franc bonds were being considered, you should know how the arrangements work. Who issues the bonds? What is their term and the interest rate? How often is interest paid? How much commission does the bank charge on the transaction? Who physically holds the bond certificates and clips coupons to collect the interest? Is there a charge for this service? Are the certificates issued in the buyer's name, the bank's, or in bearer form? Can the bonds be sold before maturity? What sort of resale market exists? Once the answers to such questions are known, a decision can be made. If a bank is instructed to handle such an investment for a depositor, it will presume that the depositor is familiar with the details of such transactions.

Essentially, there is no real problem in communicating with a Swiss bank. Keep everything as simple as possible, try to make your instructions clear, and ask as many sensible questions as necessary. Readers of this book already have a good understanding of Swiss banking practices, probably better than most foreign customers. Their understanding and their confidence will grow as they put into practice what they have learned.

12
Listing of Swiss Banks

A POTENTIAL DEPOSITOR NEEDS one essential piece of information. To establish a Swiss bank account, he must first know the name and address of a bank that accepts foreign business.

The listing of Swiss banks provided here should allow the reader an adequate choice, and give him the basic details necessary to make initial contact.

A Long Listing

The collection of Swiss banks that follows is perhaps the most extensive listing found outside of a bank directory. Why are so many banks listed? Basically, to insure that a reader will be able to find a bank suited to his needs. Individual banks may change their policies in response to varying conditions.

As an example, let's review what happened at the Foreign Commerce Bank of Zurich. Harry Browne, in his "Monetary Crisis" book, recommended the Foreign Commerce Bank. He did so with good reason; the bank is oriented toward the American depositor. All its literature and its forms are in intelligible English, and a very wide range of services is offered.

In early 1974, when Browne's book first came out, Foreign Commerce asked for moderate minimum deposits of only US$1,000 for a deposit account, and US$1,500 for a current account. By April 1974, because of a rush of new accounts, their initial deposit requirement was raised to US$4,000. Still under pressure, by August 1974 their minimum had to be increased to US$15,000. Eventually, in mid-1975, Foreign Commerce was able to lower their minimum requirement back to a more reasonable US$5,000.

An influx of American funds also caused some other banks to make adjustments upward. The Union Bank of Switzerland (Schweizerische Bankgesellschaft), for example, once had a minimum requirement of SFr 100, or about $33.50, but raised it under pressure to US$500.

A longer listing offers a wider choice. Many medium-sized and smaller banks are included that are well-equipped to handle American accounts. A longer listing will also hopefully remain accurate for a longer time, at least as far as account minimums and willingness to accept new foreign business are concerned. If 25,000 readers of this book, for example, should opt for a Swiss account, they will not overwhelm six or seven banks with their business. Instead, their accounts will be spread over 100 or so institutions.

How This Listing Was Compiled

This list is the result of a survey conducted especially to collect data for the readers of this book. After much reflection, a simple approach was used. A short letter was sent to hundreds of Swiss banks, asking for information on account types offered and current interest rates. Information was also requested on the other services available through the particular bank. The letter was similar in style and tone to a simple query by any potential American depositor.

The intention was to get a natural response, a routine answer to a routine inquiry. A more ornate survey plan was rejected, to protect the integrity of the information gathered. It was felt that some banks would overrespond, providing a quicker or more complete answer than they would regularly provide. The problem of underresponse was also considered. In Switzerland private banks are not required to publish financial statements. As a corollary to this privilege, private banks are not permitted to advertise or solicit openly for customers. This is one of the reasons private banks consistently want to know who referred you to their bank.

It was felt that sending a questionnaire, or explaining that information was being gathered for inclusion in an English-language book on Swiss banks, would turn off many banks, especially the private ones. Swiss bankers can be almost paranoid in the interpretation of the outer limits of bank secrecy. Private banks would also be reluctant, to say the least, if they thought that cooperating in such a survey project could be construed as an open solicitation of new business.

A Reassurance

This could be an appropriate place to reassure everyone concerned, readers and Swiss bankers alike. No special arrangements were made with any bank to refer customers to them. These bank listings are intended for the use of the readers of this book, and not to increase the business of any bank or group of banks.

Using the List

Every effort has been made to provide as accurate a listing as possible of banks prepared to open accounts and to accept deposits by mail from Americans. It is intended that this list be a guide to selecting a Swiss bank, based on a matching of the reader's needs and the services offered by a particular bank.

Please understand that specific interest rates, the types of accounts available, or the minimums required may change. Banks everywhere reserve the right to adjust their conditions without much notice. A Swiss bank association may recommend a change in the interest rates offered. A particular bank may no longer offer a service to new depositors because its facilities are overloaded.

There is no substitute for up-to-date information from a particular bank. However, if the reader keeps the above limitations in mind, this list will serve him well.

One recommended approach to the selection process was outlined earlier. Having determined the type of account most suitable to your needs, select about six banks that provide this service. Two from among the Big Five, and the rest from among the cantonal, commercial, or private banks would be a good mix. Send all six an identical letter requesting information and forms. From the material sent in response to your queries, select the bank you feel most comfortable with.

Details Provided

Data is provided in a standardized format for each of the banks listed. First, the name and address of the bank is given. Then, the type of bank and information on the common account types is provided. Finally, other types of services offered are covered. Sometimes, there is a special note on any unusual facts about the bank that may be pertinent.

A bank's name and address is given in the form that should be used for the first letter. Some banks, especially the big banks, use up to four translations of their name. Schweizerischer Bankverein calls itself the Swiss Bank Corporation in English, and has special stationery that it uses with its English-speaking customers. However, to the Swiss postman it is still "Schweizerischer Bankverein." By using the local language address form, delivery is certainly surer and quicker in Switzerland. In addition, a certain extra measure of privacy is obtained while the letter is in the American postal system. After all, how many American postal clerks read German?

Usually, the first address given in each listing, on the left, is the bank's street address. To the right an alternate address is sometimes provided. This is commonly a postal address; *Postfach*, or *Case Postale*, means simply "P. O. Box." In some cases the bank does not use a box number, leaving it to the postal personnel to sort the mail by name. *If no postal box number is given, it is necessary to include the bank's name* when using this short form of address.

Below the addresses, the bank's alternate names in English, French, or Italian are given, if appropriate. In many cases, the bank uses no translation. For other banks, it is not necessary to translate the name. Migros Bank is Migros Bank in German or in English.

In this listing, an indication of the bank type is given for general information. If known, the year the bank was established is also given.

For banks outside the cities of Zurich, Bern, or Geneva, the approximate location of the town is provided. (When two or more banks are listed for a smaller Swiss city the location data is given in the first listing for a bank in that town.) Who knows, someday you may want to visit your bank in person.

Account types offered are listed. After each account type, other pertinent data are given, such as minimums and interest rates. If the account is offered in currencies other than Swiss francs, this is noted.

Almost all banks provide other services for their customers. If a bank offers such special services in its initial correspondence, it is presumed that they are interested in new business of this sort. Such services are listed. Any special notes are self-explanatory.

Big Banks

In the listings that follow, the banks are grouped into categories for easy reference. Our first category consists of the Big Three, plus Bank Leu.

Each of the Big Three has upward of eighty branches apiece, and does business all over Switzerland. Each of the four banks listed is ideal for American customers, since the banks are used to dealing with foreign depositors.

Schweizerische Bankgesellschaft
Bahnhofstrasse 45
8021 Zurich, Switzerland

Union Bank of Switzerland, Union de Banques Suisses, Unione di Banche Svizzere.
Big Three, commercial bank, est. 1862.

Current accounts: SFr or convertible foreign currencies (US$, DM, £ sterling, etc.), small service charge on current accounts other than SFr. Check books available. *Cash deposit accounts:* $3^1/_2$ percent int., withdrawals to SFr 10,000 monthly. *Savings accounts:* 5 percent int., withdrawals to SFr 5,000 monthly. *Investment savings accounts:* 6 percent int., withdrawals to SFr

3,000 per half-year. Minimums on above accounts: US$500. Also offers: fixed time deposits in foreign currencies, minimum—SFr 50,000; own bonds, multiples of SFr 1,000. Forms and literature in English.

* * *

Schweizerische Kreditanstalt
Paradeplatz 8   or: see special note.
8021 Zurich, Switzerland

Swiss Credit Bank, Crédit Suisse, Credito Svizzero.
Big Three, commercial bank, est. 1856.

Current accounts: SFr, US$, Canadian $, DM, Dutch guilders, etc. *Private accounts:* 3$^1/_2$ percent int., withdrawals to SFr 10,000 monthly. *Savings books:* 5 percent int., withdrawals to SFr 5,000 monthly. *Investment books:* 6 percent int., withdrawals to SFr 10,000 per year; if holder over sixty, up to SFr 5,000 monthly. No minimums required, but would ''appreciate receiving an initial deposit of at least Fr 6,000.'' Also offers: own bonds at 6$^1/_2$ or 7 percent, multiples of SFr 1,000. As a large bank, all services available. *Special note:* Refers queries to branches which answer promptly. Lists 112 branches in Switzerland. One branch at Bülach, about five miles north of Kloten, the Zurich airport, aggressively seeks foreign accounts: Schweizerische Kreditanstalt, Bahnhofstrasse 28, 8180 Bülach, Switzerland. Also branch at Zurich airport: Schweizerische Kreditanstalt, Filiale Flughafen, 8058 Zurich, Switzerland. English-language literature and forms.

* * *

Schweizerischer Bankverein
Aeschenvorstadt 1   or: Paradeplatz 6
CH-4002 Basel, Switzerland   8021 Zurich, Switzerland

Swiss Bank Corporation, Société de Banque Suisse, Società di Banca Svizzera.

Big Three, commercial bank, est. 1872. Home office in Basel, cantonal capital of 235,000, on Rhine where Germany, France and Switzerland meet.

Current accounts: SFr or foreign currencies. *Deposit accounts:* 3¹/₂ percent int., withdrawals to SFr 10,000 monthly. *Savings accounts:* 5 percent int., withdrawals to SFr 5,000 monthly. *Investment savings accounts:* 6 percent int., withdrawals to SFr 5,000 annually. Minimums on all above accounts: US$5,000 or SFr 15,000. Also offers: Fixed term deposits, US$ or other currencies; *Cash bonds,* 6¹/₂ or 7 percent. Full services, including silver and securities, available. Literature in English, forms sent after initial deposit. Lists 106 branches in Switzerland.

*   *   *

Bank Leu, AG.

Bahnhofstrasse 32   or: Postfach 553
8022 Zurich, Switzerland   8022 Zurich, Switzerland

Big Five, commercial bank, est. 1755.

Current accounts: SFr, US$, DM, Guilders, other currencies. *Deposit accounts:* 3¹/₂ percent int., withdrawals to SFr 10,000 monthly. *Savings accounts:* 5 percent int., withdrawals to SFr 5,000 monthly. *Investment accounts:* 6 percent int., withdrawals to SFr 5,000 semiannually. No minimums stated. *Euromarket placements:* US$50,000 minimum. *Bank bonds:* 6³/₄ percent for three and four years, 7¹/₄ percent for five to six years. *Administration of discretionary accounts:* minimum of SFr 250,000. Also offers: securities, precious metals, coin transactions; Swiss franc time deposits available through subsidiary—Bank Leu International, Ltd., P.O. Box N3926, Nassau, Bahamas. *Special note:* Oldest of the Big Five, conscious of tradition, seems to have attitude of large private bank.

Cantonal Banks

Every canton has at least one cantonal bank, each with branches throughout the canton. The cantonal banks listed here are those that are able to handle overseas business in English. Other cantonal banks that will accept foreign accounts, but are not set up for English correspondence, are listed in a later category.

Zuger Kantonalbank
Bahnhofstrasse 1
CH-6301 Zug, Switzerland

Cantonal bank, est. 1892. Zug is twenty miles south of Zurich.

Current accounts: SFr or US$. *Savings accounts:* Passbook, 4$^1/_4$ percent int., withdrawals to SFr 5,000 monthly. No minimums stated.

*   *   *

Banque Cantonale du Valais
Case postale 29291
CH-1951 Sion, Switzerland

Walliser Kantonalbank (Wallis is German for Valais).
Cantonal bank, est. 1917. Sion is cantonal capital of 17,000 people, in Valais, 110 miles east of Geneva.

Current accounts. Ordinary savings accounts: 4$^3/_4$ percent int., six months' notice. *Term savings accounts:* 5$^1/_2$ percent int., one year notice, minimum deposit SFr 5,000. *Bank bonds:* 6$^1/_2$ percent for three or four years, 7 percent for five to eight years. Also offers: gold, silver, securities. *Special note:* interest rates believed due for increase.

*   *   *

Banque Cantonale Vaudoise
14, place St. François
CH-1002 Lausanne, Switzerland

Cantonal bank, est. 1845. Lausanne, cantonal capital of 140,000; thirty-six miles northeast of Geneva.

Current accounts: check book available. *Deposit accounts:* 3 percent int. withdrawals to SFr 10,000 monthly. *Savings accounts "A":* $3^3/4$ percent int., withdrawals to SFr 5,000 monthly. *Savings accounts "B":* 5 percent int., withdrawals to SFr 3,000 monthly.

* * *

Bank Cantonale de Berne
Place Fédérale
CH-3001 Bern, Switzerland

Kantonalbank von Bern, Cantonal Bank of Berne.
Cantonal bank, est. 1834.

Savings accounts: 5 percent int., minimum deposit SFr 1,000.

* * *

Banque Cantonale de Thurgovie
Bankplatz 1
8570 Weinfelden, Switzerland

Thurgauische Kantonalbank.
Cantonal bank, est. 1871. Weinfelden, town in center of Thurgau canton, thirty-four miles northeast of Zurich.

Private accounts: $3^1/2$ percent int., no withdrawal restrictions, recommended if security purchases intended. *Savings booklets:* 5 percent int., withdrawals to SFr 5,000 monthly. *Bank bonds:* $6^1/2$ percent for three or four year terms, 7 percent for five to eight years. Also offers: securities transactions, gold bullion and coins. *Special note:* emphasizes securities transactions, bonds in various European currencies.

* * *

Caisse Hypothécaire du
Canton de Genève
2, place du Molard   or: Case postale 397
1204 Geneva, Switzerland   1211 Geneva 3, Switzerland

Cantonal mortgage and savings bank, est. 1847.

Savings accounts: 5 percent int., withdrawals to SFr 5,000 monthly. *Savings accounts* (second type): 5³/₄ percent int., withdrawals to SFr 1,500 monthly. Also offers: silver or gold coins and bullion, securities transactions.

* * *

Zürcher Kantonalbank
Bahnhofstrasse 9   or: Postfach
8022 Zurich, Switzerland   8022 Zurich, Switzerland

Banque Cantonale de Zürich.
Cantonal bank, est. 1869.

Current accounts: SFr or other currencies. *Deposit accounts:* 4 percent int., withdrawals to SFr 10,000 monthly. Also offers: securities transactions and precious metals.

* * *

Basler Kantonalbank
Spiegelgasse 2   or: Postfach
4001 Basel, Switzerland   4001 Basel, Switzerland

Banque Cantonale de Bâle.
Cantonal bank, est. 1899.

Savings books: 5 percent int., withdrawals to SFr 10,000 monthly. Minimum, SFr 5. *Special note:* regulations on savings accounts in five languages, sends forms after first deposit.

* * *

Deposito-Cassa der Stadt Bern
Kochergasse 6   or: Postfach 217
3000 Bern 7, Switzerland   3000 Bern 7, Switzerland

Caisse de Dépôts de la Ville de Berne.
Cantonal savings bank, est. 1825.

Savings accounts: 5 percent int., no withdrawal restrictions, minimum deposit SFr 10. *Deposit accounts:* 6 percent int., withdrawals to SFr 1,000 monthly, minimum deposit SFr 500. Also offers: security transactions, gold coins, etc.

*   *   *

Banque Cantonale Lucernoise
Pilatusstrasse 12   or: Postfach 1043
CH-6002 Lucerne,   CH-6002 Lucerne, Switzerland
   Switzerland

Cantonal bank, est. 1850. Lucerne, cantonal seat of 75,000 people, thirty miles southwest of Zurich.

Current accounts: SFr or US$. *Savings accounts:* 5 percent int., no withdrawal restrictions, no stipulated minimums.

*   *   *

Banque de l'Etat de Fribourg
Place de la Cathédrale
1701 Fribourg, Switzerland

Cantonal bank, est. 1892. Fribourg is cantonal seat, seventeen miles southwest of Bern.

Savings accounts: 5 percent int. *Bank bonds:* $6^{1}/_{4}$ percent for three or four year terms, 7 percent for five or six years. Also offers: bonds issued by foreign companies in SFr, DM, or Dutch guilders.

*   *   *

Obwaldner Kantonalbank
6060 Sarnen, Switzerland

Cantonal bank, est. 1886. Sarnen, cantonal seat of the half-canton of Obwalden, about forty-two miles southwest of Zurich.

Current accounts. Savings accounts: 5 percent int. *Investment accounts:* 6 percent int. *Bank bonds:* three to eight year terms, $6^1/2$ or 7 percent. Also offers: usual bank services, including securities safekeeping, acting as trustees.

* * *

Caisse d'Epargne Genève
1, rue de la Tour-de-l'Ile
1211 Geneva 11, Switzerland

(Full title: Caisse d'Epargne de la République et Canton de Genève. Use short title for mail.)
Cantonal savings bank, est. 1816.

Current accounts: SFr or other currencies. *Savings books "Ordinaire":* $2^1/2$ percent int., no withdrawal limitations. *Savings books "TS":* 5 percent int., withdrawals to SFr 5,000 without notice. *Savings books "Jeunesse":* $5^1/2$ percent int., to twenty years of age, withdrawals need six months' notice. *Savings books "A":* $5^1/2$ percent int., for people over sixty years, withdrawals to SFr 5,000 without notice. Also offers: safe deposit, securities services, precious metals, etc. *Note:* forms in French, information in English.

* * *

Basellandschaftliche Kantonalbank
Rheinstrasse 7
CH-4410 Liestal, Switzerland

Banque Cantonale de Bâle-Campagne.
Cantonal bank, est. 1864. Liestal is cantonal seat of the half-canton of "Basel District", eight miles southeast of Basel.

Current accounts. Savings accounts: 5 percent int. Also offers: SFr, DM, Guilder bonds of European industries and governments.

Commercial Banks

This is a broad category. It includes all the general purpose institutions that do not fit into any of the other groupings of our list. No distinction has been made between "other banks" that are foreign-controlled and those with Swiss ownership.

Migros Bank
Seidengasse 12   or: Postfach 2826
8023 Zurich, Switzerland   8023 Zurich, Switzerland

Commercial bank, est. 1958.

Current accounts. Deposit accounts: 5 percent int., withdrawals to SFr 10,000 without notice. Minimum deposit, SFr 200. Offers full range of services, own bonds, investment counseling, trust management, precious metals, coins, securities, etc. *Special note:* Part of Migros Trust, consumer-oriented retail and service group.

* * *

Gewerbebank Zürich
Rämistrasse 23   or: Postfach 265
8024 Zurich, Switzerland   8024 Zurich, Switzerland

Commercial bank, est. 1868.

Current accounts. Savings books: 5 percent int., withdrawals to SFr 5,000 monthly. No minimums stated. Forms sent after first deposit.

* * *

Bank Leumi Le-Israel (Schweiz)
Claridenstrasse 34   or: 80, rue du Rhône
8022 Zurich, Switzerland   1211 Geneva, Switzerland

Commercial bank, est. 1953.

Current accounts: SFr, US$, DM. *Deposit accounts:* SFr—4¹/₄ percent, DM or US$—4 percent, withdrawals to SFr 4,000 monthly. *Fixed term accounts:* minimums SFr 5,000, US$1,000, or DM 5,000. Rates at market. No minimums stated on current or deposit accounts. All forms in English. *Special note:* Part of Bank Leumi group. Associate, Bank Leumi Trust Company of New York, has four offices in New York City.

* * *

Metropolitan Bank, Ltd.
Bärenplatz 7   or: Postfach 2634
3001 Bern, Switzerland   3001 Bern, Switzerland

Commercial bank. Bern, population 160,000, is national capital.

Current accounts: US$, SFr, DM. Minimum balance, US$5,000 or equivalent. *Regular savings accounts:* 5¹/₄ percent, withdrawals to SFr 10,000 monthly. *Term savings accounts:* 6¹/₄ percent, withdrawals to SFr 1,000 per year, minimum deposit SFr 2,000. *Eurocurrency fiduciary placements:* US$, DM, Guilders, French francs, £ Sterling. Minimum US$50,000. Offers usual commercial services: securities, precious metals, investment advisory, safe-custody services, etc. *Special note:* beautiful annual report in German, French, and English.

* * *

Finanzbank Luzern, AG.
Friedenstrasse 2   or: Postfach
6000 Lucerne 6, Switzerland   6000 Lucerne 6, Switzerland

Commercial bank, est. 1945.

Current accounts. Deposit accounts: 5¹/₂ percent int., three months' notice; or 6¹/₂ percent, six months' notice of withdrawal. Also offers: three-year bonds at 6¹/₂ percent. German literature.

* * *

Cosmos Bank
Dreikönigstrasse 7   or: Postfach
8022 Zurich, Switzerland   8022 Zurich, Switzerland

Commercial bank, est. 1959.

Current accounts: SFr, US$, DM. *Time deposits:* US$ or DM, rate varies according to amount, duration, and market—with Cosmos, with affiliated Bahamian bank ($10,000 minimum), or on Euromarket ($100,000 minimum). Also offers: stock brokerage, metals, advisory services. *Special note:* affiliate is Cosmos Bank (Overseas) Ltd., Nassau, Bahamas.

* * *

Foreign Commerce Bank
Bellariastrasse 82   or: Postfach 1006
8038 Zurich, Switzerland   8022 Zurich, Switzerland

Commercial bank, est. 1958.

Current accounts: SFr, US$, other convertible currencies. *Deposit accounts:* SFr and DM—4 percent; Guilders—5 percent, US$—6 percent; £ Sterling—7 percent; minimum deposit US$5,000. *Certificates of deposit:* Issued by other banks, int. rates vary. Offers very complete services: mutual funds, securities, precious metals, fiduciary Eurocurrency deposits, commodity trading, etc. *Special note:* All forms and literature in English. Deliberately geared to American customers. Affiliated with Deak-Perera International, Inc. See remarks earlier in this chapter. Branch in Geneva—Foreign Commerce Bank, 3, rue du Marché, 1211 Genève 3 Rive, Switzerland.

* * *

Handelsbank in Zürich
Talstrasse 59   or: Postfach
8022 Zurich, Switzerland   8022 Zurich, Switzerland

Commercial bank, est. 1930.

Current accounts: SFr or US$. *Deposit accounts:* SFr 4 percent int., withdrawals to SFr 10,000 monthly; US$, $3^3/_4$ percent int., withdrawals to US$4,000 monthly. *Deposit books:* 5 percent int., withdrawals to SFr 5,000 monthly. *Investment accounts:* $6^1/_4$ percent int., withdrawals to SFr 10,000 annually. *Time deposits:* US$, minimum US$20,000, interest rates "upon request."

* * *

Handwerkerbank Basel
Aeschenvorstadt 2
4001 Basel, Switzerland

Commercial bank, est. 1860.

Deposit accounts: 5 percent int., withdrawals to SFr 10,000 monthly. Also offers: Youth savings accounts at 6 percent to age twenty, cash bonds. *Special note:* Offers many types of savings accounts in German literature. Deposit account above is a special mail account, a *Postdepositenheft.*

* * *

Société Bancaire Barclays (Suisse), S.A.
6, place de la Synagogue   or: Case postale 221
1204 Geneva, Switzerland   1211 Geneva 11, Switzerland

Commercial bank, est. 1934.

Deposit passbook accounts: 5 percent int., withdrawals to SFr 5,000 monthly. *Cash bonds:* $6^3/_4$ percent for three and four years, $7^1/_4$ percent for five to eight years. *Fiduciary Euromarket deposits:* rates vary according to currency and term. Minimums—US$50,000; DM 100,000; etc. *Investment portfolio management:* US$25,000 minimum. Also offers: full commercial services, gold bullion, safe deposit boxes, company formation services. *Special notes:* Offers formation of Liechtenstein trusts. Part of British Barclays group. Cayman Islands subsidiary offers offshore banking services.

* * *

Weisscredit
Via Pioda 9   or: Casella postale 428
6901 Lugano, Switzerland   6901 Lugano, Switzerland

Weisscredit Trade and Investment Bank.
Commercial bank, est. 1949. Lugano is lakeside resort town in Ticino, the Italian canton of Switzerland. Near Italian border, only forty miles north of Milan, Italy.

Current accounts: SFr, US$, or other currencies. *Deposit accounts:* 4$^{1}/_{2}$ percent int., withdrawals to SFr 5,000 monthly. *Time deposit accounts:* US$ only, six- or twelve-month terms, minimum US$10,000. Interest will vary according to market. Suggests contacting for higher rates on time deposits over US$50,000. Signature cards and business conditions in English. *Special note:* Apparently all accounts are numbered accounts. All forms come with a number and code word already filled in. Requires personal data on card marked "Segretariato." Prospective depositor should ask on first inquiry for bank to indicate which forms require "number" signature and which standard, legal signature.

* * *

Bank Hofmann, AG.
Talstrasse 27   or: Postfach
8022 Zurich, Switzerland   8022 Zurich, Switzerland

Commercial bank, est. 1897.

Current accounts: SFr, DM, or US$. *Deposit book:* 5$^{1}/_{2}$ percent int., withdrawals to SFr 5,000 within thirty days. *Time deposits:* DM or US$ (with bank), three- to twelve-month term, minimum DM 50,000 or US$25,000. *Euromarket time deposits:* DM, Guilders, US$; minimums DM or Guilders (Hfl) 100,000,

US$35,000. Business conditions and signature card in English, "order card" for deposit book in German.

*   *   *

Overseas Development Bank
40, rue du Rhône   or: Case postale 462
1211 Geneva 3, Switzerland   1200 Geneva, Switzerland

Commercial bank.

Current accounts: SFr, US$, other currencies on request. *Regular deposit accounts:* SFr, US$, 4³/₄ percent int., withdrawals to SFr 3,000 or US$1,000 monthly, minimums SFr 3,000 or US$1,000. *Special deposit accounts:* US$, 6 percent int., withdrawals to US$500 monthly. Minimum US$5,000. *"Euro" deposit accounts:* US$, DM, French francs, variable int. based on average Euromarket rates during quarter. Withdrawals to US$500 per month. (Mid-'74 int. rate was 8¹/₄ percent.) Minimums—US$20,000; DM 50,000. Also offers: investment services, securities safekeeping, gold and silver, full services generally. Forms and information packet completely in English. Branch in England: Overseas Development Bank, Berger House, 36 Berkeley Square, London W1X 5DA.

*   *   *

Bank und Finanz-Institut, AG.
Waisenhausplatz 25   or: Postfach 1082
3001 Bern, Switzerland   3001 Bern, Switzerland

Bank & Finance Co., Inc.; Comptoir Bancaire et Financier, S.A.
Commercial bank, est. 1955. Main office in Bern, branches in Basel, Geneva, and Zurich.

Savings books: 5¹/₄ percent int. *Deposit accounts:* 5¹/₂ percent int., withdrawal to SFr 10,000 monthly. *Investment accounts:* 6¹/₄ percent int., withdrawals to SFr 3,000 monthly. Full services including current accounts, bonds, securities transactions.

Branches directly represented on stock exchanges. *Special notes:* affiliated with General Auditing Co., Ltd., of Switzerland. Requires waiver of secrecy from U.S. residents.

* * *

Wirtschaftsbank Zürich
Stauffacherstrasse 45   or: Postfach 3294
CH-8004 Zurich, Switzerland   8023 Zurich, Switzerland

Commercial bank, est. 1959.

Current accounts: SFr, other currencies. *Deposit accounts:* 5 percent int., withdrawals to SFr 5,000 monthly. *Time deposits:* currencies other than Swiss francs. *Euromarket trust deposits:* currencies other than SFr. Prevailing rates vary. Minimums US$20,000, DM 100,000. Also offers: international trade transactions; management accounts—US$100,000 minimum; precious metals; stock exchange transactions; formation and administration of companies, trusts, and family foundations; real estate investments.

* * *

Arab Bank (Overseas), Ltd.
Talacker 21   or: Postfach 958
CH-8022 Zurich,   CH-8022 Zurich, Switzerland
    Switzerland

Commercial bank, est. 1962.

Current accounts: SFr, US$, DM, £ Sterling, etc. *Deposit accounts:* SFr, 5$^{1}/_{2}$ percent int.; US$, 6 percent int.; £ Sterling, 6$^{1}/_{2}$ percent. *Trustee time deposits:* Interest according to Euromarket rates. Minimums—US$20,000, DM 100,000, £10,000. *Special note:* When querying, request forms for type of account interested in.

* * *

Banque pour le Commerce Suisse-Israélien
15–17, quai des Bergues   or: Case postale 320
1211 Geneva 1, Switzerland   1211 Geneva 1, Switzerland

Swiss-Israel Trade Bank, Bank für Schweizer-Israelischen Handel.
Commercial bank, est. 1950.

Current accounts: US$. *Savings accounts:* 4³/₄ percent int. *Certificates of deposit:* US$, interest varies according to market, minimum US$5,000. CDs are with London branch—Swiss-Israel Trade Bank, Lee House, London Wall, London E.C. 2.

* * *

American Express International Banking Corporation
Aeschenvorstadt 48–50   or: Postfach 438
4000 Basel 2, Switzerland   4002 Basel, Switzerland

Commercial bank.

Deposit accounts: 5 percent int., withdrawals to SFr 3,000 monthly. *Special note:* American Express operates as banking business overseas. Only deposit accounts available to U.S. residents. All forms in English.

* * *

Banque de Commerce et de Placements, S.A.
3, rue du Marché
1211 Geneva 3, Switzerland

Commercial bank.

Euromarket fiduciary investments: Rates vary per market, short-term for one to six months, minimums—US$25,000, DM 100,000. Also offers: "long-term investments of all kinds according to customers needs."

* * *

Bank in Gossau
Poststrasse 4   or: Postfach 35874
CH-9202 Gossau,   9202 Gossau SG, Switzerland
   Switzerland

Commercial and mortgage bank, est. 1881. Gossau is smaller town, six miles west of St. Gallen, off Autobahn, fifty miles east of Zurich.

Deposit accounts: $4^{1}/_{2}$ percent int., withdrawals to SFr 10,000 monthly. *Savings books:* 5 percent int., withdrawals to SFr 5,000 monthly. *Investment books (Anlageheft):* 6 percent int., withdrawals to SFr 10,000 per year. *Bank bonds:* $6^{3}/_{4}$ percent to $7^{1}/_{4}$ percent, three to eight years. Also offers: Youth savings account at 6 percent, other commercial services. Letters in English, other material in German.

*   *   *

Inter Maritime Bank
5, quai du Mont-Blanc   or: Postfach 423
1211 Geneva 1, Switzerland   1211 Geneva 1, Switzerland

Commercial bank, est. 1959.

Current accounts. Deposit accounts: Rates subject to agreement. *Securities safekeeping accounts. Portfolio management. Special note:* Not a typical retail bank. Specializes in "banking services to ships in ports throughout the world." Rates subject to agreement; when querying, indicate type of account desired, approximate size of deposit, and currency desired.

*   *   *

Banque de Dépôts et de Gestion
14, avenue du Théâtre
1002 Lausanne, Switzerland

Depositen und Verwaltungsbank, Banca di Depositi e di Gestioni.

Commercial bank, est. 1933.

Current accounts. Deposit accounts: 6 percent int., withdrawals to SFr 3,000 monthly. Also offers: all other banking services.

* * *

Banque Financière, S.A.
Weggengasse 1
8001 Zurich, Switzerland

Finanzbank, AG.
Commercial bank, est. 1924.

Current accounts. Ninety-day notice account: 4$^1/_4$ percent int. Also offers: security transactions, gold and silver bullion.

* * *

Nordfinanz-Bank Zürich
Bahnhofstrasse 1   or: Postfach 750
8001 Zurich, Switzerland   8022 Zurich, Switzerland

Commercial bank, est. 1938. (Since 1964, controlled by group of four big Scandinavian banks.)

Current accounts: SFr, US$. *Deposit accounts:* SFr or US$. 5$^1/_4$ percent int., withdrawals to SFr 5,000 or US$1,000 monthly. *Investment accounts:* 6 percent int., withdrawals to SFr 10,000 per year. *Fixed time deposit accounts:* US$, other currencies. Rates vary, minimum SFr 50,000. *Cash bonds:* rates vary, three- to eight-year terms. *Euromarket fiduciary deposits:* interest varies according to market, minimums SFr 100,000, US$25,000. Also offers: full services including safe deposit boxes, gold coins and bars, securities transactions, establishment of companies, all other commercial services. *Special note:* All materials in English. U.S. representative—Mr. Lars T. Radberg, Suite 1609, 1 Rockefeller Plaza, New York, N.Y. 10020.

* * *

Bank in Langnau
CH-3550 Langnau, Switzerland

Commercial bank, est. 1885. Langnau, main town in Emmental region, eighteen miles east of Bern.

Savings accounts: 5 percent int., withdrawals to SFr 15,000 per quarter. *Bonds:* 6³/₄ percent—three years, 7¹/₄ percent—five years. Also offers: all regular banking services. *Special note:* Literature in German offers full description of all commercial bank services.

* * *

Compagnie Luxembourgeoise de Banque, S.A.
Färberstrasse 6 (Seehof)   or: Postfach 64
CH-8034 Zurich,   CH-8034 Zurich, Switzerland
Switzerland

Commercial bank, est. 1967. Branch of Luxembourg bank, which in turn is wholly owned subsidiary of Dresdner Bank of Germany. Formed to participate in Euromarket.

Euromarket time deposits: US$, DM, £ Sterling, Guilders, other convertible currencies. Rates vary according to market. Minimum US$100,000 or equivalent. Also offers: private portfolio management, Eurobonds, securities transactions.

* * *

Chase Manhattan Bank (Switzerland)
63, rue du Rhône   or: Case postale 476
1204 Geneva, Switzerland   1211 Geneva 3, Switzerland

Commercial bank.

Current accounts: SFr, other currencies, minimum SFr 5,000. *Checking accounts:* SFr, other major currencies, minimum SFr 10,000. *Time deposits* (with bank): interest varies, minimum US$25,000. *Euromarket fiduciary deposits:* US$, minimum US$25,000 to US$100,000 depending on maturity. Other currencies, minimums US$100,000 equivalent. Also offers: investment management, securities transactions. *Special note:* requires waiver of secrecy for U.S. residents.

* * *

Hypothekar-und Handelsbank Winterthur
Stadhausstrasse 14
8401 Winterthur, Switzerland

Commercial and mortgage bank, est. 1865. Winterthur is industrial city of 90,000 people, about twelve miles northeast of Zurich.

Current accounts: Savings books: 5 percent int., withdrawals to SFr 3,000 monthly. *Deposit books:* 5 percent int., withdrawals to SFr 5,000 monthly. *Investment books:* 6$^{1}/_{2}$ percent int., withdrawals to SFr 5,000 quarterly. Also offers: full range of banking services, including stock exchange transactions, Euromarket investments, safekeeping services, etc.

* * *

Privat Kredit Bank
Tödistrasse 47   or: Postfach
8002 Zurich, Switzerland   8022 Zurich, Switzerland

Commercial bank.

Current accounts. Deposit accounts: 5$^{1}/_{2}$ percent int. Also offers: full services including fiduciary time deposits, portfolio management, buying and selling securities, precious metals, safe deposit boxes. Branch in Lugano: Privat Kredit Bank, Contrada di Sassello 2, 6900 Lugano, Switzerland.

* * *

First National Bank of Chicago
6, place des Eaux-vives   or: Case postale 102
1207 Geneva, Switzerland   1211 Geneva 6, Switzerland

Commercial bank.

Current accounts: SFr, US$, other currencies. Minimum balance, SFr 5,000. *Investment deposit accounts:* SFr—6 percent int., or US$—7 percent int., three-months' notice required on withdrawals. *Euromarket fixed time deposits:* SFr, US$, or other currencies. Rates according to market. Minimums, US$100,000. Also offers: securities transactions, gold coins, gold and silver bullion, portfolio management, safe deposit boxes.

* * *

Banque de Dépôts
94, rue du Rhône   or: Case rive 550
1211 Geneva 3, Switzerland   1211 Geneva, Switzerland

The Deposit Bank, Banco de Depositos.
Commercial bank, est. 1921.

Current accounts: minimum deposit, SFr 5,000. *Savings accounts:* 5 percent int., withdrawals to SFr 5,000 without notice; minimum, SFr 50. *Three months' notice savings account (Livret de placement)*: 6 percent int., withdrawals to SFr 1,000 monthly, minimum balance, SFr 5,000. *Time deposits:* US$ only, rates vary (was 8 percent), minimum deposit US$10,000. Also offers: full banking services. *Special note:* Number accounts available, SFr 10,000 minimum.

* * *

Banque Commercial de Sion, S.A.
15, rue de Lausanne   or: Case postale 28947
1950 Sion, Switzerland   1951 Sion, Switzerland

Commercial bank, est. 1874.

Ordinary savings passbooks: 5 percent int. *Savings deposit accounts:* 6 percent int., withdrawals to SFr 5,000 annually; minimum deposit, SFr 1,000. *Cash bonds:* 7 percent int., five-year term; $7^{1}/_{4}$ percent int. for six- to eight-year terms. Also offers: Youth savings accounts and savings accounts for older persons. *Special note:* forms in French.

* * *

Anlagebank Zug, AG.
Neugasse 22   or: Postfach 262
6301 Zug, Switzerland   6301 Zug, Switzerland

Banque de Placements Zoug, S.A.; Investment Bank Zug, Ltd.
Commercial bank, est. 1957.

Current accounts. Savings accounts: 5¹/₄ percent int., withdrawals to SFr 2,000 monthly. *Deposit books:* 6 percent int., withdrawals of SFr 5,000 require three months' notice. *Bank bonds:* 6³/₄ percent for three or four years, 7¹/₄ percent for five to eight years. Also offers: securities transactions, precious metals.

* * *

Adler Bank Basel, AG.
Aeschenvordstadt 48–50
4001 Basel, Switzerland

Commercial bank, est. 1921.

Current accounts. Private accounts (Einlagekontos): 4 percent int., withdrawals to SFr 10,000 monthly. *Deposit books:* 5¹/₄ percent int., withdrawals to SFr 5,000 monthly. *Investment book accounts:* 6 percent int., withdrawals to SFr 5,000 quarterly. *Bank bonds:* 6¹/₄ percent for three or four years, 7 percent for five to eight years. *Time deposits:* foreign currencies only, rates vary. Also offers: securities transactions, gold purchases.

* * *

Dow Banking Corp.
Bahnhofstrasse 24   or: Postfach 931
8022 Zurich, Switzerland   8022 Zurich, Switzerland

Commercial bank, est. 1965.

Current accounts. Deposit accounts: 5 percent int., withdrawals to SFr 10,000 within thirty-day period. *Euromarket fixed term deposits:* US$, Guilders (Hfl), £ Sterling, DM. Rates vary according to market. Minimum—US$50,000. *Bank bonds:* 6$^1/_2$ percent int. for three-year term, 7 percent for four to eight years. *Portfolio management:* minimum—US$50,000. Also offers: securities transactions. *Special note:* Requires bank reference and "statement that you will comply with IRS regulations on reporting overseas income."

* * *

Bankinvest
Brandschenkestrasse 41   or: Postfach 419
8039 Zurich, Switzerland   8039 Zurich, Switzerland

Bank for Investment & Credit, Ltd.
Commercial bank, est. 1969.

Deposit accounts: "currency of your choice," write for interest rates. *Euromarket time deposits:* minimums US$25,000 or SFr 50,000. Also offers: securities transactions, gold and silver trading, tax and estate planning advice. *Special note:* has wholly owned subsidiary in Cayman Islands.

* * *

Discount Bank (Overseas), Ltd.
3, quai de l'Ile   or: Case postale 357
1204 Geneva, Switzerland   1211 Geneva 11, Switzerland

Commercial bank.

Current accounts: available in US$. *Savings deposit accounts:* 5 percent int., withdrawals to SFr 4,000 monthly. *Fixed time deposits:* US$; three-, six-, or twelve-month terms. Minimums US$1,000 or multiples thereof. *Special note:* Bank requires "first-class bank references" to open an account. Investment accounts and portfolio management services available, but visit to bank and "detailed discussion" with investment managers necessary.

* * *

Gewerbebank Baden
Bahnhofplatz 1
CH-5401 Baden, Switzerland

Commercial bank, est. 1864. Baden, small industrial town with famous spa, thirteen miles northwest of Zurich.

Savings books: 5 percent int., withdrawals to SFr 2,000 without prior notice. *Deposit books:* 6 percent int., withdrawals to SFr 5,000 yearly. *Bank bonds:* $6^3/_4$ percent, 7 percent, $7^1/_4$ percent, depending on term.

* * *

Schweizerische Depositen-und Kreditbank
Löwenstrasse 49   or: Postfach 300
8021 Zurich, Switzerland   8021 Zurich, Switzerland

Banque Suisse de Crédit et de Dépôts.
Commercial bank, est. 1965.

Deposit accounts: 5 percent int., withdrawals to SFr 10,000 monthly. *Savings accounts:* $5^1/_4$ percent int., withdrawals to SFr 5,000 monthly.

* * *

Gewerbekasse in Bern
Schweizerhoflaube
Bahnhofplatz 7
3001 Bern, Switzerland

Caisse Industrielle à Berne.
Commercial bank, est. 1905.

Savings books: 5 percent int., currently, no withdrawal restrictions. *Deposit books:* $6^1/_4$ percent int., withdrawals to SFr 1,000 monthly. *Bank bonds:* $6^3/_4$ percent for three and four years, $7^1/_4$ percent for five- or six-year terms. Also offers: all other bank services.

* * *

Banque pour le Commerce International, S.A.

Aeschengraben 25	or: Case postale 1352
4002 Basel, Switzerland	4002 Basel, Switzerland

Bank for International Commerce, Ltd.
Commercial bank, est. 1949.

Current accounts: SFr or other currencies. *Certificates of Deposit:* US$, minimum US$15,000; one-, three-, or six-month term. *Investment funds (mutual funds):* offers INTERFIX AND INTERPLACEMENT. *Special note:* accounts can be name or numbered.

* * *

Ako Bank
Talacker 50
8021 Zurich, Switzerland

Commercial bank, est. 1934.

Deposit accounts: 6 percent int., life insurance included. *Cash bonds:* $6^3/_4$ percent for three and four years, $7^1/_4$ percent for five to eight years. *Special note:* deals mainly in consumer loans.

* * *

Banque Scandinave en Suisse

11, Rond-Point de Rive	or: Case postale 490
1211 Geneva 3, Switzerland	1211 Geneva 3, Switzerland

Commercial bank, est. 1964.

Current accounts: SFr or US$. *Deposit or Savings accounts:* SFr or US$, 5 percent int., withdrawals to SFr 5,000 or US$1,500 per month. *Notice time deposit accounts:* US$, 6 percent int., on an average balance up to US$75,000; $6^1/_2$ percent int., from US$75,000 to US$150,000. Also offers: securities safekeeping, portfolio management, precious metals, safe deposit boxes, other commercial services. *Special note:* owned by group of seven Scandinavian banks and one American bank, the Northern Trust Company.

* * *

Imefbank
6, rue Petitot   or: Case postale 59
1204 Geneva, Switzerland   1211 Geneva 11, Switzerland

Banque d'Investissements Mobiliers et de Financement.
Commercial bank, est. 1957.

Current accounts: SFr or Western European currencies. *Deposit booklets:* 4¹/₂ percent int. *Euromarket deposits:* US$50,000 minimum, rates vary. Also offers: all usual banking services, such as securities transactions. *Special note:* numbered accounts offered.

* * *

Genossenschaftliche Zentralbank, AG., Basel
Aeschenplatz 3
CH-4002 Basel, Switzerland

Cooperative Central Bank Co., Ltd.; Banque Centrale Coopérative, S.A.
Commercial bank, est. 1927.

Current accounts. Savings accounts: 5 percent int., withdrawals to SFr 5,000 monthly. *Investment accounts:* 6 percent int., withdrawals to SFr 10,000 yearly. Also offers: short-term bank bonds, securities brokerage, portfolio management, strong-room facilities, full range of banking facilities.

* * *

Neue Bank
Talstrasse 41
8022 Zurich, Switzerland

New Bank, Nouvelle Banque.
Commercial bank, est. 1960.

Current accounts: minimum average balance—SFr 5,000. *Deposit booklets:* 5¹/₄ percent int., withdrawals to SFr 5,000 monthly. *Deposit accounts:* 5³/₄ percent int., withdrawals to SFr 5,000 monthly, minimum deposit—SFr 20,000. *Bank bonds (medium-term notes):* 6¹/₂ percent int. for three and four years, 7 percent for five and six years. Also offers: "all services of a commercial and investment bank." *Special note:* requires bank references if customer does not open account personally.

* * *

Banco di Roma per la Svizzera
Paizzetta San Carlo   or: Casella postale 6444
6901 Lugano, Switzerland   6901 Lugano, Switzerland

Commercial bank, est. 1947.

Current accounts: SFr, US$, other currencies. *Savings deposit accounts:* 5 percent int., withdrawls to SFr 5,000 monthly. *Fixed term deposits:* US$, interest rates may vary, for three to twelve months. Minimum US$20,000. *Special note:* banker's reference usually required, numbered accounts available.

* * *

Banque de Paris et des Pays-Bas (Suisse), S.A.
6, rue de Hollande
1211 Geneva 11, Switzerland

Paribas Bank.
Commercial bank, est. 1872.

Current accounts: SFr or other currencies. *Savings accounts:* 4³/₄ percent int., withdrawals to SFr 3,000 monthly. Also offered: portfolio management, legal and tax services, etc. *Special note:* requires bank references.

Savings Banks

Banks listed in this category are just what the name implies, institutions devoted primarily to interest-bearing smaller accounts. Some are community banks, others are privately controlled.

Bank Neumünster
Goethestrasse 14
Stadelhoferplatz
8001 Zurich, Switzerland

Savings bank, est. 1860.

Private account: especially for mail customers, $3^{1}/_{2}$ percent int., compounded quarterly. Withdrawals to SFr 10,000 monthly, minimum SFr 20,000.

* * *

Spar-& Leihkasse Schaffhausen
Bahnhofstrasse 2
8201 Schaffhausen, Switzerland

Savings bank, est. 1866. Schaffhausen is cantonal capital of 36,000, on Rhine, thirty miles north of Zurich.

Current accounts. Deposit books: 4 percent int., withdrawals to SFr 10,000 monthly. No minimum deposit. *Savings books:* 5 percent int., withdrawals to SFr 3,000 monthly. No minimum. *Long-term deposit book:* 6 percent int., six-months notice on withdrawals. Minimum—SFr 2,000. *Bonds:* Minimum—SFr 1,000; $6^{1}/_{2}$ percent for three or four years, 7 percent for five to eight years. Also offers: all other services including metals, securities, safe deposit boxes.

* * *

Sparkasse der Gemeinde Schwyz
Herrengasse
6430 Schwyz, Switzerland

Savings bank, est. 1812. Schwyz, 11,500 population, cantonal capital about thirty-five miles south of Zurich.

Savings accounts: 5¹/₄ percent int. No stated minimums. Also offers: securities purchases.

* * *

Kreditanstalt Grabs
CH-9472 Grabs, Switzerland

Savings bank, est. 1880. Grabs, small town near Buchs in St. Gallen canton, just across Rhine River from Liechtenstein.

Deposit accounts: 4 percent int. *Savings accounts:* 5 percent int. *Investment accounts:* 6 percent int. Also offers: bank bonds.

* * *

Spar-und Leihkasse Balgach
CH-9436 Balgach, Switzerland

Savings and loan bank, est. 1868. Balgach, small Rhine valley town in St. Gallen canton, near Austrian border.

Current accounts. Savings books: 5 percent int. *Investment books:* 6 percent int. *Cash bonds:* three- to six-year terms, 6³/₄ percent to 7 percent int. *Note:* Correspondence in English, account information in German.

* * *

Esparnikasse des Amstbezirks Aarwangen
Jurastrasse 31
4900 Langenthal, Switzerland

Savings bank, est. 1971. Langenthal is town in Aare River valley, thirty miles northeast of Bern.

Deposit books: 3¹/₂ percent int., balance freely available. *Savings books (Sparheft):* 5 percent int., withdrawals to SFr 10,000 monthly. *Savings books (Sparbuch):* 5³/₄ percent int., withdrawals to SFr 20,000, require three-months notice. *Investment savings books:* 6¹/₄ percent int., withdrawals to SFr 3,000 per calender year, minimum balance SFr 1,000. *Cash bonds:* 6³/₄ percent for three and four years, 7 percent for five to eight years. *Special note:* Offers ten different savings arrangements, accounts described are typical.

* * *

Spar-und Leihkasse Steffisburg
Glockentalstrasse 6   or: Postfach 11881
3612 Steffisburg,   3612 Steffisburg, Switzerland
Switzerland

Savings and loan, est. 1863. Steffisburg, small town in Bernese Oberland, outside of Thun, twenty miles south of Bern.

Savings books: 5 percent int., withdrawals to SFr 5,000 quarterly. *Three-months' notice savings books:* 5¹/₂ percent int. *Six-months' notice savings books:* 6 percent int., *Cash bonds:* 6³/₄ percent for three or four years, 7 percent for five- or six-year terms.

* * *

Spar + Leihkasse in Bern
Bundesplatz 4   or: Postfach 2623
3001 Bern 1, Switzerland   3001 Bern 1, Switzerland

Savings and loan, est. 1857.

Savings account: 5 percent int. *Deposit account:* 6¹/₄ percent int., withdrawals to SFr 1,000 monthly. *Bank bonds:* 6³/₄ percent int. for three and four years, 7 percent for five and six years.

* * *

Schweizerische Bodenkredit-Anstalt
Werdmuhleplatz 1   or: Postfach 921
8021 Zurich, Switzerland   CH-8021 Zurich, Switzerland

Crédit Foncier Suisse.
Mortgage bank, est. 1896.

Deposit accounts: 4¹/₂ percent int., withdrawals to SFr 10,000 monthly. *Savings accounts:* 5 percent int., withdrawals to SFr 5,000 monthly. *Investment accounts:* 6 percent int., withdrawals to SFr 5,000 per year. No stated minimums on any accounts. Sends forms after first deposit. Send full identifying data and type of account desired with first transmittal.

* * *

Solothurnische Leihkasse
Westbahnhofstrasse 11
4500 Solothurn, Switzerland

Savings and mortgage bank, est. 1865. Solothurn, cantonal seat, eighteen miles north of Bern.

Savings accounts: 5 percent int., withdrawals to SFr 5,000 monthly. *Savings accounts:* 5¹/₂ percent int., withdrawals to SFr 2,000 monthly. *Savings accounts:* 6 percent int., withdrawals to SFr 10,000 yearly. (Note: bank makes no distinction between types of savings accounts in English translation.) *Bank bonds:* 6³/₄ percent for three- or four-year terms, 7¹/₄ percent for five to eight years. Also offers: all usual bank services.

* * *

Caisse d'Epargne du Valais
place du Midi
1951 Sion, Switzerland

Savings bank, est. 1876.

Current accounts. Deposit accounts: 3¹/₂ percent int., withdrawals to SFr 10,000 monthly. *Ordinary savings books:* 5 percent int., withdrawals to SFr 3,000 without notice. *Cash bonds:* three-year term, 6¹/₂ percent int., 6³/₄ percent for four or five years, 7 percent for six to eight years. Also offers: other types of savings accounts, securities transactions. *Special note:* brochures in French.

* * *

Esparniskasse Nidwalden
6370 Stans, Switzerland

Savings bank, est. 1827. Stans is cantonal seat of half-canton of Nidwalden, about thirty-seven miles south of Zurich.

Savings books: 5 percent int., no withdrawal limitations. *Deposit accounts:* 6 percent int., withdrawals from SFr 1,000 to SFr 10,000: three-months notice. *Bank bonds:* 6¹/₂ percent int. for three-year term, 7 percent for five years. Also offers: all standard services.

* * *

Eigenheim Bank Basel
St. Jakobsstrasse 18   or: Postfach 440
4002 Basel, Switzerland   4002 Basel, Switzerland

Savings bank, est. 1931.

Savings accounts: 5¹/₄ percent int., withdrawals to SFr 5,000 monthly. *Deposit accounts:* 5³/₄ percent int., withdrawals to SFr 3,000 monthly. *Bank bonds:* three- to eight-year terms, units of SFr 1,000, 5,000, or 10,000. Also offers: securities transactions on Swiss exchanges, gold and silver bullion.

Private Banks

Technically, in Switzerland a true private bank is not incorporated. Another type of institution might also be called a private bank, except that it does not fit the legal description. Many were genuine private banks in the past, but have since incorporated, either to increase their capital base or to continue to use a prestigious name. In practice, in character, in style of operations, there is little to distinguish these two types of banking houses.

For simplicity, in this listing both types are grouped together, but under separate categories. Banks in Category I are the "true" private banks; Category II includes banks that describe themselves as "private" banks in bank directories, but that are incorporated and not technically private.

Banks in both categories will generally want to know who referred you to them, or how you came to find out about them.

Category I Banks

Pictet & Cie.
6, rue Diday
1211 Geneva, Switzerland

Private bank, est. 1805.

Portfolio management: for institutions or individuals, descretionary or per client's instructions. Minimum—US$100,000.

* * *

Bordier & Cie.
16, rue de Hollande   or: Case postale 298
1211 Geneva, Switzerland   1211 Geneva 11, Switzerland

Private bank, est. 1844.

Specializes in the management of funds, either on "safekeeping" basis, with client giving instructions, or with general management powers. Offers short-term DM & US$ deposits, minimum US$50,000, rates varying according to market. Prefers to discuss client's objectives and account details in person.

* * *

Darier & Cie.
4, rue de Saussure
1211 Geneva 11, Switzerland

Private bank, est. 1837.

Specializes "in international money management for private individuals." Accounts may be either regular or numbered. Provides foreign exchange, gold, checks, etc.

* * *

Armand Von Ernst & Cie.
Bundesgasse 30   or: Postfach 1081
3001 Bern, Switzerland   3001 Bern, Switzerland

Private bank, est. 1812.

Portfolio management: on discretionary basis or per client's instructions. Minimum securities value—US$100,000. *Deposit accounts:* 2 percent int., withdrawals to SFr 10,000 without prior notice. (Deposit accounts are maintained only for customers who maintain securities management accounts.) *Special notes:* Reference from "a bank of good standing" required. Signature verification required from same bank. Remittances should be made through a bank. Waiver of bank secrecy from Americans.

* * *

Falck & Cie., Banquiers
Schwanenplatz 2
CH-6002 Lucerne, Switzerland

Private bank, est. 1875.

Current accounts: SFr or "better known Western currencies." *Deposit accounts:* $3^{1}/_{4}$ percent int. Also offers: negotiable certificates of deposit, minimum US$25,000; gold and silver; creation of companies. *Special notes:* main concern is asset management. Requires some information on client background.

* * *

J. Vontobel & Co.
Bahnhofstrasse 3   or: Postfach
CH-8022 Zurich,   CH-8022 Zurich, Switzerland
Switzerland

Private bank.

Investment accounts: Initial deposit—US$50,000. No interest paid, apparently bank will place funds in other investments, per agreement with client. *Deposit account:* 4^1/$_4$ percent int., initial deposit—SFr 10,000. May only be opened in connection with investment account. *Portfolio management:* minimum—US$100,000. Also offers: formation of companies, trusteeship services, etc. *Special note:* issues English-language booklet describing Swiss banking practices in general.

* * *

Sturzenegger & Cie.
St. Jakobsstrasse 46   or: Postfach
4002 Basel, Switzerland   4002 Basel, Switzerland

Private bank, est. 1920.

Current accounts only. Also offers: securities transactions, administration of customers' securities, "all the usual banking operations." *Special note:* wants to meet new customers, all customers are known personally.

* * *

Wegelin & Co.
Bohl 17   or: Postfach 10
9004 St. Gallen, Switzerland   9004 St. Gallen, Switzerland

Private bank, est. 1741. St. Gallen is cantonal seat of 80,000, forty-seven miles east of Zurich.

Specializes in portfolio management. Can also assist in company formation, many other banking services.

*   *   *

Ferrier, Lullin & Cie.
15, rue Petitot
1211 Geneva, Switzerland

Private bank, est. 1795.

Specializes in "security investment business" and in investment management for clients. Requires waiver of secrecy from U.S. residents and citizens.

*   *   *

Lombard, Odier & Cie.
11, rue de la Corraterie   or: Case postale Stand
1211 Geneva 11, Switzerland   1211 Geneva 11, Switzerland

Private bank, est. 1798.

Current accounts (Cash accounts). Investment accounts: portfolio minimum, US$100,000. *Discretionary accounts:* minimum, US$250,000.

Category II Banks

Von der Muehll & Weyeneth Bankers, Ltd.
Utoquai 37
8022 Zurich, Switzerland

Private bank, est. 1940.

Deposit accounts (Time deposits): 6 percent int., withdrawals on ninety-days notice. *Portfolio management* is main activity. Also offers: gold & silver transactions, and safekeeping. *Special note:* policy to require bank or broker's reference from new customers.

*   *   *

Guyerzeller Zurmont Bank, AG.
Genferstrasse 6–8
8027 Zurich, Switzerland

Private bank, est. 1939.

Specializes in portfolio management. Minimum for accounts, US$300,000.

* * *

Bank Von Ernst & Cie, AG.

Marktgasse 63–65	or:	Postfach 2622
CH-3001 Bern,		CH-3001 Bern 1, Switzerland
Switzerland		

Private bank, est. 1869.

Current accounts: SFr, or other convertible currencies. *Deposit accounts:* $3^1/_2$ percent int., freely available. *Savings accounts:* $5^1/_4$ percent int. *Investment savings accounts:* $6^1/_4$ percent int., withdrawals to SFr 5,000 annually. Minimum deposit, SFr 3,000. *Cash bonds:* SFr 1,000, 5,000, or 10,000 denominations. $6^3/_4$ percent for three- and four-year terms, $7^1/_4$ percent for five years. Also offers: Euromarket time deposits, investment management. *Special note:* wholly owned subsidiary of Hill Samuel Group, Ltd., London merchant banking and financial group.

* * *

Julius Bär & Co.

| Bahnhofstrasse 36 | or: | Postfach 992 |
| 8022 Zurich, Switzerland | | CH-8022 Zurich, Switzerland |

Private bank, est. 1890.

Current accounts: any negotiable currency. *Deposit accounts:* $4^1/_2$ percent int., withdrawals to SFr 3,000 monthly. *Eurobonds:* various currencies, rates vary, minimum—US$5,000. *Euromarket short-term investments:* rates vary according to currency and term, minimum—US$10,000. *Stock transactions:* minimum—US$5,000. *Silver bullion:* minimum—1,000 oz. *Gold coins:* minimum—US$4,000. *Fully managed accounts:* US$300,000 minimum. Also offers: own investment trusts (mutual funds). *Special note:* wants to know who referred new clients, and would like to know investment goals of customers. Formerly one of the largest private banks, Bär & Co. became a joint-stock bank in January 1975.

* * *

Cambio + Valorenbank
Utoquai 55   or: Postfach 535
8021 Zurich, Switzerland   8021 Zurich, Switzerland

Private bank, est. 1959.

Current accounts (*Regular account*): SFr, US$, Canadian $, DM, Guilders, £ Sterling. Minimums—US$1,000. *Deposit accounts:* SFr, $4^{1}/_{2}$ percent int., withdrawals to SFr 5,000 monthly, minimum SFr 1,000. *Eurocurrency fixed time deposits:* minimum US$50,000. Also offers: securities transactions (also on margin); South African gold mining stocks; currency futures on margin (minimum trade US$100,000); gold coins, available on margin; silver for delivery in Zurich or in London. Sends forms after receipt of first deposit; requests initial deposit by cashier's check. *Special note:* Harry Browne, in his investment seminars, has been said to be recommending this bank because of its high liquidity (reportedly 86 percent); possibility of a rise in minimums.

* * *

Maerki, Baumann & Co., AG.
Dreikönigsstrasse 8   or: Postfach Fraumünster
8002 Zurich, Switzerland   8022 Zurich, Switzerland

Private bank, est. 1932.

Current accounts: various currencies, name or numbered. Specializes in portfolio management, securities transactions as member of Zurich stock exchange. Also offers: gold, Euromarket transactions.

* * *

Banque Galland & Cie., S.A.
8, avenue du Théâtre   or: Case postale 39960
1002 Lausanne, Switzerland   1002 Lausanne, Switzerland

Private bank, est. 1889.

Current accounts. Also offers: placement of funds in bonds or in time deposits. Portfolio safekeeping.

* * *

Banque Pariente
12, rue de Rive   or: Case postale
1211 Geneva 3,   1211 Geneva 3 Rive, Switzerland
    Switzerland

Investment bank, est. 1957.

Current accounts. Euromarket time deposits: US$ or DM, rates vary according to market and term. Usual minimum US$25,000, but "amounts as small as US$5,000" from different clients can sometimes be grouped to reach minimums. Also offers: deposit accounts, by arrangement for three-month periods; numbered accounts; gold; securities transactions; mutual funds; formation of foreign corporations; and portfolio management. *Special notes:* Requires bank references. Minimum balance required is US$3,500.

* * *

Banque Pasque, S.A.
10, rue de Hollande
1211 Geneva 11, Switzerland

Private bank, est. 1885.

Portfolio management only: minimum US$35,000. Requires waiver of bank secrecy from U.S. residents.

* * *

Banque Courvosier, S.A.
21, faubourg de l'Hôpital
2001 Neuchâtel, Switzerland

Private bank, est. 1926. Neuchâtel, lakeside cantonal capital, about twenty-five miles south of Bern.

Current accounts. Deposit books: type "A"—5¹/₂ percent int., withdrawals to SFr 10,000 monthly; type "B"—6 percent int., withdrawals to SFr 2,000 per month. Cash bonds: three-year term at 6³/₄ percent; five years at 7¹/₄ percent.

* * *

Banque d'Investissements Privés
7, place de l'Université   or: Case Stand 138
1211 Geneva 11, Switzerland   1211 Geneva 11, Switzerland

Private bank, est. 1951.

Current accounts: any currency. *Fiduciary time deposit accounts:* interest per Euromarket rates, minimums—US$100,000; DM, guilders, or French francs—100,000; Belgian francs—500,000. *Special notes:* Requires waiver of secrecy from U.S. residents. Correspondence in English, all other forms in French.

* * *

Privatbank & Verwaltungsgesellschaft
Barengasse 29
8001 Zurich, Switzerland

Private Bank & Trust Company, Société Privée de Banque et de Gérance.
Private bank, est. 1932.

Specializes in trading securities and portfolio management. No savings-type accounts. *Current accounts only:* as base for investment program. Minimums: US$50,000 or equivalent in securities. Also offers: tax-exempt Swiss franc bonds, $7^1/_2$ to $7^3/_4$ percent int.; gold bullion and coins, silver bullion.

* * *

Banque Romande
8, boulevard du Théâtre   or: Case postale 180
1204 Geneva, Switzerland   1211 Geneva 11, Switzerland

Private bank, est. 1954.

Current accounts: check books available. *Deposit accounts:* $5^1/_2$ percent int., no minimums or withdrawal restrictions specified. (Ask when querying.)

Banks That Correspond in French or German

Some banks are not equipped to correspond in English. Their replies will be informative and polite, but in German or French. Such banks, however, should present an interesting challenge to many Americans. They are listed here for the use of those readers who have a workable command of French or German.

For help with banking terms, you can refer to the translations in this book, or to one of the fine paperback dictionaries now on the market.

"French Only" Banks

Banque A. Tardy & M. Baezner, S.A.
6, place de l'Université   or: Case postale
1211 Geneva, Switzerland   1211 Geneva 4, Switzerland

Private bank, est. 1914.

Only activity is the management of funds, *la gestion de fortunes,* operating on instructions of client. Requires waiver of secrecy from U.S. citizens.

* * *

Caisse d'Epargne et de Prévoyance de Lausanne
1, galeries Benjamin-   or: Case postale 670
Constant   1002 Lausanne, Switzerland
1002 Lausanne, Switzerland

Savings bank, est. 1817.

Savings books: 5¹/₄ percent int., name or bearer form, withdrawals to SFr 1,000 monthly.

* * *

Banque Cantonale Neuchâteloise
4, place Pury
2001 Neuchâtel, Switzerland

Cantonal bank, est. 1883.

Ordinary savings account: 5 percent int., withdrawals to SFr 5,000 monthly. *Placement savings account:* 6 percent int., to SFr 20,000; 5¹/₂ percent int. over SFr 20,000. Withdrawals to SFr 5,000 yearly. *Cash bonds:* 6¹/₂ percent for three- and four-year terms, 7 percent for five to eight years.

* * *

Piguet & Cie.
14, rue de la Plaine
1400 Yverdon, Vaud, Switzerland

Private bank, est. 1856. Yverdon, industrial town and trading center, forty-five miles Southwest of Bern.

Places client's funds to earn interest. Also: brokerage and safekeeping services, portfolio management, other banking services.

"German Only" Banks

Volksbank in Schüpfheim
Dorfstrasse 81
CH-6170 Schüpfheim, Switzerland

Commercial bank, est. 1927. Schupfheim is small town near Lucerne, forty-eight miles southwest of Zurich.

Savings deposit accounts: 4 percent int. *Deposit books:* $5^1/_4$ percent int., three-months notice. *Investment books:* 6 percent int., one-year notice. *Cash bonds:* $6^3/_4$ percent for three to four years, 7 percent for five or six years, $7^1/_4$ percent for seven- and eight-year terms.

* * *

Bank in Niederuzwil
CH-9244 Niederuzwil, Switzerland.

Savings bank, est. 1858. Niederuzwil, in St. Gallen canton, thirty-four miles east of Zurich.

Private accounts: 5 percent int., withdrawals to SFr 20,000 monthly. *Savings books:* 5 percent int., withdrawals to SFr 5,000 monthly. *Investment books:* 6 percent int., withdrawals to SFr 10,000 yearly. *Cash bonds:* $6^3/_4$ to $7^1/_4$ percent, three to eight-year terms. Also offers: youth savings accounts (*Jugend-Sparheft*).

* * *

Basellandschaftliche Hypothekenbank
Rheinstrasse 8
4410 Liestal, Switzerland

Mortgage bank, est. 1849.

Savings accounts: 5 percent int., withdrawals to SFr 15,000 per month. *Deposit accounts:* $5^1/_2$ percent int., withdrawals to SFr 5,000 monthly. *Cash bonds:* $6^3/_4$ percent to $7^1/_4$ percent, three to six-year terms. Also offers: *Zinspramien,* under certain conditions; youth savings accounts (*Jugend-Sparheft*).

* * *

Kantonalbank Schwyz
Bahnhofstrasse 3
6430 Schwyz, Switzerland

Cantonal bank, est. 1890.

Current accounts. Savings books: 5 percent int., withdrawals to SFr 10,000 monthly. Name and bearer accounts available. Minimums—SFr 10 for name, SFr 500 for bearer. *Youth savings books:* 6 percent int., withdrawals to SFr 1,000 yearly. *Cash bonds:* 6½ percent for three- and four-year terms, 7 percent for five to eight years. SFr 1,000 minimum. Also offers: securities transactions, and full gold services. *Special note:* issues informative German-language pamphlets on available securities and gold.

* * *

Urner Kantonalbank
Hauptplatz   or: Postfach 52556
6460 Altdorf-Uri,   6460 Altdorf-Uri, Switzerland
   Switzerland

Cantonal bank, est. 1915. Altdorf, cantonal seat of Uri, about thirty-seven miles south of Zurich.

Savings accounts: 5 percent int., name or bearer accounts available.

* * *

Schaffhauser Kantonalbank
Vorstadt 53   or: Postfach 1843
8201 Schaffhausen,   8201 Schaffhausen,
   Switzerland   Switzerland

Cantonal bank, est. 1883.

Current accounts. Savings books: 5 percent int., withdrawals to SFr 5,000 monthly. *Investment accounts:* 6 percent int., withdrawals to SFr 5,000 yearly. Also offers: gold and gold coins, securities, Euromarket time deposits, investment advice.

* * *

Nidwaldner Kantonalbank
6370 Stans, Switzerland

Cantonal bank, est. 1879.

Current accounts. Savings books: 5 percent int., withdrawals to SFr 3,000 monthly. *Deposit books:* three distinct types, $5^1/_4$ percent to 6 percent, depending on restrictions. *Cash bonds:* $6^1/_2$ percent for three- or four-year terms, 7 percent for five to eight years.

* * *

Amtsersparniskasse Burgdorf
Technikumstrasse 2
3400 Burgdorf, Switzerland

Savings bank, est. 1834. Burgdorf, in canton of Berne, thirteen miles northeast of city of Bern.

Savings accounts: 5 percent int., withdrawals to SFr 10,000 monthly. *Savings books:* 6 percent int., withdrawals to SFr 5,000 yearly. *Youth savings accounts (Jugend-Sparheft):* 6 percent int., withdrawals to SFr 2,000 annually. *Cash bonds:* $6^3/_4$ percent for three and four years, $7^1/_4$ percent for five and six years.

* * *

Esparnisanstalt der Stadt St. Gallen
Gallusstrasse 14
9001 St. Gallen, Switzerland

Savings bank, est. 1811.

Deposit accounts: $4^1/_2$ percent int., withdrawals to SFr 10,000 monthly. *Savings accounts:* 5 percent int., withdrawals to SFr

2,000 bimonthly. *Investment accounts:* 6 percent int., withdrawals to SFr 5,000 yearly. Also offers: youth savings accounts and cash bonds.

* * *

Spar + Leihkasse Belp
Dorfstrasse 55   or: Postfach Nr. 4
3123 Belp, Switzerland   3123 Belp, Switzerland

Savings and loan bank, est. 1906. Belp is suburb of Bern, five miles south of center of city.

Offers all usual savings accounts and bonds. *Special note:* issues leaflet that describes all accounts; however, when querying ask specifically for interest rates since are not printed in leaflet.

13

Some Background on Foreign Exchange

MOST AMERICANS HAVE HAD LITTLE CONTACT with any currency other than the U.S. dollar. Dealings in foreign currencies, if only because there are so many of them, have often been perplexing. Many a tourist, before setting out on a trip to Europe, has armed himself with a currency converter. These were simple, pocket-sized calculators, printed on cardboard, that could be set to provide dollar equivalents for any local currency. Reassuring though they were, currency converters are now obsolete. They became almost useless in 1971, when fixed exchange rates between the various national currencies were abandoned.

Currency converters were simple devices, suitable for a simpler era. Times are now more complicated and Americans are now interested in foreign monies for more than sightseeing expenses. Hard currencies are now an important defense against inflation and a weakening dollar. To utilize another nation's money for this new purpose, more than a pocket converter is needed. The key to success is a clear understanding of foreign

254

exchange and why exchange rates fluctuate. The purpose of this chapter is to provide some background on the subject, so that, in the process of keeping abreast of developments, news pertinent to the foreign exchange market will be more comprehensible.

To begin with, the term *foreign exchange* has several common but overlapping meanings. Currency outside its country of origin is foreign exchange. An example would be a Mexican 100-peso note in St. Louis. A balance of 10,000 rials in an Iranian bank account of someone who lives in Philadelphia is only money to the Iranians, but foreign exchange to the Pennsylvanian. Foreign exchange is also used to describe both the converting of an amount of one national currency into its equivalent in another, and the international movement of bank drafts and other money instruments.

The Value of a Currency

Most nations have their own currencies, their own special national standard of exchange. A national money is considered as important a mark of sovereignty as a national flag, and an essential tool of economic policy. A few countries, because of their small size or their dependence upon a larger nation, are content to utilize that nation's money as their own official currency. Andorra uses both French francs and Spanish pesetas, while Liechtenstein transacts its business in Swiss francs. The rand, from neighboring South Africa, is the official currency of both Botswana and Lesotho. Liberia, on the west coast of Africa, has adopted the U.S. dollar as its own.

The major problem of foreign exchange is to decide the price of one currency in terms of another. Although a national money may simplify the financing of a nation's budget deficits, the sheer number of currencies complicates international trade.

While there are over 130 different national monies, fortunately, for our purposes, we can ignore all but a halfdozen or so, the currencies of the major industrial nations.

A currency's reputation is all important to its future. The eminence of the issuing nation in the world community is a factor. But a currency's reputation is finally built by the behavior of its home country over a period of time. Excesses, living beyond apparent means, overambition, faulty judgments, and irresponsibility all cheapen a nation's money. Prudence, conservatism, hard work, modest ambitions, and strong financial reserves help build a good reputation and make a currency more desirable. Over the long term, the value of a currency depends primarily on the opinion held of it by the rest of the world.

Over the short term, two factors are of prime importance in determining how much a currency is worth in terms of other monies. The relative purchasing power of a currency, and its general supply and demand, weigh most heavily. Sometimes, speculation becomes a very important factor, too.

"Relative purchasing power" is simply how much one currency will buy when compared with another. Perhaps a thousand U.S. dollars will now pay for approximately the same amount of goods and services as 2,500 West German deutsche marks. Consequently, 2.5 deutsche marks should equal a dollar, and forty cents, one DM. These relationships are not stable, of course. The rate of inflation directly affects relative purchasing power. As prices rise within a national economy, a unit of that nation's currency will buy less and less. As soon as this is recognized internationally, the exchange value of the inflation-weakened currency will decline. Suppose that the United States suffers from a 20 percent rate of inflation, while in West Germany inflation is held to 3 percent. At the end of a year, it will take US$1,200 to buy about what DM 2,625 buys. A dollar, then, should sell for only 2.1875 deutsche marks and it will take 45.71 U.S. cents to obtain one DM.

Supply and demand conditions in the foreign exchange marketplace can act to force a currency either up or down. An excessive supply of a particular money will push its price down, while increased demand will pressure its price upward. Exchange values change constantly, daily, even hourly, and it all depends upon what currency is needed and how much of it is available. The funds needed to finance imports, exports, and foreign travel are all obtained through the foreign exchange market. Suppose a New York wine importer brings in a shipment of fine French wines. The importer pays for the wine with U.S. dollars, buying a draft from a New York bank. When the French wine house receives the dollar draft, it must be sold to obtain French francs. The dollars from the draft are then available in France for sale to someone else. While imports add to the supply of dollars overseas, exports bolster the demand for them, since dollars are needed to pay for American products.

Economists use the phrase balance of trade to describe the net relationship of imports to exports. If a country exports more than it imports, it creates a balance of trade "surplus." Excessive imports can create a balance of trade "deficit." Tourism is a factor, too; tourists spending money abroad can destroy a surplus won by heavy exports. This is one reason that, periodically, governments attempt to discourage their nationals from traveling in other countries. But even if an economy's business community can achieve a surplus in the balance of trade account, a government can turn it into a balance of *payments* deficit by its own heavy expenditures in foreign lands. The United States government has done this many times in the last few decades with two major wars in Asia, by maintaining large troop forces in many countries, and by profligate foreign aid. Continued U.S. balance of payments deficits have sent huge amounts of dollars overseas. Too many dollars available on the foreign exchange markets have forced the dollar down in relation to many other currencies.

Speculation is another force that periodically affects exchange values. Speculators are betting on what a currency will be priced at some time in the future. They are trying to make a profit by anticipating trade surpluses, official devaluations, or other changes that will affect the value of a currency. This is where a currency's reputation becomes important; market opinion as to a money's future underlies much speculation. Sometimes, when there is widespread recognition of a money's deterioration, there are mass movements out of a weakening currency into stronger ones. These flights are not speculation really, but only people anxious to protect their remaining capital. Nevertheless, such panics do affect the exchange prices of the involved currencies, often drastically.

An example of this sort of thing is the flight from the British pound. Once worth $4.85 in American money, it was devalued to $2.80 in 1949, and to $2.40 in 1967. By mid-1975, it had floated down to $2.17, one day in July losing a full four cents. With inflation in Britain running between 25 and 30 percent, the economy hamstrung by strikes, and the Bank of England no longer able to afford to support the pound, capital flight began in earnest. Despite strict exchange controls, making bank transfers abroad illegal for most people, Britons were finding ways. Some Englishmen were reported to be carrying suitcases full of banknotes out of the country. As this money hits the exchange market, the pound is sure to plummet. In the near future, there is a good chance a pound sterling will not command US $2, and it must be remembered that the dollar itself has depreciated severely in relation to such harder currencies as the deutsche mark and the Swiss franc.

The Gold Standard

World monies now float, the relative value of each currency determined by market forces. For most of the last hundred years, though, exchange values have been fixed, maintained within relatively narrow limits.

Until the 1930s, the price of a foreign currency was determined under the rules of the "gold standard." Under this arrangement, each nation valued its paper money in terms of gold, not in terms of other currencies. Each land established a "mint parity," fixing the legal gold content of its money. For the United States, this was $20.67 per troy ounce of gold; British sterling was set at 3 pounds, 17 shillings, 10½ pence an ounce. Each central bank bought and sold gold at parity, freely redeeming its paper currency for gold or issuing fresh banknotes in exchange for gold. Gold coins also circulated—this was the era of the U.S. $20 "double eagle" and the British sovereign.

The main advantage of the gold standard was that it more or less automatically kept foreign exchange rates stable and inflation under control. A nation could acquire gold either through trade or from its mines. As it added to its gold stock, a government was required to issue enough additional currency, no more or no less, to cover the new gold acquisitions at parity.

If the money supply expanded faster than the economy, price levels would rise; internal inflation would inevitably make exports less competitive. A balance of trade deficit would eventually result, with the nation spending more in other countries than it was earning abroad. In this situation, supplies of the nation's money in the hands of foreigners would soon exceed the demand for it, and the exchange rate would begin to drop. Whenever the exchange rate fell far enough below parity to cover transportation costs, gold traders could redeem currency for gold and sell it abroad at a profit. In fact, the exchange rates could fluctuate only within narrow limits, defined by the costs of moving gold to another country. When enough banknotes had been taken out of circulation by the redemption process, deflation would cause price levels to ease back to acceptable levels. Exports would again be priced competitively, and the exchange rate would return to normal. And all this would happen without any conscious decision or action on the government's part.

The heyday of the gold standard was between 1879 and 1914. England inaugurated the arrangement in 1816, with the United States adopting the practice only in 1873. It was not until 1879, however, that enough major nations acquiesced to the rules for the gold standard to become important internationally. Until about 1900 the system worked, but not as effectively as it could have had there been enough gold available.

The opening of South Africa's gold mines in the 1890s improved the situation. Eventually, as gold became more plentiful, most nations increased their gold stocks, and national money supplies grew proportionately. Trade and industry expanded, financed by the new supplies of gold. The period from 1900 to 1914 was truly the monetary golden age; all important countries were on the gold standard, and, nourished by the new gold, the system functioned superbly. Unfortunately, World War I put an end to this prosperous period. Faced with the costs of war, and anxious to use deficit financing and the printing press to pay these expenses, most governments abandoned the gold standard. Only the United States, safe behind its ocean barriers, kept its currency convertible into gold.

By the end of the war, the supplies of wartime-issued paper money were so inflated that it was impossible to return to a strict gold standard. None of the ex-belligerents had nearly enough gold left to resume convertibility at the old mint parities. It was not feasible to deflate by shrinking the money supplies, for this would hinder reconstruction. Powerful property-owning interests in most countries also prevented devaluation, the lowering of parities to realistic levels. Instead, at Genoa in 1922, a new international arrangement was worked out. Called the "gold exchange standard," it permitted both gold-backed currencies and gold itself to be used as reserves for national currencies. Since Britain had already returned to a full gold standard, with sterling again convertible into gold, the British pound became the major reserve currency of the new system.

The gold exchange standard lasted only until the 1930s. While it survived, it was characterized by a great number of "competitive devaluations," by which nations sought to increase their exports and limit their gold outflow. In 1931, the great worldwide depression forced the British to abandon convertibility for sterling. With the key currency gone, the system collapsed, and central banks took their currencies off gold. In 1933, the United States barred its citizens from owning gold, limiting the right to convert dollars into gold only to foreign central banks.

The Bretton Woods System

All governments paid for World War II in the normal manner, with printing press money, confiscation of alien property, and massive budget deficits. Because the need seemed so obvious, before the war ended the Allied nations began to plan a new postwar international monetary system. In July 1944, forty-four nations met in conference at Bretton Woods, a New Hampshire resort. One of the organizations conceived at this meeting was the International Monetary Fund, or IMF. Later, in 1945, when the United Nations came into being, the IMF became one of its specialized agencies.

The IMF was created to help resolve foreign exchange problems and to encourage freer world trade. Member nations were officially discouraged from using tactics that would restrict trade or the free flow of foreign exchange. Each IMF member established a "par value" for its national currency, in terms of both gold and the U.S. dollar, the world's dominant money after World War II. The dollar, of course, was the key currency of the new arrangement, being freely convertible to gold, at $35 an ounce, by the central banks of the IMF nations. Members agreed not to allow the exchange rate for their currency to move more than 1 percent up or down from the established par or "pegged value." Central banks were required to "intervene" if market forces were about to drive exchange rates beyond the narrow 2 percent allowable range.

Intervention meant that a government had to support its paper money whenever its exchange value threatened to drop, by buying back its excess currency with dollars or gold from the national reserves. In the rare event of upward pressure, a government needed only to issue additional money to meet the demand. Most nations, recuperating from the economic destruction of the war, continually faced the problem of holding their currencies within the required 1 percent of the pegged value. The United States, the only major nation to end the war with undiminished industrial capacity, faced the opposite problem, meeting world demand for its dollars.

Whenever a nation was unable to continue to support its currency, to keep its exchange value from dropping below its pegged limits, it had two choices. Devaluation, lowering the peg, was one solution, but this option carried the onus of failure with it, and was considered a last resort. In 1949, however, there was a wave of devaluation by several European nations. More often, as national monetary reserves approached the vanishing point, governments turned to the IMF. Reserves could be borrowed from the IMF, which, acting as a central bank for central banks, maintained an international reserve fund of gold, dollars, and other currencies. This fund, created by assessment of all member nations, was designed to help governments bridge over periods of payment deficits. A loan from this pool was really an exchange; the borrowing nation put in a sum of its own money equal, at par, to the amount of dollars or other currencies it withdrew. Eventually, the borrowing nation was expected to buy back its currency with dollars. Since the U.S. dollar was the key currency of the system, in the event the United States borrowed from the IMF, it was required to repay with gold.

Looking back and making a judgment, it must be admitted that the Bretton Woods system worked. Its major objective, the recovery of the war-damaged economies, was achieved. But, in retrospect, as Sidney E. Rolfe and James L. Burtle have noted in their book, *The Great Wheel, the World Monetary System,* the goal was achieved by temporarily ignoring the working rules agreed upon at Bretton Woods.

The International Monetary Fund began operation in 1945. For the first dozen years of its existence, IMF agreements and objectives were more often ignored than honored by most European nations. Strict exchange controls hindered world trade, contrary to IMF's stated goals. Free exchange, the convertibility of one European currency into another, was restricted. Profits in foreign currencies were often frozen and could only be spent within the country where they were earned. Typical of the times were the many American movies made in Europe, the only way American motion picture companies could use the blocked foreign exchange they had earned from European bookings of U.S.-made movies.

Until 1958, European recovery fed on a flow of U.S. dollars, just as the gold standard nations thrived on newly mined gold in the years before 1914. American trade deficits, overseas expenditures for the Korean and Cold Wars, spending by American tourists and military personnel stationed abroad, and heavy foreign aid, all supplied essential dollars that financed European recovery. But all through the IMF's first years dollars remained scarce and in great demand.

In 1958, the European Economic Community was formed, establishing the so-called Common Market. As part of the effort to promote internal European trade, restrictions on the free exchange of the various European currencies were eased. It quickly became apparent that European nations were holding far more dollars in their reserves than were actually needed. This soon led to the wholesale redemption of dollars for U.S. gold. In only two years, America's gold reserves were depleted by $5.1 billion. Still the dollar remained the key currency of the Bretton Woods system; central bankers were gradually becoming worried about the future of the dollar, but for a few more years its value held.

By 1965, confidence in the dollar was fading, largely because of U.S. inflation and the continued budget and payment deficits caused by the Vietnam war. European central bankers, led by the French, were now quite nervous about the dollars they still held. Afraid of losses from a future dollar devaluation, they continued to convert their dollars into American gold whenever possible.

As the 1970s approached, the American government was being viewed from abroad as irresponsible. From a central banker's viewpoint, forgetting about America's Asian misadventure, there were two main reasons for this. First, there were by now so many dollars overseas that it was impossible for the United States ever to meet its obligation to exchange them for gold on demand. In 1950, U.S. gold reserves had been about $25 billion; in 1971, only $10 to $11 billion in gold was left.

Second, and perhaps of more immediate concern, the United States was exporting its inflation. Under the Bretton Woods system, the U.S. dollar was the key reserve currency. Foreign central banks treated dollars just as they had gold under the gold standard; they were required to issue more of their own currencies, increasing their national money supplies, as they added dollars to their reserves. Because of U.S. balance of payments deficits, the river of dollars flowing abroad had become a flood. In 1971 alone, according to *Fortune* magazine, foreign central banks were forced to absorb $29.8 billion dollars, more than they had added to their official reserves in all the years since 1945.

The accumulation of dollars overseas finally brought the post-war fixed exchange rate system to the brink of collapse. On August 15, 1971, when President Nixon announced the end of the dollar's convertibility into gold, the Bretton Woods arrangement was pushed over the edge to a quick death.

Floating Rates

With the American dollar, the kingpin of the system, no longer convertible into gold, the Bretton Woods system could not operate, but no other workable mechanism to regulate fixed rates was available as a substitute. The only option was to allow foreign exchange rates to float, letting supply and demand set the relative value of each currency.

Despite some initial consternation, world trade did not collapse when the fixed rate system ended. The international movement of money continued, even increased, although some nations applied controls in an attempt to dampen the surges of short-term money from one currency to another. Foreign governments were no longer forced to expand their money supplies to accommodate the inflow of unwanted dollars; if they still inflated, it was at their own initiative. The dollar remained the primary international money, although still suspect, if only because no satisfactory substitute had been found. In fact, many authorities believe the floating rate system is an improvement over the previous fixed rates; the periodic crises and the monetary panics common under the old arrangements have been conspicuously absent now that price adjustments are left to the free market.

But there are still calls for "reform," for a reworking of the Bretton Woods rules, for a return to some sort of fixed rate system. First of all, the International Monetary Fund still exists; bureaucracies being what they are (and make no mistake, the

IMF is a bureaucracy), it is a source of pressure to return to some sort of administered system. The natural allies of the IMF in this quest are the central bankers. Many governments would like to return to fixed rates, if only because such a system helps protect from the consequences of loose fiscal and monetary practices. By their standards, floating exchange rates indicate too clearly and too quickly when a central bank is mismanaging its affairs.

Since 1971, the bureaucrats have called for reform, but little progress has been made. Reform, as they seem to think of it, would require only a modification of the Bretton Woods rules. But that would require a currency convertible into gold. The logical candidate is the U.S. dollar, but American Treasury officials are not keen on entering into any arrangement that might deplete the remaining $11 billion U.S. gold stock. The French have suggested revaluing gold reserves to the free market price, $140 to $165, but the Americans continue to be antigold, preferring some system in which they will not be the ultimate losers. There appears to be no immediate solution, no easy end to the impasse. For the time being, governments will just have to try to live with their mistakes. After all, the floating system works.

Dirty Floats

The reader should not assume that since foreign exchange rates are now floating, that they are "freely" floating. This is not the case.

During the twenty-six years that the Bretton Woods system was operative, governments were required to intervene to support their currencies when necessary. Such intervention became a habit, and habits are hard to break. Although the relative values of currencies are determined largely by market forces, national governments do interfere from time to time. Such tactics create what monetary officialdom calls a "managed float," and the traders at bank foreign currency desks, a "dirty float." Rolfe and Burtle, in *The Great Wheel,* describe dirty floats as "interventions by the central banks to distort the true, i.e., market-determined, value of a currency for some political reason."

If a currency's value is trending down, a nation may intervene, buying up its money with dollars or other currencies to create an artificial demand and help to support the price. Britain consistently did this for its pound, even borrowing to obtain the funds, until its reserves and credit were gone. Intervention may also be used to hold the price of a currency down. If the exchange value of a nation's currency rises too far, the world market price of its export goods becomes too high and its export business suffers. The nation's manufacturers lose money and unemployment rises. Switzerland faced such a situation in late 1974 and early 1975, when the Swiss franc jumped in value relative to the dollar. The Swiss National Bank attempted to hold the line at 2.5 francs to the dollar ($0.40 per franc) by buying dollars and selling francs on the exchange market.

But there is a limit to what Switzerland or any other nation can do when the free market threatens to price its national currency up in relation to the dollar. Sometimes, if pressure is light, buying up a few hundred thousand or a million extra dollars is sufficient to hold the exchange rate down. But occasionally, the dollar flow can be massive; in 1973, for instance, $6 billion moved into German marks in only a few days. An intervening government runs the risk of fueling internal inflation when it trys to absorb dollars on such a scale. The national money supply must be increased, new currency issued, to pay for the dollars bought on the free market. Most smaller nations, faced with this situation, will attempt to deal with the problem in other ways. The Swiss approach, in 1974, was to impose a negative-interest tax on new Swiss franc bank deposits to try to dampen the dollar inflow.

A more ambitious attempt to regulate exchange values is the European "joint float system," which for some reason has been nicknamed the "snake." Eight European nations have agreed to float their currencies as a bloc against the dollar, while maintaining fixed exchange rates between themselves. In mid-1975, the members were: France, West Germany, Belgium, the Netherlands, Luxembourg, Denmark, Norway, and Sweden. Each of these nations intervenes as necessary to hold the value of their currency, relative to the other seven in the "snake," within an allowable range of 2.25 percent. Whether this venture will succeed is still a question; nations have joined and then dropped out as they jockey for a more advantageous rate within the snake. A more important question is whether or not Switzerland will join. It seems unlikely, for the Swiss were never even IMF members, but the subject has arisen. If the Swiss do enlist in the joint float, it will dampen the antiinflationary value of Swiss francs for American hedgers.

Special Drawing Rights

In 1944, John Maynard Keynes, the British economist whose writings were the ideology of Roosevelt's New Deal, led the British delegation to the Bretton Woods conference. One of his suggestions at the time, which was not accepted, was for "bancors," monetary units to replace gold in international reserves. In 1970, this idea finally became reality, when the IMF issued its first Special Drawing Rights, or SDRs. Called "paper gold," SDRs are not an international banknote; they exist only as a bookkeeping fiction and were intended primarily to make settlements between the IMF and member central banks.

As originally conceived, SDRs were designed to partially

replace gold as the principal international reserve and to give some additional liquidity to the world monetary system. Unfortunately, when they finally appeared after years of preparation, the world needed nothing less than more liquidity. As Rolfe and Burtle have remarked, in 1970 "the world was figuratively drowning in excess dollar liquidity."

SDRs are mentioned in this chapter on foreign exchange because it appears they will become increasingly important in the future. New, unplanned uses have been found for SDRs. They are beginning to be accepted as an international accounting unit. Saudi Arabia, Iran, and Burma now state the value of their currencies in SDRs, rather than in gold or dollars. In October 1975, the Organization of Petroleum Exporting Countries began to price its members' oil in SDRs, and Egypt has set Suez Canal tolls in SDRs. In June 1975, the first private loan denominated in SDRs was made; Alusuisse, the Swiss aluminum producer, successfully marketed an issue of five-year notes totaling 50 million SDRs.

The value of an SDR now fluctuates daily, depending on changes in foreign exchange rates. When first issued, each SDR was declared equal to $1/35$ of an ounce of gold, or US$1. After two devaluations of the dollar in terms of gold, one SDR became worth US$1.20635. In June 1974, the "standard basket" technique of computing SDR value was adopted by the IMF. The "basket" consists of sixteen different national currencies, weighted for their importance in world trade; it is used as the input for a complicated calculation to determine the value of an SDR in terms of standard currencies. On August 13, 1975, to pick a day at random, the official IMF rate for an SDR was US$1.18618.

Though it appears that SDRs have a future as an international accounting unit, their future in their intended role as a substitute for gold is unclear. The idea of paper money being backed by paper gold has gathered only meager support, and that mainly from nations with little actual gold in their reserves. Naturally, the IMF has continued to push for SDR acceptance since the success of SDRs can only increase the importance of the IMF bureaucracy. To win wide acceptance as a reserve unit, SDRs must first achieve credibility. But the obvious, potential disadvantage of SDRs is the same as for paper currency—there are no real limits as to how many can be issued and to the economic trouble they can cause.

Eurodollars and Petrodollars

In 1963, in an effort to help limit chronic balance of payments deficits, the U.S. government initiated the interest equalization tax. Designed to discourage private American investment in overseas securities, the tax did just that. Levies of up to 11.25 percent effectively closed the American financial market to foreign corporations and governmental bodies that had traditionally sought dollar financing through New York investment bankers. However, there was another effect, completely unanticipated by the American government. The new tax stimulated the formation of an important financial industry in Europe, the "Eurodollar" market.

Frozen out of New York, foreign borrowers began to seek dollars elsewhere. They found that there were large dollar holdings overseas, held in liquid form for a variety of reasons, not the least of which was that there were few choice dollar investments outside of the United States. There was also a fear that foreign dollar holdings in American banks ran the risk of being seized or frozen by the U.S. Treasury; the Russians, for one, kept their dollars in London, well out of reach of the Americans.

European governments soon began to float bond issues, called "Eurobonds" and denominated in dollars, drawing upon these newly discovered pools of overseas dollars. Soon international corporations, including some American blue chips, entered the Eurobond market. In the 1960s, the American government made it very difficult for U.S.-based corporations to make capital transfers overseas. To carry out their expansion plans, these companies now formed financial subsidiaries in such cooperative places as Luxembourg. Eurobonds issued by such well-known and credit-worthy names as Ford, Mobil Oil, Procter and Gamble, or IBM sold quickly. For the Americans, it turned out to be a wonderful arrangement; foreign expansion was financed with foreign money.

Technically, a Eurodollar is just a dollar deposited in a bank outside of the U.S. banking system. It may be owned either by a foreigner or an American resident, but it is still a Eurodollar. Called Eurodollars only because the market was centered in Europe, the dollars might actually be on deposit in a bank in Curacao or Singapore. Although most activity was in dollars, loans could be denominated in Eurosterling, Eurofrancs, Euromarks, or Euroyen. Collectively called Eurocurrency, the common denominator was that these currencies were outside their countries of issue, beyond their native government's exchange restrictions. A mark is only a mark in Germany, but it becomes a Euromark once it finds its way to a Swiss, Dutch, Cayman Island, or London bank.

Eurocurrency issues ran an estimated $200 to $300 million annually at first, mainly in ten- to twenty-year-term Eurobonds. As its advantages become obvious and new methods came into use, the Euromarket expanded manyfold. There is no central authority, hence no source of statistics, but the Bank of International Settlements estimated Eurocurrency loans had reached $200 billion by mid-1974.

Much of the growth in the Euromarket has been in medium-term loans, for perhaps three to seven years, and not in bonds. There is only a total of $25 billion outstanding in Eurobond issues. By contrast, in 1974 alone, a reported $60 billion in medium-term loans was made to governments and large corporations by international syndicates of banks. *Barron's,* the weekly financial newspaper, has observed that $100 million loans have been organized in two days or less. Massive loans have been made to such underdeveloped nations as Senegal, Costa Rica, and Gabon, often with scant regard for their ability to repay. Furthermore, many of these loans were made with what might be politely described as "bankers' bookkeeping dollars," Eurodollars created out of thin air. Just as American banks extend loans totaling five or six times their deposit base, Eurobankers have taken to making loans totaling many times their "prime deposits" of Eurodollars. A Eurodollar "prime deposit" is a deposit based on a dollar transfer from the United States. The same prime deposit may be the basis for several loans, each of which increases the potential hazard.

In the last year or so, the funds available as Eurocurrency have increased dramatically. "Petrodollars," dollars owned by the Arab oil states, have flooded the market. Coincident with the rise in oil prices and a jump in the dollar reserves of the petroleum producers, there has been an increased demand from borrowers. Many smaller nations have needed Eurocurrency loans to help pay deficits caused by the rising costs of their oil imports.

The Eurocurrency market, by its very nature, is unregulated, with little agreement on lending standards. Because of its past excesses and the conditions under which this money market operates, many observers are worried about its stability and viability. The consequences to the world banking system of a collapse in the Eurocurrency market from a series of loan defaults could be very grave. Only time will tell.

Keeping Informed

For the reader who has persevered this far, one thing should be clear—foreign exchange practices are constantly being modified. So many factors bear on the exchange market, including economics, politics, government decisions, and new methods of doing business, that what we may learn about foreign exchange one year might not be valid the next. For the reader trusting part of his assets to foreign currencies, it obviously is important to keep abreast of developments.

Of priority interest to most people with foreign accounts is prices, the current exchange rates. Newspapers throughout the United States carry listings of foreign exchange quotations, usually printed five days a week and reporting currency prices for the previous two business days. Illustration 13–1 (p. 274) shows a typical listing from the *Wall Street Journal*. This paper, available in several regional editions, provides the most comprehensive listing available on most newstands. The Associated Press also reports on a short list of twenty-four currencies. AP's foreign exchange column is carried in the business section of many daily newspapers. If your local paper does not print this feature, but is an Associated Press member, perhaps a phone call to the paper's financial editor would persuade him to use it regularly.

A caution: typographical errors are common in the price listings. If the reported value of the Swiss franc goes from .3950 one day to .0395 the next, don't have heart failure. The typesetters just don't know (or care) where the decimal point belongs.

Some newspapers occasionally provide short news stories on the prior day's exchange market activity. If you have money in Switzerland, this news should often be discounted; in some papers the stories seem to be quickly summarized from teletype copy, perhaps by a junior reporter who doesn't have the sophistication to understand market developments. Minor, and quite normal, fluctuations in exchange rates can be played up out of proportion. Local daily newspapers can provide the first news of important developments, such as devaluations, balance of payments deficits or surpluses, or new transfer restrictions. For more detailed explanations, it will generally be necessary to turn

Foreign Exchange

Tuesday, June 24, 1975

Selling prices for bank transfers in the U.S. for payment abroad, as quoted at 3 p.m. Eastern Time (in dollars).

Country	Tuesday	Monday
Argentina (Peso)	.0375	.0375
Australia (Dollar)	1.3375	1.3400
Austria (Schilling)	.0603	.0604
Belgium (Franc)		
Commercial rate	.028595	.028575
Financial rate	.027410	.027500
Brazil (Cruzeiro)	.1270	.1270
Britain (Pound)	2.2600	2.2719
30-Day Futures	2.2542	2.2665
90-Day Futures	2.2420	2.2494
180-Day Futures	2.2160	2.2209
Canada (Dollar)	.9751	.9753
China-Taiwan (Dollar)	.0270	.0270
Colombia (Peso)	.035	.035
Denmark (Krone)	.1836	.1836
Ecuador (Sucre)	.0407	.0407
Finland (Markka)	.2838	.2836
France (Franc)	.2504	.2502
Greece (Drachma)	.036	.036
Hong Kong (Dollar)	.2025	.2025
India (Rupee)	.1220	.1220
Iran (Rial)	.0153	.0153
Iraq (Dinar)	3.41	3.41
Israel (Pound)	.1670	.1670
Italy (Lira)	.001595	.001596
Japan (Yen)	.003387	.003396
90-Day Futures	.003386	.003393
180-Day Futures	.003385	.003392
Lebanon (Pound)	.4510	.4510
Mexico (Peso)	.08006	.08006
Netherlands (Guilder)	.4126	.4130
New Zealand (Dollar)	1.3175	1.3175
Norway (Krone)	.2038	.2041
Pakistan (Rupee)	.1030	.1030
Peru (Sol)	.024	.024
Philippines (Peso)	.1440	.1440
Portugal (Escudo)	.0412	.0413
Singapore (Dollar)	.4380	.4382
South Africa (Rand)	1.4750	1.4750
Spain (Peseta)	.0180	.0180
Sweden (Krona)	.2554	.2552
Switzerland (Franc)	.4009	.4008
Uruguay (Peso)	.0006	.0006
Venezuela (Bolivar)	.2338	.2338
West Germany (Mark)	.4275	.4267
30-Day Futures	.4279	.4273
90-Day Futures	.4292	.4285
180-Day Futures	.4317	.4310

Supplied by Bankers Trust Co., New York.

Prices for foreign banknotes, as quoted on the last business day (in dollars):

	Buying	Selling
Argentina (Peso)	.02	.03
Australia (Dollar)	1.27	1.34
Austria (Schilling)	.058	.065
Belgium (Franc)	.026	.028
Brazil (Cruzeiro)	.09	.11
Britain (Pound)	2.24	2.30
Canada (Dollar)	.96	.98
China-Taiwan (Dollar)	.025	.035
Colombia (Peso)	.02	.04
Denmark (Krone)	.17	.19
Finland (Markka)	.27	.29
France (Franc)	.23	.25
Greece (Drachma)	.028	.033
Hong Kong (Dollar)	.19	.23
India (Rupee)	.08	.14
Italy (Lira)	.00145	.00165
Japan (Yen)	.0033	.0035
Malaysia (Dollar)	.39	.45
Mexico (Peso)	.078	.082
Netherlands (Guilder)	.41	.43
New Zealand (Dollar)	1.08	1.15
Norway (Krone)	.1850	.21
Pakistan (Rupee)	z	z
Philippines (Peso)	.1250	.15
Portugal (Escudo)	.035	.0395
Singapore (Dollar)	.40	.46
South Korea (Won)	.0013	.0018
Spain (Peseta)	.017	.019
Sweden (Krona)	.23	.26
Switzerland (Franc)	.39	.41
Turkey (Lira)	.055	.07
Uruguay (Peso)	.0003	.0005
Venezuela (Bolivar)	.2275	.24
West Germany (Mark)	.41	.44

Supplied by one major New York bank.
z-Not available.

Illustration 13–1: Foreign exchange quotations from the *Wall Street Journal*

to more specialized publications such as the *Wall Street Journal*. The *Journal of Commerce,* which is hard to find except on large newstands, carries an excellent daily foreign exchange story, usually on its first page. Newsletters, such as those listed in chapter 15, are a help in interpreting the effect of new developments on foreign currency prices.

The ultimate source of information on foreign currencies and exchange rates is Franz Pick, who *Fortune* magazine has described as making "a career out of denouncing government inflationists." He is the publisher of *Pick's Currency Yearbook,* an annual, and *Pick's Currency Reports,* a monthly service. These publications are quite expensive (again, see chapter 15), but definitely worthwhile if a significant hard currency investment is involved.

Switching Currencies

This chapter would be incomplete without a warning about a great danger in the field of foreign exchange, the temptation to speculate. Sooner or later, someone becoming familiar with foreign currencies will recognize that they are only commodities, and that there is a great potential profit to be made by anyone who can anticipate price moves.

In theory, the profits are there to be made. In practice, a part-time speculator cannot take advantage of short-term movements in currency prices. By the time information on changes likely to affect the market filters down to him, via the press or newsletters, it is too late. The market has already adjusted to the news. Currency speculation is a hazardous game, even for professionals. In 1974, two large banks collapsed because of losses they suffered trying to outguess the foreign exchange market. West Germany's Bankhaus I.D. Herstatt suffered losses that ran an estimated $150 million before it went under; the losses of the

Franklin National Bank of New York were over $45 million. Even the Union Bank of Switzerland took a reported $150 million loss in the currency market. With assets of over $14 billion, the Union Bank did not fail, but this demonstrates that even the most seasoned professionals can get burned occasionally in the currency markets.

It is one thing to speculate on minor exchange price movements and another to ride with long-term price trends, ignoring small dips in the currency's exchange prices. Against the U.S. dollar, the long-term prospects for the Swiss franc are only up, but the franc moves up and down in spurts along the main trend line. From September 1974 to January 1975, the franc rose by 19 percent in relation to the dollar. In February 1975, it gained about 5 percent more, which it promptly lost again in about two weeks, but in July 1975, on news of an American balance-of-trade surplus, the franc fell another 7 percent in about ten days, and then leveled off, presumably before starting another slow climb. The problem with trying to pick up a few extra points by switching back to dollars during a franc drop is that the price movements occur suddenly. Since the basic goal of a hard-currency account is to hedge against inflation, it would seem a better strategy to ride with the Swiss franc or another hard currency until a permanent change in its price trend is recognized.

It is hazardous to try to anticipate short-term exchange fluctuations; it is also a mistake to stay with a currency too long, for sentimental reasons, because it once was the best hedge currency. At some future time, the Swiss franc will no longer offer the protection it does now. Perhaps the American economy will settle down, inflation will be licked, or the U.S. dollar again become a hard, gold-backed currency. Perhaps the Swiss will "peg" the exchange rate of the franc. When a change like this occurs, it is time to reconsider strategy; maybe assets in Switzerland should be converted back to dollars, or perhaps to Dutch guilders, German marks, or even French francs.

When the time comes to make such a switch, though, it is not necessary to give up the other advantages of a Swiss account. Swiss franc deposits can be converted to another hard currency and left on deposit with the same bank.

No matter what currency your Swiss account is denominated in, as a depositor you may be able to benefit from some of the many other services available through Swiss banks, and described in the next chapter.

14

Liechtenstein Trusts and Other Services

SWISS BANKS ARE one-stop financial shopping centers. They are able to provide services to their customers that are unusual by American banking standards. To Americans, banks are primarily institutions that accept deposits and make loans. We look to other specialists to set up investment programs, to gain advice on estate and tax matters, or to buy securities. The Swiss expect their bankers to handle most of their financial needs.

In Switzerland, as everywhere, bigness has its advantages. As might be expected, the largest banks offer the widest variety of specialized services to their depositors. Nevertheless, smaller Swiss banks provide a wide range of what we might consider "special services" to their local customers. As a matter of course, at big banks or small, most of these services are also available to their overseas depositors.

Usually, if a bank is interested in selling certain services, they will be described in the material sent a prospective depositor. If in doubt as to whether your bank is active in areas that interest you, write and ask for a clarification.

Securities Brokerage

It usually surprises Americans to learn that Swiss banks handle the purchase and sale of securities for their depositors. In the United States, such activities are the exclusive domain of specialized brokerage firms. Once upon a time, American banks were involved in the securities business, too. But, in 1933, as part of Roosevelt's restructuring of the financial community, commercial banking was separated from investment banking. Investment banks were no longer allowed to accept deposits, and commercial banks gave up their underwriting and brokerage business.

In Switzerland, banks dominate the securities industry. Not only do they buy and sell stocks, but many banks are members of the stock exchange, of *Börse,* in their own right.

There is no federal regulation of stock exchanges in Switzerland. Three exchanges, in Zurich, Basel, and Geneva, are regulated by the cantonal authorities. Zurich's Börse is the largest and most active. Five smaller exchanges, in St. Gallen, Lausanne, Bern, Chur, and Neuchâtel operate privately.

Swiss banks can easily handle transactions in almost any security regularly traded in the Western world. American, Canadian, and European securities are listed on the Zurich exchange along with Swiss issues. The American issues are primarily those of blue chip companies, whose shares are in international demand; Xerox, IBM, General Electric, AT&T, and Eastman Kodak are typical. Such non-Swiss shares are sponsored on the Swiss exchanges by the Big Three banks, or by an association of Geneva banks, in whose names the shares are registered on the corporations' books. The stock certificates are endorsed in blank, and then traded in bearer form.

Other American and European securities, not listed on Swiss exchanges, are also available through Swiss banks. Many of the larger American brokerage houses maintain branches in Zurich and Geneva whose business consists mainly of executing transactions on behalf of Swiss banking houses. There is also a large internal over-the-counter market in Swiss securities, handled largely by telephone between the banks.

Commissions on Swiss exchanges are low by American standards. As of 1972, a uniform commission schedule allowed charges of $5/8$ of 1 percent on shares selling above SFr 150, 1 percent on those below SFr 150, $3/8$ of 1 percent on Swiss bonds, and $1/2$ of 1 percent on foreign bonds. There are also Swiss federal and cantonal transfer taxes and stamps on each transaction; these transfer charges run SFr 0.30 per SFr 1,000 on Swiss securities, and SFr 0.65 per SFr 1,000 on foreign issues.

For foreign securities not listed on a Swiss exchange, the total commissions and charges are somewhat higher. To buy an American stock, for example, the customer must pay charges that include the regular commission to an American brokerage house, and a service charge to the Swiss bank. Buying most American stocks, those not listed on a Swiss exchange, through a Swiss bank will cost one and a half to two times the usual American commission rates. If an American depositor uses a Swiss bank for this purpose, he should have the bank explain all the costs involved.

Swiss banks, because of the strict requirements of secrecy, complete all securities transactions in their own name, not the customer's. Bonds or shares, if registered, will be carried on the issuing company's stockholder register only in the name of the Swiss bank handling the transaction.

Most Swiss securities, however, are not registered in the shareholders' names. The most common type of stock certificate is the "bearer" share, or *Inhaberaktie*. Bearer shares are like cash; possession is presumed ownership. The issuing corporation does not maintain a register of shareholders. Bearer shares can be voted, but the owner/bearer must take the initiative; he will not receive notices of annual meetings and the like because the issuing company doesn't know who its true shareholders are.

Some companies issue registered shares, called *Namensaktien* in German. This is a relatively new custom, dating back to the Second World War. At that time, Swiss companies were under pressure from the belligerent nations to prove that their shareholders were actually Swiss. Registering shareholders was a reluctant solution to this problem. Some companies will only allow Swiss residents to purchase their registered shares.

Partizipationsschein, or participation certificates, are another unique type of security. Dividends are paid, but the holder has no voting rights; foreigners are allowed to own them, since they are usually used to limit outside control.

Some Swiss companies issue two or more types of these securities. The Swiss value anonymity so highly that often the bearer shares sell at a premium over the other available types of shares in a company. Bearer certificates, as issued in Switzerland, resemble bond certificates. Coupons are attached, which must be clipped and presented to collect dividends. On registered shares, dividend payments are usually remitted directly to the registered owner.

One of the difficulties of trading in Swiss securities is in obtaining quotations. Listings of ten to twenty "selected issues" from the Zurich exchange are carried in *The New York Times* and the *Wall Street Journal.* For comprehensive listings it is necessary to see the *Neue Zürcher Zeitung,* Zurich's daily newspaper. This is a German-language newspaper, but the stock market quotations should be understandable to anyone with a little effort.

Generally a foreign investor will have to depend on his Swiss bank for quotes, and for execution at the best price. A few Swiss banks provide lists of recommended stocks; *Kantonalbank Schwyz,* for one, periodically issues a pamphlet, entitled

"Kursliste und Mitteilungen," which lists the most popular stocks, *Aktien,* and bonds, *Obligationen,* traded in Switzerland.

Securities may be bought on margin through a Swiss bank; the customary margin requirement is 50 percent. In the past, many American traders have used Swiss banks to avoid the generally higher SEC margin requirements. If your stock drops, the Swiss bank will not issue a call for extra margin, as is American custom, unless special arrangements have been made beforehand. Because the bank has the shares in bearer form, this is time-consuming and unnecessary; the bank will simply sell the stock to avoid further loss.

Most transactions on Swiss exchanges are spot or cash deals; these transactions are similar to American practice, i.e., transfer and payment are completed quickly. A large portion of Swiss stock transactions, however, are "forward" deals. This is basically a sort of option arrangement. The buyer pays a variable premium, called a *dont* by the Swiss, to delay completion of the purchase until "settlement day," four trading days before the end of each month. The buyer can choose between settling at the end of the current month, or at the end of the next month. On settlement day, the purchaser must decide to take the stock or to abandon his claim to it, losing only his premium. His decision, of course, is based on price movement in the interim. A down payment of at least half the total transaction is expected at the start of a forward deal; payment of the balance is made on settlement day, if the stock is taken.

Although Swiss banks can handle almost any sort of securities transactions for a depositor, there are practical limitations. Because of the six-hour difference in time zones between New York and Zurich and because of language and other communications problems, Swiss banks are not geared to the quick in-and-out trader who does not live in Switzerland. Swiss banks are better suited for the individual investing for the long term;

they are ideal for the investor who utilizes their expertise to build a diversified international portfolio.

Securities Safekeeping

The predominance of bearer certificates and the custom of handling stock transactions in the bank's name causes complications in the storage and administration of securities. Foreign investors find it impractical to take physical possession of their stock certificates. As a result, Swiss banks provide for the safe storage and routine paperwork connected with their customers' securities. This is usually described as "safekeeping services" or "portfolio administration" in their English literature. In German it is called *Aufbewährung von Wertschriften* (safekeeping of securities), or *Wertschriften-Verwaltung* (securities administration). Banks in French-speaking areas call the service *Garde de titres*.

Under this type of arrangement, the bank keeps the certificates in its vaults and handles all the detail work. The customer makes his own investment decisions. Bank employees clip coupons, and collect stock dividends or bond interest as they become due. The bank also notifies customers when matters such as rights to new issues arise. Both stock dividends and bond interest payments on Swiss securities are liable to the same 30 percent Swiss federal withholding tax as interest from savings accounts; these taxes are also handled by the bank. Periodic statements of the customer's holdings are provided as part of this service.

Customers utilizing a bank's safekeeping services must also maintain a regular bank account with the bank. Dividends, costs of purchases, proceeds from sales, and commissions or fees for services are all run through this base account. Many banks will also handle securities transactions and perform custodial services on a numbered account basis.

Fees charged for securities administration services vary but are always reasonable. One bank quotes a charge of SFr 1.25 per year for administration of SFr 1,000 worth of securities, with a minimum fee of SFr 20 per year. Charges for this service through a numbered account arrangement run slightly higher, the same bank charging SFr 1.50 per SFr 1,000. Another bank quotes $2/10$ of 1 percent as its charge, with SFr 200 the minimum annual charge. For purposes of determining safekeeping charges, stocks are valued at market, and bonds at face value.

Discretionary Accounts

Swiss banks will also undertake full management of a customer's investments. Americans commonly call this service "portfolio management." Swiss banks describe it as *Vermögensverwaltung* in German, or *Gestion de fortunes* in French. Under such an arrangement, the bank makes the investment decisions, buying and selling as it sees fit.

Full portfolio management is a specialty of the private banks, although many other banks offer this service. Substantial minimum funds are usually required for a discretionary account. A few banks will undertake management of sums as small as US$25,000, but more typically at least $100,000 is expected.

Some banks charge a separate fee for account management, others do not. One foreign-controlled commercial bank quotes a management fee of $1/10$ of 1 percent over its safekeeping fee of $2/10$ of 1 percent, with a minimum charge of SFr 300 annually for a fully managed account. The banks that do not charge formal management fees generally expect the investment fund to be of sufficient size to generate worthwhile brokerage commissions. Again, a base account is a necessary adjunct; some banks will also handle discretionary accounts on a numbered basis.

Many of the banks, especially the private ones, who specialize in discretionary management of investments like to meet personally with their customers. This makes sense to both parties; investment goals can be agreed upon, the customer can be familiarized with the bank's procedures, and mutual confidence can be established.

A personal meeting to establish rapport is certainly recommended. One reason is that Swiss bankers think differently from American investment counselors. Less salesmanship seems to be involved. An investment manager in this country generally makes an effort to explain or at least justify his decisions to his clients. Most Swiss bankers traditionally take a different view; once a customer grants management powers to his bank, they are often reluctant to explain the decisions made under that authority. There are exceptions, of course. Many Swiss bank officers, in private banks and elsewhere, have received part of their business education in an American graduate school, and are more attuned to the psychology of American investors.

Discretionary management accounts are obviously not for everyone. They are probably advantageous only to Americans who lack the time or expertise to manage their own investments, or to those who want large sums handled professionally, conservatively, and, for whatever reason, in complete secrecy.

It is not necessary to open a discretionary account to take advantage of your banker's investment advice. Any bank will generally offer specific recommendations upon request of a depositor. An investor can then make his own decisions, have the bank execute the transactions, and handle the paperwork under a regular safekeeping arrangement.

Mutual Funds

Yes, Switzerland has mutual funds, too, although the Swiss usually describe them in English as "investment trusts" or "investment funds." *Anlagefonds* is the German word for "investment funds" and is used to describe all types of mutual funds. Most Swiss funds invest their assets in securities; these are called *Wertschriftenfonds* (securities funds). Real estate investment funds are called *Immobilien-Anlagefonds* in German.

Over one hundred different funds are based in Switzerland and are available through Swiss banks. Some concentrate their investments in Swiss securities or real estate, while others have an international portfolio. All are sponsored by Swiss banks and are managed by the banks or by bank-organized management companies.

As in the United States, the appeal of mutual funds is mainly to investors with limited capital who, nevertheless, seek to diversify their investments. There are Swiss funds designed to generate income, others geared to capital growth. In addition, some Swiss banks offer American mutual funds. Swiss banks can also buy shares for investors in other European funds, such as the Dutch Robeco investment trust, or in the bank-run funds of West Germany.

An investor considering mutual funds will probably have to rely on the advice of his Swiss bank. He should bear in mind that, if the bank sponsors a mutual fund, it will tend to recommend that fund. However, advice can be solicited from two or more banks, if desired, before making a decision.

Information in English on European investment funds is scanty. One source is Rainer Esslen's *How to Buy Foreign Securities,* which is listed in chapter 15.

Liechtenstein Trusts

The Principality of Liechtenstein, *Fürstentum Liechtenstein* in German, is a tiny country nestled in the upper Rhine valley between Switzerland and Austria. Liechtenstein has only eleven villages, an area of sixty-five square miles, and some 22,000 inhabitants. Although it is a politically independent nation with its own ruling prince and an elected legislature, Liechtenstein is associated with Switzerland in many ways. Their mutual boundary is open, and the two nations are joined in a customs union. Since 1921, the Swiss franc has been Liechtenstein's official currency.

Liechtenstein's importance to the world lies mainly in its unique "Company Law." This act, the *Personen- und Gesellschaftsrecht* which dates from 1926, allows many types of companies to be formed. No special government permission is required to organize a Liechtenstein registered company, except to form a bank. Companies based in Liechtenstein and controlled by nonresidents pay no taxes on their earnings from abroad. Bank secrecy is as strict as in Switzerland, and Liechtenstein has no tax agreements with any nation except Austria. Because of these liberal practices, many thousands of companies have been founded and registered in Liechtenstein.

To most Americans, a "Liechtenstein Trust" is even more mysterious than a Swiss numbered account. Any sort of company based in Liechtenstein is generally referred to as a "trust" by our press. In actuality, trusts are only one of the many forms of organizations that can be created under Liechtenstein corporate law. The most important are corporations, establishments, foundations, and trusts, although several sorts of partnerships and cooperative associations are also possible.

An *Aktiengesellschaft,* or company limited by shares, is similar to a corporation as we know it, and is commonly abbreviated to *AG*. in German. This form of organization is suitable when large amounts of capital are involved, when there are a number of shareholders, or when public participation is anticipated. At least SFr 50,000 capital is necessary, but an AG can be formed by a single shareholder. Ownership may be kept secret, if so desired; shares can be issued in bearer form or in registered form.

An "Establishment," or *Anstalt* in German, is perhaps the most flexible and interesting form of organization. Establishments are unique to Liechtenstein; they are normally nonshare companies, with liability limited to their capital. A minimum capital of SFr 20,000 is required; these funds may be held in Liechtenstein or abroad. An Establishment can be formed by a private person, a legal person such as a corporation, or a trustee. The legal life of an Establishment is unlimited. At a later date, if desired, an Anstalt can be converted from a non-share company to a share company or even to a foundation merely by amending its articles of establishment.

Anstalts are often personal holding companies, but they can engage in almost any sort of business. Their objectives, as stated in their articles of establishment, are usually broadly written. The following statement of purpose, from a specimen set of articles furnished by a Liechtenstein bank, is typical: "Trading, financial and legal business of any kind, property management, purchase and sale of chattels and realty, and participation in other business organizations."

The usefulness of a Liechtenstein Establishment lies mainly in that it is much more flexible than a plain, numbered account. A numbered account can screen ownership of bank deposits or securities well enough, but becomes awkward when real estate, works of art, or other tangible property is involved.

Anstalts may be formed and controlled through Swiss banks. The first step in organizing a personal Liechtenstein Anstalt is to visit Switzerland and have a private meeting with an officer of a

Swiss bank. After this discussion, the Swiss bank arranges with a Liechtenstein bank or lawyer to form and register the Establishment. A name must be chosen that includes the word "Anstalt," "Establishment," or the French "Etablissement." The name selected must be unique, and not duplicate any other firm name in the Public Register of Liechtenstein. The Swiss bank opens an account in the name of the new Establishment, and certifies to the Liechtenstein authorities that the minimum capital has been paid into this account.

The intermediary in Liechtenstein who acts as the official "founder" does not know the name of the real owner of the Establishment. This "founder" then transfers his rights to a "successor" with a "declaration of cession." The name of the successor is usually left blank on this document, which is kept by the Swiss bank in its vault. A board of directors for the Establishment is appointed, one of whom must be a Liechtenstein resident. There is no requirement as to the number of directors, but the Swiss bank will usually appoint one or two of its staff members as directors. This board has the duty of carrying out the instructions of the "successor" who now controls the Establishment.

In practice, only the Swiss bank officer who handled the details knows the identity of the person who controls the Liechtenstein Establishment. The controlling owner communicates his instructions to the bank officer, who handles the necessary transactions through the Swiss bank. With the exception of the confidential papers in the bank's vault, all the bank's records show only the firm-name of the Establishment. All property bought through the bank shows the Establishment as the legal owner. Confidentiality is further protected by the legal restrictions of Swiss bank secrecy.

A foundation, or *Stiftung,* is another common form of legal structure. It is usually used to conserve and administer a family fortune and to provide for members of the family. A Stiftung differs from an Establishment in that it has no owner. Assets are transferred to the foundation for a specific purpose and for certain designated beneficiaries. This type of foundation may be formed during the lifetime of the founder, or after his death by an endowment made in his will. It can be set up to be either irrevocable or revocable by the founder. A foundation board, appointed by the founder, controls the Stiftung. To maintain anonymity, an intermediary can be used to form the foundation. Minimum capital is again SFr 20,000.

There are two basic kinds of "trusts" under Liechtenstein law. One is called a *Treuhänderschaft,* the other a *Treuunternehmen.*

A *Treuhänderschaft* is a trusteeship, or a "trust settlement." Legal title to property is granted to a trustee who has the responsibility of administering the property for the benefit of one or more beneficiaries. The designated trustee may be an individual or a corporate body such as a bank. Under Liechtenstein law, the trust funds remain independent of other assets owned by the trustee. This type of Liechtenstein trust is popular in Europe because in other countries, such as Switzerland or France, trust funds may be endangered by claims against a trustee's other assets. Also, once a trust is established, trust funds are legally beyond the reach of any creditors of the principal who established the trust. A trust settlement can be set up in ways that keep the founder's identity and the financial details secret.

A *Treuunternehmen* is a "trust undertaking." This type of trust is notable because of the various ways it can be organized. Basically, a Treuunternehmen is an independent enterprise, functioning in its own name under the supervision of one or more trustees. Liabilities are limited to its funds. It can function as a business trust, a family trust, or a holding company, depending on how the articles of organization are drafted. Again, it can be anonymously created. Minimum capital for both types of trusts is SFr 20,000.

A Liechtenstein Anstalt, Aktiengesellschaft, Stiftung, or trust can provide a tax-free haven and a secret financial operating base. However, because of the costs involved in creating and administering such a company or trust, something over US$100,000 is needed to make it worthwhile. While there is no tax on foreign income, there are stamp duties, registration fees, annual capital taxes, and fees to be paid to both the Swiss bank and to its Liechtenstein agent. As an example, an Anstalt must pay a registration free of SFr 250, and a stamp duty of 2 percent of capital (SFr 400 on the minimum SFr 20,000) when formed. Bank charges vary, but one bank quotes SFr 4,500 as an initial charge. An Anstalt also pays an annual tax on capital of $^1/_{10}$ of 1 percent with a minimum of SFr 1,000. This is paid in advance, on registration, and annually thereafter. The Swiss bank will also collect an annual fee for "representation." It will therefore cost about US$2,500 to organize an Anstalt, and about US$1,200 each year to maintain one. To be practical, the potential benefits of using Liechtenstein as a secret base must outweigh the costs of administration.

Many Swiss banks provide service in this area, although they seldom advertise it. If a bank offers "trustee services," or "formation of foreign companies" in its literature, this is a definite clue. Companies and trusts can also be organized directly through a Liechtenstein bank, but this approach does not provide the double screen of privacy created by operating a Liechtenstein haven through a Swiss bank.

Liechtenstein corporate law is a specialty unto itself, a legal mirror-maze comprehensible only to the most dedicated student. Forming a Liechtenstein trust is not something to be done by mail. At a bare minimum, a visit to Switzerland and a consultation with a knowledgeable bank officer is essential. Because of the wide variety of possible legal structures, it would seem advisable to have a fairly frank discussion of the planned uses of the projected Liechtenstein entity; only in this way can the most efficient legal setup be arranged.

Booklets in English that describe the various forms of Liechtenstein companies are available from the banks listed below. The material they provide is generally heavy reading, more suitable for a lawyer than a layman, but useful as an introduction to the topic. If you are seriously considering forming an Anstalt or whatever, write them on your letterhead and ask for information.

Société Bancaire Barclays (Suisse), S.A.
6, place de la Synagogue
1211 Geneva 11, Switzerland

Verwaltungs-und Privat-Bank, AG.
Postfach 34672
FL-9490 Vaduz, Liechtenstein

Liechtensteinische Landesbank
Stadtle 44
FL-9490 Vaduz, Liechtenstein

Bank in Liechtenstein, AG.
FL-9490 Vaduz, Liechtenstein

Any speculation on the possible uses of a Liechtenstein trust always reminds me of the common childhood fantasy of being an "invisible man," able to go anywhere and do anything and yet not be seen. A Liechtenstein arrangement is the equivalent for monied adults, as close as they will ever get to being financially "invisible." No one really knows what sort of financial maneuvers are made from behind Liechtenstein screens; the successful strategems remain anonymous forever.

Only occasionally do any reports of the uses of this sort of arrangement reach the press. In June 1975, Christina Onassis announced that her father, Aristotle Onassis, had arranged in his will for a "public welfare foundation" to be set up in Liechtenstein, into which half of his estate was to be placed; I wonder if we will ever know for whose "welfare" this money will be used. For the last few years, Liechtenstein companies have been heavy buyers of investment-grade art. In 1974, in a New York court case, a famous art dealer was alleged to have sold two paintings to a Liechtenstein firm for $140,000, and later to have bought the same pieces back for $420,000 for resale to a wealthy collector. Somehow I doubt that any government will ever collect taxes on the $280,000 profit someone made from this deal.

Swiss Corporations

Many of the larger Swiss banks are also equipped to help form Swiss corporations. Because of its central location in Europe, its stable government, its free exchange regulations, and the highly developed banking system, Switzerland has become a favored location for holding companies and for European headquarters of firms doing business internationally.

Corporate laws vary from canton to canton. Some cantons, such as Zug and Chur, are noted for their accommodating laws; they are centers for corporate registration in much the same way that Delaware is in the United States. Most commercial banks will be able to help a customer find the best canton for his purposes and to handle the details of corporate creation. If need be, a banker can also introduce a depositor to a Swiss lawyer or accounting firm.

Safe Deposit Boxes

Safe deposit boxes are called *Tresorfächern* in German and *coffres-forts* in French. Except for the name, this service is the same in Switzerland as it is in this country. Normally, safe deposit facilities are of little interest to a mail depositor. In special situations, however, if periodic visits to Switzerland were made, such a box could be used for long-term storage of valuables. Boxes are normally rented by the year, with a small box renting for perhaps SFr 40 annually. A box may also be taken for shorter terms, perhaps to store important papers temporarily while traveling in Europe.

Gold

In Switzerland, private ownership of gold is not only legal, but respectable. There are no restrictions on owning or trading gold, or on transferring gold in or out of the country.

Such Swiss attitudes have helped to make Zurich one of the most important gold markets in a world where many governments fear gold in the hands of their citizens. One of the major tourist attractions of Zurich is the Bahnhofstrasse, a street where gold bullion and gold coins are displayed in the windows of bank after bank.

Gold coins and gold bars are sold to all comers at Swiss bank counters. The larger banks offer every variety of gold coin imaginable; most banks are able to provide the more common coins. Bullion is usually offered in metric bars, from ten grams to a kilogram. The larger banks with their own gold refineries can provide gold in more exotic measures, such as the *tael* of Southeast Asia, or the *tola* of India.

Many Swiss banks offer special gold accounts to their customers. Under this arrangement, the more popular coins, such as US$20 gold pieces, British sovereigns, or Austrian 100 coronas, are available for minimum investments of US$1,000 or more. Bullion is also available, in either metric or ounce measures, with ten ounces as a typical minimum buy. For this sort of "gold account," the bank holds the gold in its vaults, charging about $^{15}/_{100}$ of 1 percent annually for insurance and storage. There is also a brokerage fee of about $^{3}/_{8}$ of 1 percent on bullion purchases and sales. Bullion stored by the bank may be resold without an assay charge.

Gold coins can also be bought on margin, generally 50 percent or so. Futures are also available through Swiss banks; a Swiss gold contract is usually for fifty kilograms, or 1,607 ounces. Margin requirement is about 20 percent, with commission $3/8$ of 1 percent per contract.

Gold ownership became legal again for Americans at the end of 1974. Before legalization, however, there were apparently many U.S. citizens who owned gold through a Swiss bank. Though gold is now readily available in the United States, there remain certain advantages to Swiss gold. The most important, of course, are privacy and security. Some Americans will always prefer to acquire their gold through a Swiss bank, and to leave it in the bank's safekeeping, well out of reach of Uncle Sam.

Other Services

Established customers will often find Swiss banks willing to serve in ways not normally described in a bank's promotional literature. Introductions and discreet inquiries are examples. A letter of introduction from a Swiss bank to a correspondent bank in another part of the world can be a useful tool. Please note, however, that a Swiss banker's introduction carries weight precisely because such letters are not casually issued. A Swiss bank may also be able to use its international network of contacts to explore commercial possibilities or third-party reputations on behalf of one of its substantial customers.

Swiss banks are not insurance brokers, but they might be willing to refer a depositor to a Swiss insurance agent. Life insurance policies are available from Swiss companies whose proceeds are payable in Swiss francs. A hard-currency policy such as this is a valuable hedge against the future. Arrangements often can be made with the bank for automatic payment of the premiums on such a policy from the depositor's Swiss franc account.

Swiss banks are not real estate brokers either, but they can often assist in overseas realty transactions. Payments for a second home in Ireland or a condominium in Spain could be made through a Swiss account. The bank may be able to help find mortgage money for a foreign property, either through a Swiss mortgage institution or through a source in the country where the property is located.

In general, a Swiss bank is always a good place to start if help in foreign financial matters is needed. Their services are so diverse, and their international connections so broad, that the chances are always good they can be of some assistance. If a bank cannot handle the problem directly, it can often act as a source of referrals to other institutions. At the very least, a depositor can expect sound financial advice.

15
Sources of Further Information

MANY READERS, especially those who have not read other books on the new economic situation, may wish more information. The books, newsletters, and other materials described here are listed to encourage you to read further. The more information you have, the better equipped you will be to protect your assets in the uncertain times that lie ahead.

Actually, to acquire sufficient information to manage your affairs intelligently and prudently, a two-stage reading program is essential. Books will provide necessary background on the world economy, on developments likely to occur, and on personal planning in a changing economic environment. To keep current, as the situation develops, supplementary reading is also important. A good daily newspaper, one or two weekly news magazines, and at least two newsletters are basic. *The New York Times* is perhaps the best newspaper for general world news and background stories on developing shortages, etc. The *Wall Street Journal* is very good for its wrapups of developments in the economy, banking, and the foreign exchange market. Both the *Journal* and the *Times* carry daily foreign exchange listings. Either *Newsweek* or *Time* magazines, supplemented by *U.S. News & World Report,* will provide summaries of trends as they develop. Newsletters are necessary to obtain the hard-nosed, specialized commentary and advice not found in publications intended for the general public.

You should not expect to agree completely with all the opinions and advice contained in these publications. Sometimes, individual writers will express contradictory viewpoints. Newsletters, especially, will often offer differing interpretations. You must form your own opinions, based on your own special situation and upon your personal objectives.

Books listed in this bibliography may be ordered through any bookstore, if not already in stock. If you prefer, or if a bookstore is not convenient, they may be bought directly from the publishers, by mail; some newsletters and bookstores also provide mail order service, selling these and similar books by mail. On books, the prices indicated are for editions available when this listing was prepared.

Books on Swiss Banks

The Swiss Banks, by T. R. Fehrenbach. When this book was published in 1966, the dollar was still sound; Swiss accounts were not yet desirable nor necessary for Americans. Times have changed, but still a very readable explanation of Swiss banking. Excellent for background. Hardcover: McGraw-Hill Book Company, 1221 Avenue of the Americas, New York, N.Y. 10020; $7.95.

Switzerland: an International Banking and Financial Center, by Max Iklé. Takes the broad view and covers Swiss conglomerates, industrial companies, insurance companies, etc., as well as Swiss banks. Dr. Iklé was formerly general manager of the

Swiss National Bank. Translated from the German in 1972. Hardcover: Dowden, Hutchinson & Ross, Inc., Box 699, Stroudsburg, Pa. 18360; $7.

The Banking System of Switzerland, by Hans J. Bär, 1973. Originally written as a thesis for an M.A. in economics at New York University. Has been updated several times since first publication in 1950; now in fourth revision. Herr Bär is now a senior partner of Julius Bär & Co. and one of the Swiss bankers most quoted in the English-language press. A logical presentation on the types of Swiss banks, the banking system, and the financial markets of Switzerland. Paperback, available by mail from Swiss publisher: Buchhandlung Schulthess Polygraphischer Verlag, AG., Zwingliplatz 2, 8001 Zurich, Switzerland; SFr 19, plus SFr 3.30 for airmail postage. (Multiply 22.30 by latest rate for Swiss francs listed in *The New York Times* or *Wall Street Journal.* Send money order and ask them to mark package LUFTPOST or AIRMAIL so it won't be sent by surface mail.)

What the Prudent Investor Should Know About Switzerland and Other Foreign Money Havens, by Harry D. Schultz, 1970. Discusses reasons for investing abroad and the many uses of a Swiss bank account. Hardcover: Arlington House, 165 Huguenot Street, New Rochelle, N.Y. 10801; $7.95.

The Swiss Bank Connection, by Leslie Waller, 1972. An exposé of how organized crime supposedly uses Swiss banks, interwoven with an explanation of the Swiss banking system. Paperback: New American Library, 1301 Avenue of the Americas, New York, N.Y. 10019; 95 cents.

Money, Inflation, and the Economy

You Can Profit from a Monetary Crisis, by Harry Browne, 1974. This is the new classic on protecting your assets and your future from continued devaluation of the dollar. Notable for its clear explanation and its analysis of the possible directions in which our economy can move. A "must read" for anyone anxious about inflation or depression. Hardcover: Macmillan Publishing Co., 866 Third Avenue, New York, N.Y. 10022; $8.95. Paperback: Bantam Books, Inc., 666 Fifth Avenue, New York, N.Y. 10019; $2.25.

How You Can Profit from the Coming Devaluation, by Harry Browne. This is the book that established Browne's reputation; he correctly predicted the devaluation of the dollar. Originally published in 1970, its recommendations are of course outdated. However, still worth reading for its masterful expositions on money and how government causes inflation. Paperback edition still around: Avon Books, 250 West 55 Street, New York, N.Y. 10019; $1.75.

Nothing Can Replace the U.S. Dollar . . . and It Almost Has, by M. Martin Rom, 1975. Investment strategies for the new economy, with emphasis on techniques applicable in an "inflationary depression." Evaluates many types of investments in the light of what lies ahead. Well worth reading. Hardcover: Thomas Y. Crowell, Inc., 666 Fifth Avenue, New York, N.Y. 10019; $7.95.

The Great Wheel, the World Monetary System, by Sidney E. Rolfe and James L. Burtle, 1973. Makes sense out of foreign exchange and Eurodollars. Explains how and why the dollar deteriorated. Several chapters on forecasting foreign exchange rates. Hardcover: Quadrangle/New York Times Book Co., 10 East 53 Street, New York, N.Y. 10022; $9.95.

How to Beat the Depression That Is Surely Coming!, by Robert H. Persons, Jr., 1973. A manual on the tactics of investment in an era of uncertain conditions. Covers many types of investments. Soft cover, large format: C.B.C. Company, 485 Fifth Avenue, New York, N.Y. 10017; $10.

Economics in One Lesson, by Henry Hazlitt, 1946. An enlightening book and a classic. Takes an irreverent look at popular economic theories and fallacies. Makes a complicated subject understandable. Still in print in paperback: Manor Books, Inc., 329 Fifth Avenue, New York, N.Y. 10016; 95 cents.

The Decline and Fall of the American Dollar, by Ronald Segal, 1974. Chronicles the rise and fall of the dollar. Interesting explanations of inflation and government's manipulation of money. Well worth reading. Paperback: Bantam Books, Inc., 666 Fifth Avenue, New York, N.Y. 10019; $1.95.

Inflation, the Permanent Problem of Boom or Bust, by Robert Lekachman, 1973. Covers the inflationary process and its causes, and the factors that led to the current inflation. Paperback: Vintage Books Div. of Random House, 201 East 50 Street, New York, N.Y. 10022; $1.50.

The International Money Game, by Robert Z. Aliber, 1973. "A primer in international finance," written for the nonspecialist. Highly readable. Hardcover: Basic Books, Inc., 10 East 53 Street, New York, N.Y. 10022; $6.95.

Panics & Crashes and How You Can Make Money Out of Them, by Harry D. Schultz, 1972. If you still don't believe that economies collapse and currencies become worthless, this book will convince you. Hardcover: Arlington House, 165 Huguenot Street, New Rochelle, N.Y. 10801; $7.95. Paperback: Pinnacle Books, 275 Madison Avenue, New York, N.Y. 10016; $1.50.

Smart Money in Hard Times, by Ronald L. Soble, 1975. Discusses many types of investments for an inflationary economy, ranging from Swiss bank accounts to Samurai swords. Paperback: New American Library, Inc., 1301 Avenue of the Americas, New York, N.Y. 10019; $1.75.

The Kondratieff Wave, by James B. Shuman and David Roseman, 1972. All about the "long-wave" economic cycle, first observed by the Russian economist, Nikolai D. Kondratieff. If the theory is valid, there is a fifty-year cycle to economic events and we are now entering a deep trough. Soft cover: Dell Publishing Co., Inc., 1 Dag Hammarskjold Plaza, New York, N.Y. 10017; $2.45.

Investing Overseas

How to Buy Foreign Securities, by Rainer Esslen, 1974. Subtitled, "The Complete Book of International Investing," this work takes the view that Americans can no longer ignore foreign investment opportunities. Covers foreign markets, country by country; good chapter on Swiss exchanges. Hardcover: Columbia Publishing Company, Inc., Frenchtown, N.J. 08825; $14.

Neue Zürcher Zeitung. Zurich's daily newspaper, it is one of the few available sources of comprehensive quotations on Swiss securities. This is a German-language paper, so it is only for the investor competent enough in German to read the financial news, or for someone content with only the stock quotation columns which anyone should be able to understand with a little effort. For mail subscription prices, write to: Neue Zürcher Zeitung, Falkenstrasse 11, 8021 Zurich, Switzerland.

Gold and Silver

Until recently, there were few books available on investing in gold and silver. Since the legalization of gold ownership for Americans, there have been many new books issued on the topic. The following should serve as an introduction to the field.

The Coming Profit in Gold, by Charles Curley, 1974. The writer was an associate director of the National Committee to Legalize Gold. Covers the theory and history of gold, money, coins, bullion, and gold futures. A chapter on the advantages of buying gold through a Swiss bank. Paperback: Bantam Books, Inc., 666 Fifth Avenue, New York, N.Y. 10019; $1.95.

Everything You Need to Know About Gold and Silver, edited by Louis E. Carabini, 1974. Advice from nine contributing authorities, including Harry Browne, on much more than gold and silver. Hardcover: Arlington House, 165 Huguenot Street, New Rochelle, N.Y. 10801; $8.95.

How to "Wheel & Deal" in Gold and Silver, by C. M. Allen, 1974. The how-to of investing in these precious metals. Paperback: Allen Advertising Company, Inc., 118 East 93 Street, New York, N.Y. 10028; $3.95.

How to Invest in Gold Stocks and Avoid the Pitfalls, by Donald J. Hoppe. Essential reading for anyone interested in investing in gold mining shares. Hardcover: Arlington House, 165 Huguenot Street, New Rochelle, N.Y. 10801; $9.95.

The Root Causes

A worried American, concerned with current economic problems, should understand the basic underlying causes. Incompetent governments, and Arab oil states beginning to feel their power are just complicating factors, symptoms of the root problem. Primarily our troubles are caused by overpopulation, too many people competing for the limited resources of our planet. As an introduction, the books listed here will help the reader comprehend the magnitude of the problem. Hopefully, they will impress him with the need to act now, to make plans for his own future security.

The Population Bomb, by Dr. Paul R. Ehrlich. First printed in 1968, this book had a major impact on population trends in the United States. Worth reading to understand the "too many people, too little food" equation, that underlies the changes in our world economy. Paperback: Ballantine Books, 201 East 50 Street, New York, N.Y. 10022; $1.25.

The Limits to Growth, by Donella H. Meadows, Dennis L. Meadows, Jørgen Randers, and William W. Behrens III. Published in 1972, this is a report on the Club of Rome's "Predicament of Mankind" project. This study ran all available data through a computer to determine the carrying capacity of the planet. Dire predictions about shortages, etc. Paperback: The New American Library, Inc., 1301 Avenue of the Americas, New York, N.Y. 10019; $1.25.

The End of Affluence—A Blueprint for Your Future, by Paul R. Ehrlich and Anne H. Ehrlich. Issued in 1974, this book's theme is "America's economic joyride is coming to an end." Emphasizes that the world is changing, permanently, and that people must depend on themselves more than on the government. Many suggestions on adapting to the new era of shortages. Paperback: Ballantine Books, 201 East 50 Street, New York, N.Y. 10022; $1.95.

The Eco-Spasm Report, by Alvin Toffler, 1975. Insights on the new era of global change: the "breakdown of industrial civilization" and the transition to a new "super industrial civilization." Paperback: Bantam Books, 666 Fifth Avenue, New York, N.Y. 10019; $1.50.

Suicide of the West, by James Burnham. Not a book about population and resources, this, nevertheless, belongs on the reading list of those who seek to understand the origins of our problems. First published in 1964, this is a brilliant analysis of the causes "of the weakening of the West's will to survive." Available in a new edition. Hardcover: Arlington House, 165 Huguenot Street, New Rochelle, N.Y. 10801; $7.95.

Fiction

The Billion Dollar Sure Thing, by Paul E. Erdman, 1973. A novel about speculation in gold by London and Swiss bankers. Notable because the writer started this book while confined in a Swiss prison. Erdman was formerly the president of the United

California Bank in Basel, AG., whose downfall was described in "Adam Smith's" *Supermoney*. Hardcover: Charles Scribner's Sons, 597 Fifth Avenue, New York, N.Y. 10017; $6.95. Paperback: Pocket Books, 630 Fifth Avenue, New York, N.Y. 10020; $1.50.

The Silver Bears, by Paul E. Erdman, 1974. Another novel by the same writer. This one is about manipulation of the silver market. Hardcover: Charles Scribner's Sons, 597 Fifth Avenue, New York, N.Y. 10017; $6.95. Paperback: Pocket Books, 630 Fifth Avenue, New York, N.Y. 10020; $1.95.

The Dogs of War, by Frederick Forsyth, 1974. An adventure yarn about mercenaries taking over a small African country. Instructive, because operation is financed through Swiss and Belgian bank accounts, and hidden in a maze of dummy corporations. An insight into the way control of a company is concealed in Europe. Entertaining, too. Hardcover: The Viking Press, 625 Madison Avenue, New York, N.Y. 10022; $7.95. Paperback: Bantam Books, 666 Fifth Avenue, New York, N.Y. 10019; $1.95.

Miscellaneous

Supermoney, by "Adam Smith," 1972. Observations on the end of the great 1960s stock market boom. Chapter 4 covers the rise and fall of an American-controlled Swiss bank. The author was a shareholder in the United California Bank in Basel, AG., that went bankrupt because of speculation in commodities. Hardcover: Random House, Inc., 201 East 50 Street, New York, N.Y. 10022; $5.95. Paperback: Popular Library, Inc., 355 Lexington Avenue, New York, N.Y. 10017; $1.95.

The Money Tree, by Catherine Crook de Camp, 1972. Although written before inflation had its full impact, still lots of good advice on managing personal financial affairs. Paperback:

New American Library, Inc., 1301 Avenue of the Americas, New York, N.Y. 10019; $1.50.

Reason. A monthly magazine with a libertarian viewpoint and many distinguished contributors. Includes articles on current economics, financial tactics, etc. Especially noteworthy is issue of June 1975 on "Surviving Inflation and Depressions." Back copies usually available: P.O. Box 6151, Santa Barbara, California 93111.

Laissez Faire Books is a New York bookseller who specializes in books of the sort that are listed here. Write for their "Free Market Economics and Investment Catalog" of books available by mail. 206 Mercer Street, New York, N.Y. 10012.

Pick's Currency Yearbook. A reference book on world currency and foreign exchange, updated annually. The 1974 edition, the nineteenth, was $120. Pick Publishing Corporation, 21 West Street, New York, N.Y. 10006.

The April Game, by "Diogenes," 1973. An account of the Internal Revenue Service from the inside, written by an anonymous IRS agent. Enlightening, and an insight into what a taxpayer who decides to cheat is up against. Reissued every year at tax time. Paperback: Playboy Press, 919 North Michigan Avenue, Chicago, Ill. 60611; $1.25.

Tax Revolt, by René Baxter, 1975. An introduction to the art of avoiding taxes while staying within the outer limits of the law. Well worth reading, if only to assess the mood of the tiny minority who are determined to stand on principle and not give another cent to the IRS; an indication of the resentment that exists against big government and confiscatory taxes. Pamphlet: RBPress, 4045 East Palm Lane, Phoenix, Ariz. 85008; $2.

Switzerland as a Place to Visit

Fodor's Switzerland 1975, edited by Eugene Fodor. Comprehensive tourist guide to Switzerland and Liechtenstein. Introductory essays on Swiss life and customs, then district by district tour guide. Revised yearly. Hardcover: David McKay Company, Inc., 750 Third Avenue, New York, N.Y. 10017; $8.95.

TWA Getaway Guide, Zurich, Geneva. For reader planning a trip to either Geneva or Zurich, perhaps to visit his bank. Much information about hotels, restaurants, and night life. Revised annually. Paperback: distributed by TWA and Simon & Schuster, Inc., 630 Fifth Avenue, New York, N.Y. 10020; $1.50.

Swiss National Tourist Office will provide free brochures and booklets on Switzerland in general and on specific resort areas. Just ask and you will be inundated with material. Write or visit at: 608 Fifth Avenue, New York, N.Y. 10020; or 661 Market Street, San Francisco, Calif. 94105. Representative office: 104 S. Michigan Avenue, Chicago, Ill. 60603.

Swissair, the national airline of Switzerland, provides an information packet on available tours. Ask for the latest edition of "Alpine Highlife." Beautifully illustrated, and free, too. Swissair, 608 Fifth Avenue, New York, N.Y. 10020.

Swiss Consulates in the U.S.

The Swiss Embassy is located at 2900 Cathedral Avenue, N.W., Washington, D.C. 20008. Consulates are at: 444 Madison Avenue, New York, N.Y. 10022; 307 N. Michigan Avenue, Chicago, Ill. 60601; 535 Boylston Street, Boston, Mass. 02116; 1106 International Trade Mart, New Orleans, La. 70130; 235 Montgomery Street, San Francisco, Calif. 94104; and 3440 Wilshire Boulevard, Los Angeles, Calif. 90005.

Obtaining a Passport

To visit Switzerland, or a Swiss bank, a U.S. citizen will need a passport. Once issued, passports remain valid for five years. Application forms and information on requirements may be obtained by mail from: Department of State, Passport Office, Washington, D.C. 20524.

Newsletters

To keep up to date on developments that may affect your investment plans, regular reading of a newsletter or two is important. They are essential to anyone contemplating anything fancier than a plain savings account.

Newsletter subscriptions can be expensive, in some cases running $100 a year or more; with one exception, subscription prices are not listed here, since many are now being increased because of inflation and rising postal charges. It is suggested that the interested reader ask a few services for rates and a sample copy. The most promising can then be evaluated further by means of a trial subscription.

Inflation Survival Letter. Biweekly. Broad range of information on personal financial and survival tactics in a difficult period. Highly recommended. 410 First Street, S.E., Washington, D.C. 20003.

The International Harry Schultz Letter. Issued every three weeks. Much quoted, strong opinions, covers a broad range of topics. Hard to describe, see for yourself. Dr. Schultz has been living in Germany, but the service is printed in Switzerland. Write to: Financial and Economic Research Corp., Postfach 2523, 1002 Lausanne, Switzerland.

The Dines Letter. Biweekly. Oriented toward the stock market. Called the market correctly all the way down. Dines is an analyst who led his clients into gold stocks very early. If interested in gold stocks or in knowing when the stock market will again offer an opportunity, this is the letter for you. James Dines & Co., Inc., 18 East 41 Street, New York, N.Y. 10017.

Harry Browne's Special Reports. Ten issues yearly. Good way to keep in touch with Browne's thinking between books. Periodically reports on liquidity of individual Swiss banks. Highly recommended. P.O. Box 5586, Austin, Tex. 78763.

The Kiplinger Washington Letter. Weekly. Perhaps the largest and best-known American newsletter. Bland, but good for political trends—most U.S. economic decisions will be politically motivated. The Kiplinger Washington Editors, 1729 H Street, N.W., Washington, D.C. 20006.

Tax Haven Review. Monthly. Just what the title implies. This publication also runs a book service that is a central source of material on foreign tax havens, etc. Kompagnistraede 6, DK-1208 Copenhagen, Denmark.

The Forecaster. Forty-four issues annually. Covers speculative opportunities in many fields, all outside of the stock market. Forecaster Publishing Co., Inc., 19623 Ventura Boulevard, Tarzana, Calif. 91356.

International Moneyline. Twice a month. Reports on international monetary affairs, gold markets, oil and the Middle East, other matters likely to affect U.S. economy. Good for its analysis of developing situation. 21 Charles Street, Westport, Conn. 06880.

Swiss Economic Viewpoint. Issued by a bank with many American customers. Foreign Commerce Bank, Bellaristrasse 82, 8038 Zurich, Switzerland.

Kaffir Trac. Specializes in South African gold mining stocks. Box 4127, New Orleans, La. 70178.

National Coin Reporter Hard Asset and Currency Review. Monthly. Formerly oriented toward the coin investor, now reports on foreign exchange and currency futures as well. P.O. Box 7212, Chicago, Ill. 60680.

London Gold Report. Biweekly. Continuing update and analysis of developments affecting investments in gold and gold stocks. Published in London, but has U.S. office, too: Advisory

Information Services, Ltd., 30 East 42 Street, New York, N.Y. 10017.

The Inflation Early Warning System. Monthly. A new letter being sponsored by *Free Enterprise* (formerly *Capitalist Reporter*) magazine. Too early to tell as this is prepared, but worth checking out. 150 Fifth Avenue, New York, N.Y. 10011.

McKeever's Multinational Investment and Survival Letter. Twenty issues yearly. Another newcomer. Edited by Jim McKeever, who has become a popular speaker at recent seminars on financial survival. 726 Richards Street, Vancouver, B.C., Canada.

International Wealth Protection Newsletter. Twenty-four issues annually. Another interesting letter that seems particularly adept at explaining economic trends in plain English. Financial Services, Ltd., N.V., Box 1000, Grand Cayman, Cayman Islands, B.W.I.

Pick's World Currency Report. Monthly. Published by currency expert Franz Pick, this is a sophisticated source of information and opinion on developments in the foreign exchange market. It is also expensive, $350 a year; it has been reported that there are *no free sample copies* but that a single copy can be obtained for $35. Pick Publishing Corporation, 21 West Street, New York, N.Y. 10006.

The Freedom Fighter. Twice a month. A new letter by René Baxter, a well-known investment adviser who formerly published *The René Baxter Letter*. Dedicated to "the restoration of our constitutional liberties," this publication would make Thomas Paine feel at home. Emphasis on making the IRS sweat for every cent of taxes it tries to collect. RBPress, 4045 East Palm Lane, Phoenix, Ariz. 85008.

The Ruff Times. Twice a month. Published by Howard Ruff, offers advice on protecting yourself from the periodic problems that will beset us in the years to come. Moderate viewpoint. Target Publishers, P.O. Box 172, Alamo, Calif. 94507.

16
In Closing

By now, the reader should be well-versed in the lore of Swiss banks, and familiar enough with Swiss banking practices to be able to open and use a hard-currency account with confidence.

For the last thirty years, there has been no more enduring myth than that of secret Swiss accounts. Many readers, because of the aura of mystery and exclusivity surrounding Swiss banks, are undoubtedly excited at the prospect of opening their own Swiss account. At this stage, I am certainly not about to discourage anyone from doing so. I would, however, like to remind the readers that a hard currency bank account in Switzerland is only a tool, a device to help protect his savings from inflation and the uncertain future of the U.S. economy. A Swiss account is perhaps the simplest way to diversify investments internationally, to spread the risk by moving some assets out of dollars and the American economy. The world economy, though, is in such an unsettled condition that even international diversification is an imperfect solution; if the age of interplanetary commerce were already here, I would recommend investments on other planets, other worlds, the widest possible hedge.

Our world is not about to collapse, but it is about to change; in fact, it is already changing. Historians of the future will look back upon these years and write of the period of monumental transition that began about the time of the Second World War; they will consider the events of this era as important historically as the Fall of Rome, the Renaissance, or the Industrial Revolution. What our descendants will call this era in unknown. Some observers today write of "the birth of a new civilization," or of the "transition to a postindustrial society." I prefer to think of it as the new "World Reformation," because I hope rational men will prevail.

Basically, the population load of our planet and our technology have gotten ahead of our social systems. Our politics, our economics, our religions can no longer cope. We can put men on the moon, but we cannot provide an adequate diet for billions of people. We can televise a presidential speech or tally election results with a computer, but we do not seem to able to agree on national goals. We can perform open-heart surgery and install atomic pacemakers in human chests, but we have not persuaded hundreds of millions of women to practice birth control. We can transmit a bank transfer across an ocean in seconds, but we cannot stop governments from overspending and inflating national money supplies. We speculate on the existence of civilizations on other planets and send out space probes bearing messages from Earth, yet most of our people worship gods prescribed by ignorant prophets who walked the earth thousands of years ago.

Our world society will change, inevitably, but the alterations will not be accomplished smoothly or peacefully. It is too late for that, the built-up stresses are already too great. In the next hundred years, there will be revolutions, civil and international wars over resources, religious differences, and political systems. Children now living, today's teenagers even, will witness the main acts of this spectacle, but probably not the climactic final scene, which might feature the tentative establishment of a "world order," the dream of conquerors and revolutionaries for millennia.

America will probably be spared the worst of this upheaval; the Third World is the likely bloody arena. In the process, the social structures of the underdeveloped nations of Latin America, Asia, and Africa will be ripped apart and reassembled; their populations will be thinned, and a new economic and political order forcibly imposed. In the United States, there will be a further extension of government power and control over our everyday lives. Periodic economic chaos, of the sort predicted by the "Prophets of Doom," will serve as an excuse; so will occasional political crises.

Despite all this, there is a good chance that the U.S. economy will remain the world's largest and strongest; other nations will have their own problems and are not likely to surpass us economically. Regardless of shortages, temporary economic breakdowns, or other problems of adjustment to a changing world, Americans will probably remain among the most prosperous inhabitants of the planet.

Most people will accept additional restrictions on their freedoms, thinking it the price to be paid for security. A small minority, a self-reliant and clear-thinking group, will seek their own financial security by maintaining Swiss accounts. It can be expected that the government will try to use moral pressure against those who use such methods to preserve their economic independence, branding them as unpatriotic or worse. Already the Treasury Department, by implication, by requiring foreign accounts to be reported at tax time, has seemingly managed to get most citizens to believe that Swiss accounts are improper. Such is the power of subtle brainwashing that many of my acquaintances, while this book was being prepared, reacted with astonishment upon discovering its topic; they were startled to learn that Swiss accounts were not actually illegal for Americans.

No matter how immoral a foreign account is made to seem, it would be a grievous mistake to yield to this sort of persuasion. Americans have been forced by an irresponsible government to turn to Swiss banks and hard currencies to protect their assets; it would be foolish to trust the same government when it uses patriotism to appeal to us to cease using foreign accounts. The prosperity of this nation depends on the financial strength of the people; government does not create wealth, it only redistributes it or wastes it. If there is an economic patriotic duty, it is to strive for your own financial security; as the individual benefits, so does the nation. If an economic breakdown comes, the recovery will depend on the capital that has been protected and preserved by individuals acting in their own self-interest.

Many of the publications listed in the previous chapter were written from a right-wing, conservative, or libertarian viewpoint. This is only natural; conservatives normally are the first to criticize an overpowerful federal government for its shortcomings. What is interesting, however, is that lately liberal voices have been joining in the chorus calling for a more financially responsible national government; liberals have traditionally favored a highly centralized, bureaucratic administration, with heavy spending on social programs, paid for by budget deficits if necessary.

There seems to be a growing awareness that overgovernment and overspending will ruin us all; a recognition that liberals and conservatives, Kansas farmers and San Francisco porno czars, Harlem hustlers and Houston oil equipment distributors, Florida retirees and Wisconsin graduate students, all are in the same economic boat. The opponents to big and callous government and proponents of self-reliance and decentralization now range across the entire political spectrum. The right and the ultra-right are well represented by many who advocate investments in gold and foreign currencies and suggest the preparation of individual retreats. Paul R. Ehrlich, who could probably be classified as an activist-liberal on the basis of his work in population control, currently recommends self-sufficiency and the building of family food reserves; he tells us we can expect "precious little help" from the government when the "crunch" comes and we need it the most. Karl Hess, a former Goldwater speechwriter who is now a left-wing libertarian, refuses to pay taxes to what he terms a "predatory government"; he now lives by barter, his tax resistance being punished with a 100 percent IRS lien on all his earnings.

As a result of having written this book, I would not be surprised if the Internal Revenue Service calls me in for a retaliatory audit every year from now on. I only hope that enough readers, regardless of their political beliefs, benefit from this information on Swiss accounts to make it all worthwhile.

Let me now close with a quote from a talk given by Senator James L. Buckley of New York:

> "Government is the enemy—government
> is necessary, but it must be kept at bay."

Index